SOUTHWEST CI[illegible]

A WALKABOUT IN THE AMERICAN OUTBACK

by

Brett A. LeCompte

A solo pilgrimage from the bottom of the Grand Canyon to the top of the Rockies and back again.

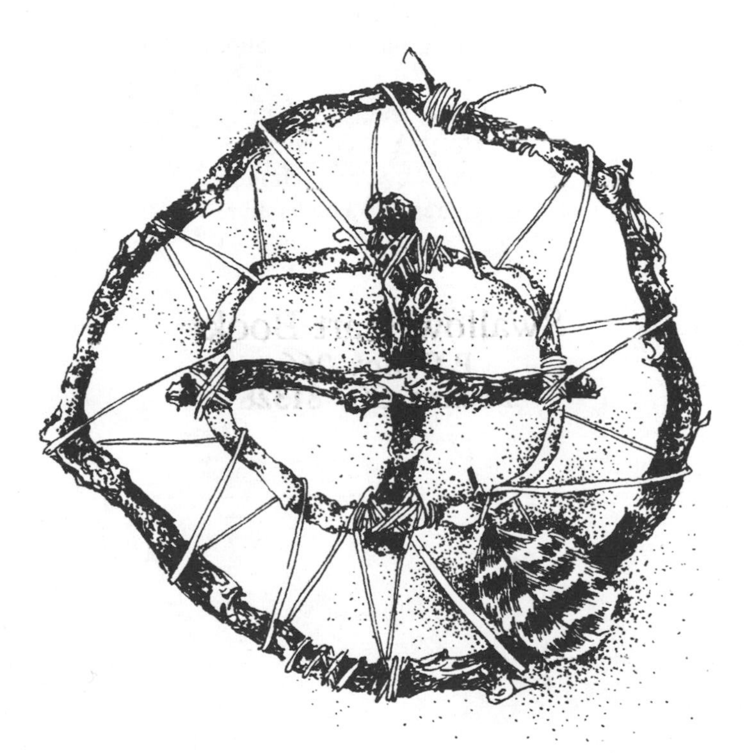

1998
Canyon Country Publications

Walk in Beauty!
Brett A. LeCompte

Maps and artwork by Kathi Sutton

Published 1998 by
Canyon Country Publications

ISBN 0-925685-34-8
Library of Congress Catalog Number 97-74934

SwallowHeart Books
P. O. Box 266
Mancos, CO 81328

CONTENTS

Dedicated to those who find the courage and persistence to follow their dreams.

In Memory of
Kenison Smith
1938 - 1997
who always believed in me
and
Steve Arrowsmith
1961 - 1992
who slipped away too soon.

ACKNOWLEDGMENTS

Many friends have helped me "carry the pack" before, during, and after my walk and throughout the birthing of this book. Abby Schreiber offered me seven years of loving support and companionship. Kitty and Brian Benzar, Don and Barbara Rosner, Steve Arrowsmith, and Chick Wayne opened their homes to me during my trek and brought the human touch to my walkabout. Kitty and Brian also helped make the Four Corners my home and this book a reality; they deserve special thanks. Greg Moore, Rob Meltzer, Mary Lyn Ray, Dr. Ronald Koetzsch, Hubert Ferguson, Steve Allen, and Shaine Gans offered valuable feedback during the evolution of my manuscript. Fran Barnes of Canyon Country Publications graciously shared his expertise on book production, after his wife, Terby, polished the final script. Kathi Sutton's drawings and maps beautifully captured the spirit of the land and my words. Douglas and Beverly Capelin of Deer Hill Expeditions and Janet Ross of The Four Corners School have given me the opportunity to live my vision in the years following my walk.

Finally, I must deeply thank my mother, Kenison Smith, and my father, Ernest LeCompte, for always having the trust, fortitude, and wisdom to encourage me to follow my dreams. All my love.

SOUTHWEST

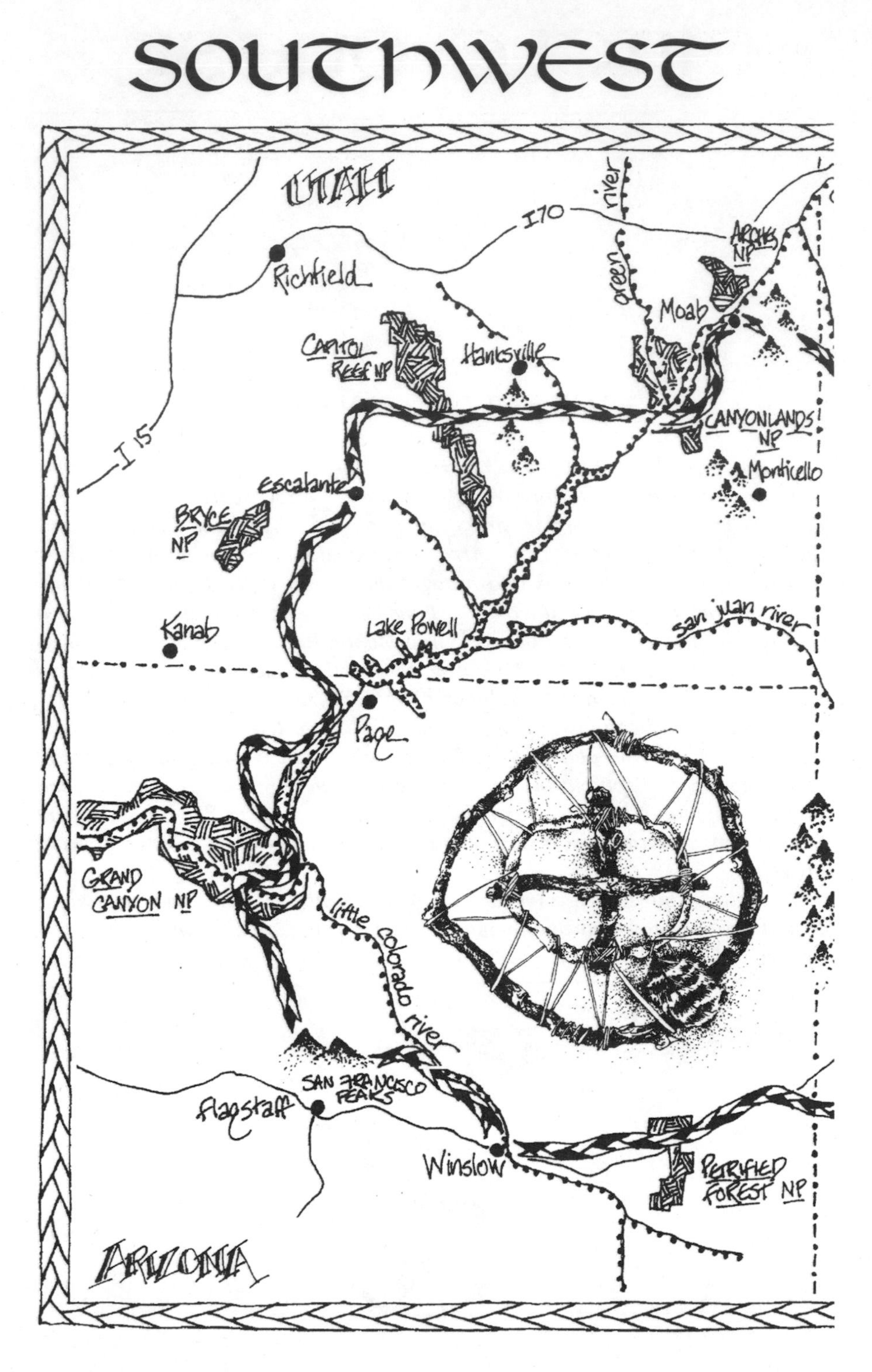

UTAH
I 70
green river
Richfield
ARCHES NP
Moab
CAPITOL REEF NP
Hanksville
I 15
CANYONLANDS NP
Monticello
Escalante
BRYCE NP
Kanab
Lake Powell
san juan river
Page
GRAND CANYON NP
little colorado river
SAN FRANCISCO PEAKS
Flagstaff
Winslow
PETRIFIED FOREST NP
ARIZONA

CIRCLE QUEST

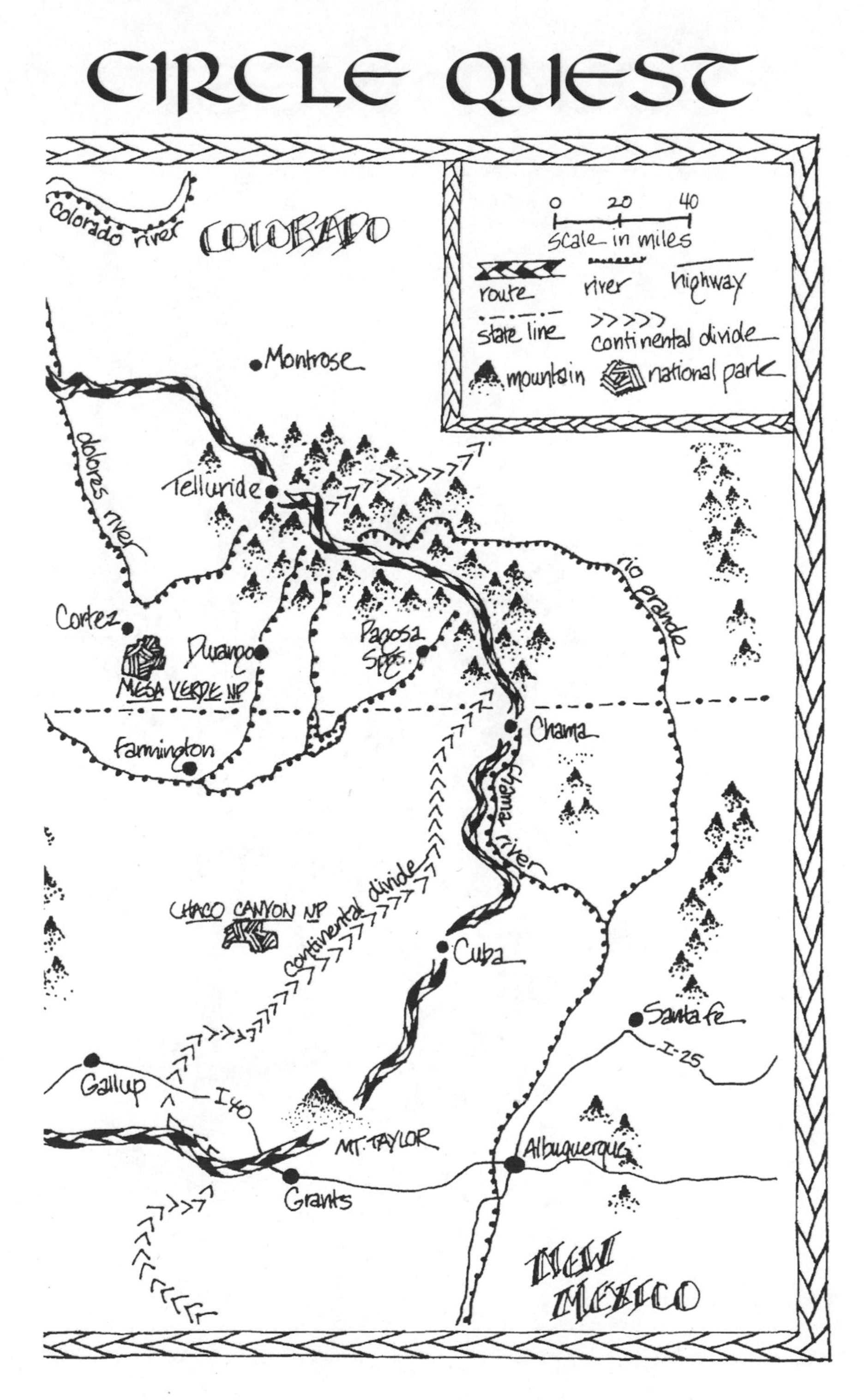

PROLOGUE

A Quest Is Born

A man must go on a quest
to discover the sacred fire
in the sanctuary of his own belly
to ignite the flame in his heart,
to fuel the blaze in the hearth,
to rekindle his ardor for the earth.

Sam Keen
Fire in the Belly

Gravel clatters noisily beneath my boots as I stumble down the dry bed of Vishnu Creek. Imposing ramparts of granite, schist, and sandstone rise a thousand feet on either side to form a seemingly impressive canyon. Yet here, near the bottom of the mighty Grand Canyon, the gorge is but a chord lost in the symphony of erosion. Greedily, I scan the creekbed for any sign of water: a seep, a puddle, anything to ease my raging thirst. Around another bend, the streambed of pebbles turns to slickrock and disappears over a lip. Dropping my pack, I lie on the hot bedrock and peer over the precipice with a silent prayer for water. A silky smooth tongue of stone slides away to a pool of dusty cobbles a hundred impassable feet below.

Pour-off.

Dead end.

Big Trouble.

Rolling onto my back, I squint up at the ribbon of hard blue Arizona sky fluttering between the jaws of rock and wonder if I should laugh or cry. This can't be happening again -- not here, not now. Only a week remains in my summer-long, fourteen hundred mile solo trek around the Southwest. I should be coasting to the finish, savoring my triumph after surviving the blazing deserts of the Navajo Reservation, the lightning storms of the Continental Divide and the maze of Utah's redrock country. Instead, I'm stuck in a forgotten corner of the Grand Canyon, trapped, nearly out of water, and wilting fast.

My gaze drops to the faded blue backpack and the weathered walking stick that lean against a boulder -- my sole companions for the last fifteen weeks. Perhaps only they will ever understand what this walk, my vision quest, has meant to me. This solitary exploration of the wilderness and the boundaries of my mind, body, and spirit has forever changed my life. As the miles have unfolded, I've danced in riotous beauty, trudged through many hostile terrains, and traversed the full myriad of emotions. I've come so far in so many ways....

This crazy, wonderful journey actually began over a year earlier, during the summer of 1990, in a tiny cabin only a couple dozen miles (as the raven flies) from Vishnu Creek. I was working as a hiking guide at the Kaibab Lodge, a rustic outpost on the vast plateau of spruce, aspen, and silence near the Grand Canyon's remote North Rim. By day, I led tourists on interpretive hikes and an occasional backpacking trip. Each evening, I roamed much farther, spending quiet hours lost in my collection of adventure travel books. In my imagination, I paddled down the Yukon, trekked across Tibet, and sailed singlehandedly around the world.

Late one night, after setting aside yet another exciting tale, I lay in bed staring at the ceiling and wondered what became of my dream of someday undertaking a major expedition. True, my life had been centered in the outdoors since my childhood in rural New Hampshire. The past three years had been a delightful exploration of the American West through a series of seasonal jobs and wilderness trips with my girlfriend, Abby. Career-bound friends already considered my freewheeling lifestyle adventurous enough, but I'd always secretly hoped to wind up in the pages of National Geographic magazine. Now approaching thirty, I saw marriage, a permanent home, maybe even a "real" job looming down the road. Would my grand adventure soon be impossible? Was I ready to let go of my dream?

No, it's never too late. I could dedicate the next summer to a real expedition -- a unique journey more challenging and far-flung than any of my earlier travels. But where? Trip possibilities flashed temptingly before me: the Pacific Crest Trail, circling New England in a canoe, a bike tour across Australia. Nothing quite fit, but by morning, I'd resolved to make my expedition dreams into a reality.

In the weeks that followed, my motivations as well as the expedition itself were greatly clarified. I knew that people in other cultures sometimes undertook an epic journey as a rite of passage. I considered my own life: a carefree, drifting ramble where the question "What am I doing with my life?" often surfaced like an annoying itch. Perhaps a long, introspective journey would be just what I needed to advance to the next phase of my life. I decided to use the trip as a time for self-examination and personal growth. My expedition grew beyond a mere adventure into a vision quest.

Concurrently, the perfect journey hit me like a lightning bolt. Staring at the United States map on my cabin wall, my eye focused on the Four Corners region of the Southwest. Here the Colorado Plateau meets the Rocky Mountains. What if I connected the plethora of national parks and wilderness areas of the region with a walking trek? I could hike from the Grand Canyon to the Continental Divide...and back again. Yes, a thousand-mile grand circle around the diverse country where Utah, Colorado, Arizona, and New Mexico come together! I would traverse both the redrock canyon country and the high mountains -- my two wilderness passions. The route felt so right in my mind and, more importantly, in my heart. The Southwest Circle Quest was born.

When the aspens of the North Rim blazed yellow, I left the Grand Canyon, reunited with Abby, settled into a friend's cabin near the inspiring mountain wall of the Grand Tetons. As the bitter cold blanket of a Wyoming winter settled upon us, I earned my keep as a carpenter, but concentrated my energy into getting ready for the upcoming summer. I bought and studied maps, dried and packaged trail food, and double-checked backpacking gear. My mental and spiritual preparations were equally as comprehensive. Voraciously, I read everything I could find on the ritual of the vision quest. I studied Eastern, Western, and Native American philosophies and drew lessons from Joseph Campbell's study of comparative mythology. As my learning continued, I realized that this quest for a guiding vision was exactly what my spirit required. Like Thoreau, I longed to "live deep and suck all the marrow of life". What better opportunity than when alone in the wilderness!

By late April, winter was just beginning to loosen its grip on Wyoming, but I was ready and eager for the summer to begin. My tentative route was drawn, my boots were greased, and my kit was assembled. Thirteen cache boxes, each containing food rations and supplies for ten days, sat on the cabin floor awaiting delivery to obscure points south. Time had come to close the books and experience lessons directly. Once again, Abby and I packed our scant belongings into our trusty, rusty Toyota pickup and bade another town goodbye. We drove south and visited friends while leaving my cache boxes in stores and visitor centers in carefully spaced towns along my route.

This road trip revealed the full scope of my trek and tempered my enthusiasm with a heavy dose of reality. Barren desert plains flowed by the truck window for hours. How would I survive walking alone through this empty landscape? My first major mistake might be my last.

I spent my final days before the quest with Abby as she began another summer as a national park ranger in Colorado. My dear friend understood my need to spend the summer alone in the wilderness, but she knew the risks I faced. The bus driver waited patiently during our long final embrace. "Come back safe," Abby whispered emotionally. I tried to assure her with a smile, but we both knew there were no guarantees. I wiped aside tears as the bus sped me towards Arizona where the journey through the wilderness and into my heart would finally begin.

Kathi Sutton 11/97

THE OPENING CIRCLE

The trick is what one emphasizes.
we either make ourselves miserable
or we make ourselves strong.
the amount of work is the same.

Carlos Castaneda
The Teachings of Don Juan

Day 1, Twelve miles

With a hiss of pneumatic brakes, the Greyhound shutters, then sighs to a standstill in its slip. "Flagstaff," intones the driver. Groggy from twenty-one hours in buses and their grim terminals, I step down into a brilliant May morning and suck in a huge lungful of northern Arizona air. The pine-scented breeze smells sweet, full of promise. I retrieve my luggage, a faded blue backpack and a walking staff, and ease out of the bus station. Sixty-five pounds of food and camping gear settles heavily on my back, but I smile. My Southwest Circle Quest has begun.

Waiting for the crosswalk light at busy Santa Fe Avenue, my gaze climbs beyond the traffic and brick buildings to the snowy summits of the San Francisco Peaks towering above this university town. Among those beautiful sacred mountains I will begin and end my summer-long circular trek through the deserts, canyons, forests, and mountains of the Southwest. The wilderness will be my home, my school, and my church. Standing at the brink of my grand expedition at last, the possibilities seem as endless as the Arizona sky. The flashing signal commands me to "WALK" and taking aim at the frosted peaks, I obey.

City street becomes country lane which fades to dirt road and then trail. Downtown Flagstaff is already a memory when I pause for lunch on the mountainside. The flaky, pumpkin-red bark of a ponderosa pine feels rough against my sweaty back, but I lean close and savor the tree's pleasant vanilla scent. The previous weeks of roadways and relatives, cities and cement begin to dissipate as my body and soul relax.

Closing my eyes, I review my plan to begin the summer with an opening ceremony -- a four-day vision quest. This ritual, drawn from Native American and other indigenous cultures, is deceptively simple. The seeker leaves family and community to journey into the wilderness. Upon reaching a "place of power," such as a mountaintop, the quester constructs a small circle of stones and sits inside without the comforts of food or fire for four days and nights. Alone and focused, the seeker searches for guidance and insight from within and from the natural world and the spirit realms through the use of prayers, songs, drums, and dreams. Commonly, the goal is a vision of one's proper path through life.

Returning home to follow and share any wisdom learned is the final, and often most difficult, act of the ritual.

I have not entered the woods to "play Indian." The ritual of the vision quest is an archetypal experience that transcends background and culture. It is the personal enactment of "the hero's journey" which forms the basis of myths and teachings around the world. Anyone willing to put forth the effort can benefit from the vision quest. A recent revival of the vision quest has a growing number of organizations offering guidance in modern versions of this ancient ritual. As an Outward Bound student in college, I experienced a three-day "solo" as part of my course. Since then, I experimented with other solo rituals and always found them to be difficult, but insightful and empowering. A traditional vision quest seems an ideal way to center and focus myself before my Circle Quest journey. Before exploring the outback, I shall sit still and gaze inward.

A chill gust pulls me back to the present. Pines give way to budding aspens as I continue climbing the eastern flank of the peaks to seek my vision quest site. By sunset, I am exhausted. The sleepless night on the bus haunts me as a headache. Winter-white legs ache and shoulders throb with first-day tenderness. Creeks where I'd planned to get water are dry and I'm dangerously low on water. Day One and I'm already a wreck!

But now, as I lie in my warm goosedown sleeping bag under a canopy of brilliant stars and listen to the gentle night sounds, I feel content, relaxed, and genuinely at peace for the first time in months. My journey into the wilderness has begun and I wouldn't trade places with anyone.

Day 2, Five miles

I sleep like the dead my first night, awakening surprised, then delighted, to find myself in the middle of nowhere. Continuing around the shoulder of the mountain, I approach a richly forested valley known as the Inner Basin. A large hill, Sugarloaf Mountain, stands guard over the mouth of the valley. A careful study of area maps last winter revealed that this trailless mountain might serve as an excellent vision quest site. The first glimpse of the flat-topped dome proves that my instincts were good.

I struggle up steep elk paths to the summit and discover that Sugarloaf is everything I'd dreamed. The 9000 foot high forest of pine dotted with aspen and spruce seems devoid of human intrusion. Dropping my pack, I clamber atop a limestone outcrop and savor the magnificent vista. Eastward, the cinnamon-brown plains of the Navajo Reservation roll away towards New Mexico. The Grand Canyon is visible fifty miles to the north as a subtle break in the forested Coconino Plateau. Most impressive is the cluster of winterbound summits rising another 3500 feet a few miles to the west. I've found my place of power.

The San Francisco Peaks have likely been considered a sacred place since human eyes first spied the massif rising 7000 feet above the Painted Desert. To the local Navajo people, the San Francisco Peaks are Dooko'oosliid -- the

Mountain of the West -- one of the four southwestern mountains that delineate their physical, spiritual, and mythic world. To the Hopi, whose ancient pueblo cities sit atop stony mesas facing the peaks, the mountains are Nuva'tuky'ovi -- home to their life-sustaining Kachina gods for half of the year. To this day, the Hopi make pilgrimages from their desert home to this high tundra world to leave offerings and gather herbs and ceremonial spruce boughs. Arizona's Yavapai and Walapai people also consider the San Francisco Peaks to be sacred mountains. However, one need not be of Native American heritage to feel a spiritual attraction to this place. Years ago, my first excursion into northern Arizona was a drive from Denver to the Grand Canyon. After passing through the entire chain of the majestic Rocky Mountains, it was the San Francisco Peaks, glowing crimson at sunset, that made the deepest impression on me. I have been drawn to and fascinated by these mountains ever since. When I needed to find a place along my circular route to begin and end my quest, the choice was easy.

I continue exploring my new-found sanctuary. Animal tracks lead to a dying snowbank -- my water source. In a small clearing, I stumble across an unusual formation. Two large boulders are connected by low stone walls to form a circle about five feet across. The crude dry-laid masonry is ancient, yet too big for a fire pit and too small for a shelter. Suddenly, my heart races. Similar circles of stone on the Nevada desert have been identified as prehistoric quest sites. Is this an ancient vision quest circle? Could Navajo or Hopi youths have climbed to this same spot generations ago in search of their visions? The thought rocks me back on my heels. The coincidence of stumbling across this circle while searching for my own vision quest site seems too unbelievable...or is it?

Tentatively, I enter the circle and replace those stones that have fallen. Sitting down in the center, I quiet my mind and look around. This spot feels right. I offer thanks for this first gift of the summer and set up camp nearby.

Now, watching the flames of the fire, I'm excited finally to begin the experience which my spirit has cried out for during the long, dark winter. With the next dawn, I shall bare my flesh and my soul to the natural world. Tonight, I pray that I shall be worthy of whatever I receive.

Day 7

At dawn this morning, I ended my vision quest. As I recover in my base camp surrounded by familiar gear, everything that has happened in the last four days and nights has an intense dreamlike quality to it. Being now snowbound in my tent on this first day of June adds to the mystical atmosphere. A lifetime seems to have passed since I last wrote ....

At first light four days ago, I secure my base camp and walk quietly to the ring of stone. Standing at the edge of the circle, I remove all my clothing and my eyeglasses and tuck everything under one of the boulders. Into the circle I will take only three items: a thin wool blanket, a metallic "space blanket," and my homemade cedar and rawhide drum. Six quarts of drinking water lie within my grasp just outside. Naked in the chill morning air, I vow aloud to remain within the confines of the ring of rocks until dawn of the fifth day. Then I step purposefully over the the low wall and begin the toughest challenge I have ever faced.

The first day is the easiest in all ways. Time becomes the movement of the rising sun as I sit wrapped in the black blanket. Warm light filters through the pines until the sun clears their crowns. Caught in the direct burning rays, I go from chilled to cooking in a matter of minutes and the wool blanket became an umbrella shielding me against the brilliant sun arcing slowly across the flawless sky.

I don't remember many thoughts from the first day, but I'll never forget the appearance of my first teacher. It is a beetle. I am drinking in the beauty surrounding me; feeling happy, relaxed, and open. A lizard dances around the opposite rock wall pursuing black ants. A big-eyed chipmunk pops up an armslength away and approaches my feet in halting scurries before disappearing back into the stonework. Then I notice a large black beetle between my outstretched legs frantically clambering to escape my deep heelprint in the dust. His hectic climbing only spills him upside down where he struggles mightily to right himself and start all over again. I speculate idly how this beetle might succeed if only he'd slow down and concentrate!

During one of his self-righting attempts the beetle quite suddenly quits fighting altogether and lies still, belly-up in the hot sun. Am I witnessing the end of a life right in front of me? I pick up the minute creature. Three legs make feeble reflex movements but my companion seems to have given up the ghost. Cradling the insect in my palm, I think about how this tiny being acted like so many people who scramble and struggle without much thought only to fail and give up. Don't I also often act irrationally when angered or upset? I resolve to not struggle blindly, but live in awareness of my actions. Never will I give up so easily.

The desert below becomes awash in late afternoon flame and there is a brief moment of perfect comfort between the fire and ice. Yet at 9000 feet, the growing evening breeze soon cuts into my naked body. With dusk quickly approaching, I decide on a ritual to end the day. I will drum down the sun and dance up the moon!

I have only recently created my drum and playing it is still a new experience. I find a satisfying beat and keep repeating it until a new rhythm spontaneously evolves. Vibrations travel through my hands, over my body, and fill my circle. I begin chanting; nothing in particular, just deep guttural sounds that rumble up naturally from my belly. Drumming and chanting in the fading light alone on a mountaintop, I relax into a pulsating universe. The deafening silence that swallows me when I pause is even more amazing.

Once I "properly" set the sun, I huddle in my blanket and await the moon. As darkness gathers, I feel deep anxiety over the night ahead. I am naked in the mountains with no sleeping bag, no tent, no fire. Never before have I faced the natural world on these terms. Will I become totally hypothermic? Is sleep possible? Can I resist the temptation to break my vow and use the warm clothes an armslength away? I think of the beetle. With a nervous laugh, I realize that my fear, like all fears, is primarily a dread of the unknown.

Suddenly, a patch of blood-red appears on the southeastern horizon. Time to dance! With the blanket around my shoulders and hanging to my bare knees, I shuffle in place and begin chanting: "positive mental attitude, positive mental attitude ...." A gorgeous tangerine moon climbs into the indigo sky above the Painted Desert and these simple words filled my soul.

I reach a crescendo. With a final screaming whoop, I stand trembling and panting, ready to take on the cold, unknown night. Crouching again against the stones, I pull the space blanket over the wool one and sit cozy and pleased. Perhaps I'll survive this night after all. But my optimism evaporates as I quickly cool down and fingers of icy air begin to probe beneath my covers. I curl up in a ball, sandwiched between the blankets on the uneven, rock-studded earth. With careful tugs on the thin covers, I try desperately to plug each airhole and gap. The cold night just snickers and hugs me tighter.

The shivering begins. Uncontrollable shuddering spasms sweep through my body. Sleepless hours pass. Cramped muscles and the unforgiving ground drive me to my feet several times. I look pleadingly up at the full moon, but the cold, platinum light offers no solace. Sometime in the early morning hours, I steal a few snatches of troubled sleep. When the new day finally dawns, it's a dirty, weary, but very grateful face that stares eastward through bloodshot eyes. The first twenty-four hours of the vision quest have felt like a year.

Time to dance up the sun. The now-familiar shuffle comes easily as I stretch stiff muscles. What a glorious moment when the golden warmth finally penetrates my blanket and ends the agony of shivering. Within an hour, however, this blessing becomes a curse. Gentle warmth again grows to scalding heat until the harsh rays pin me to the mountaintop like a butterfly in a collector's case. Seeking solace, I consider the ancient questers who proceeded me, perhaps on this very spot. They often denied themselves a blanket and sometimes even water. Will I receive the full intensity of the experience when protected, however meagerly, from the elements? The sun bores into my head and shoulders with renewed fury.

The sizzling heat finally abates when strong gusts of wind buffet the mountaintop in late afternoon. Savoring this respite, I noticed that I am experiencing none of the expected foggy-headedness; indeed, I have an exceptional clarity of mind. My fast is becoming easier as well. I feel empty, yet not really hungry.

This vacation from discomfort slips away as the cooling winds turn biting cold. I drum down the sun from within a tiny "tent" of blankets and allow the moon to rise without my help. My second night passes like the first: shivering, stillness, more shivering. Islands of sleep in a sea of discomfort.

The wind howls fiercely all night and the third day. Great zephyrs roar down from the peaks, blast my mountaintop, and then sweep down to swirl into dust devils in the desert. The endless white noise swallows me; concentration or relaxation almost impossible amidst such chaotic energy. My placid surroundings seem to come alive.

For most of the day, I huddle in the windbreak of the low wall, barely finding enough energy to sit up. I stare at the tall ponderosa pines swimming through the storm. The highest trees lack windward branches and many of the crowns are missing entirely. These pines must have grown up in the face of the punishing wind and yet they survive, even thrive. Another lesson forms in my mind. The resilient trees teach me that my situation, good or bad, is not as important as how I deal with it. Here, dancing to the rhythm of the tempest, are fine examples of adaptability, flexibility, and courage. My teachers are appearing most unexpectedly.

As the sun sets, I pray for the wind to cease. The arrival of another nightfall no longer terrifies me, but I dread the hours of misery that lay ahead. Reluctantly, I crouch into my "survival ball" -- my arms hugging my knees that were crunched up under my chin -- in an attempt to conserve whatever feeble body heat I produce. Dreams are instantaneous whenever sleep overtakes me, yet I remember only fragments: the presence of someone in the circle with me, images of an earlier age where I am surrounded by beaded buckskin objects. Very unusual, like undecipherable pieces of an ancient vision thrown at me. This dreamscape is repeatedly shattered when violent shivering shakes me awake.

During the night, the wind finally subsides. My relief, however, is short-lived when, to my horror, I feel a gentle pitter-patter upon my outer blanket. Panic shocks me fully awake as I realize I might not survive getting soaked in my hypothermic and enfeebled condition. Deep fear grips me for the first time since entering the circle.

The gentle tap of precipitation continues as a gray dawn breaks. Keeping my head wrapped under the blankets, I await the inevitable and deadly touch of water reaching my skin. It never comes. Confused, I poke my head free of its shroud and discover I'm slowly being blanketed by snow-like pellets of sleet. Ironically, I burst out laughing. Here I am: naked, starving, freezing, and balled up under two thin blankets in a hailstorm. And who's responsible for this torture? ME! At least I am staying dry since the sleet bounces off my covers. I smother myself back under the blankets.

Hours crawl by and my thoughts drift towards calling it quits. What more can I accomplish lying here enveloped too cold and miserable to think straight? Just go back to the base camp, build a fire, eat some ....

"Nooooo", I roar, rising suddenly from my sodden nest. I remember the lessons of the beetle and the trees. No longer shall I cower under the blankets and wallow in self-pity. The sun must hear my frantic cry as the clouds break up and rays of life-giving warmth begin to thaw my body and my attitude. I renew my sacred vow to remain in the stone circle -- come hell or high water -- and wonder to what further punishments I am sentencing myself.

I've made it to the final day and feel as much animal as human. My hands are black with dirt and a second skin of grime covers me from head to toe. I reek of urine, sweat, and filth while my breath would wilt flowers. Feeling helpless as a newborn, I am content to merely lie in the sun and listen passively to the sounds that float up to my mountaintop from below: distant traffic, the rumble of a nearby gravel pit, the rustle of dried needles. I don't analyze or contemplate; I drift.

My teacher during this hazy final day is one of the most easily overlooked, yet most important members of the natural community. Surrounding me on my ring of rocks is a great profusion of lichens, those crusty growths which are a synthesis of algae and fungus. Resting my cheek against the stones, I spend hours focusing on these remarkable beings. Lichens play the crucial role as the first colonizers of the harshest environments, dissolving stone into soil. They are the very foundation for the glorious succession of life that follows them. Here are the true champions of endurance. They live on bare rock in both direct sunlight and deep shade. From a noselength away, I'm struck by their variety and beauty -- from gaudy pea greens capped with black and gold to inconspicuous gray dots which seemed at first to be part of the rock. What tough, yet unassuming beings, quietly changing their world to make it better for others. Unexpectedly, I've found another role model.

As the final day winds down, my favorite afternoon light is stolen by ashen clouds that begin dusting me with snowflakes. Back to my prison of blankets on the floor of the circle. Although weak and numb, I mentally begin preparations for the last and greatest challenge of the vision quest -- the final night's vigil. In both the ancient and modern traditions of the vision quest, the seeker spends the final night awake and vigilant. Over the previous three and a half days, the quester has broken down barriers of separation from the natural world and peeled existence to its precious core. Ideally, by the final night, the seeker has become so emotionally open, mentally cleansed, and physically exhausted that the hard-sought vision is received. Will I slip into a visionary trance? I vow to remain vigilant through the night, ready for whatever awaits me.

My anticipation grows with the shadows. Somehow, the entire Southwest Circle Quest seems dependent on the night's outcome. If I can see this night through, I'll be able to handle all the obstacles of my long summer's journey. If I can't uphold my vigil, my trek will also end in failure. Listening to the dusk calls of the forest birds, I pray for no wind as the most important night of my life begins.

I sit upright in the center of the circle. The snow stops, but ominous thunder rumbles atop the San Francisco Peaks. As the nervous tapping of my feet keeps the shivering at bay, my thoughts turn to all those people who supported my decision to undertake this Southwest Circle Quest. Family and friends around the country have given me encouragement with their loving words and actions. I decide to dedicate the night's vigil to them. Slowly and carefully, I thank each person aloud as if he or she is standing before me. I hug my thighs as I would the individuals. In offering my thanks, I do not forget Earth, Sky, Sun, Moon, or the mountain plus those who had chosen this path before me. Gratitude flows like tears. My soul is at peace.

Eager to escape the thick darkness and sharp chill, I decide to dance up the moon. Under my breath, I chant my "positive mental attitude" mantra to the easy shuffle of my bare feet while my eyes yearn eastward. Finally, a speck of apricot light appears above the clouds. The moon pulls free of the Painted Desert as I stomp with renewed vigor, then collapse back to the circle's center.

My second round of sitting is much more difficult. The lust for sleep is such a seductive desire. Spoken prayers and thoughts become gibberish. The metronome of my tapping feet barely keeps me warm and awake. The moon, my sole means of marking progress through this eternal night, slips back behind clouds. The battle has begun.

I fall over onto my side. Immediately, two internal voices begin arguing. My conscience screams, "No excuses! You did this on purpose. This is no trance. Get up or you will fail!" The rest of me just sighs with the relief of being horizontal. My will to continue begins to succumb to the lure of surrender.

Neither sleep nor a vision appears. Instead, my mind clears and my conscience calls more loudly. The cold becomes my ally, its icy bite forcing me to move. Up I sit, ashamed, yet with a renewed determination. When the siren of sleep again sings softly in my ear minutes later, I rise unsteadily to my feet. Snowflakes begin drifting past my shrouded face as I start to dance. My breath moves in and out to the shuffle of my feet. My mind tries to doze, but a rip of adrenaline shakes me awake as I begin to topple. For several brutal hours this cycle repeats itself until I crumble once more to the ground.

Again, an internal battle rages. Again, reality remains intact. With the cold snapping at my exposed flesh, I drag myself reluctantly to my feet, burning with disappointment and angry resolve. In the silvery half-light, the large boulder that forms one side of my circle looks like a massive laughing face mocking my feeble efforts. I remember the three days I've endured to reach this night. I recall all those who believe in me and ponder the lessons of Beetle and Ponderosa and Lichen. My determination reaches new heights. Around and around I shuffle, glaring resolutely at the cruel face of stone.

A cold mist envelops the mountaintop. Without a clear horizon, the brightening of the false dawn will have to signal the end of my ordeal. The battle to stay upright intensifies. I consider the sacred songs of seekers in ancient times. Lacking these, I face east and begin to hum whatever folk songs pop into my brain. Perhaps these aren't as appropriate as prayer chants, but I need a plan.

The eastern sky finally appears to brighten. I sing louder. The brightening intensifies. Suddenly, I hear the sweetest song of all -- the dawn singing of the forest birds. As the endless night peacefully dies, my heart rejoices. I've made it! Relief gives way to exhaustion. Trying to step outside my stony womb/tomb, my painful knees finally buckle. Lying helpless in two inches of snow, I laugh uneasily, realizing I could freeze to death at my moment of triumph. The protective energy I've miraculously found to keep moving is nearly gone and I'm racing hypothermia and a total collapse. I clamber into my chilled clothes, stick my numb feet into unlaced boots, and stumble towards base camp. My vision quest is over. An even greater adventure lies ahead.

Day 8, Five miles

Only a day and a half have passed since I stepped forth from my vision quest circle, yet the memory of dancing naked through a snowy night seems like a dream. How quickly I have returned to dependency on my base camp equipment. For better or worse, my world has resumed its normal rhythm.

After escaping the ring of rocks, I stagger back to my base camp to find my tent collapsed and my foam sleeping pad missing. The snow is falling heavily. Working with an efficiency that my survival demands, I reset the tent, recover the nearby pad, and dive into my warm, dry sleeping bag. Ahhh -- it is a glorious moment of simple comfort. Soon, however, my adrenaline rush wears off and I shiver uncontrollably even while wrapped in my bag wearing most of my clothes. Only then do I realize how close I've come to the edge. When the shivering subsides, I break my four-day fast with an apple and some trail mix and spend the remainder of my recovery day dozing, writing, and eating.

Late in the afternoon, I rouse myself and return to the stone circle. Standing outside the ring of rocks, I try to imagine myself huddled here, but the picture is already fuzzy and remote. Although all the lessons I have learned may take years to unravel and I feel more grizzled than enlightened, my vision quest has been a success. I know I'm ready to face the difficulties and unknowns on the trail ahead. Back in the sleeping bag that I shall never again take for granted, a whispered thanks for life itself is all I manage before plummeting into a blissfully solid sleep.

I awaken to a sunny, warm, and snowless morning. Below, the earthtone corduroy of the Painted Desert beckons, but one task remains before setting sail from this mountaintop sanctuary. I fish out a packet of letters from the bottom of my pack. These are the responses from family and friends to my formal announcement of my Southwest Circle Quest months ago. I carefully read each letter one final time, and after such an intensely solitary experience, the warm words soothe me like a loving embrace. I also peruse my journal of inspiring quotes and thoughts gathered last winter, but the words fail to satisfy me now. Seeking my own knowing over another's knowledge, I realize my truth must come from within. To this end, I stow both letters and journal in a protected cache to be left behind on the mountain. I have decided to carry no reading material and receive no letters during my quest. The natural world and experience shall be my teachers.

My base camp is broken down and everything is stuffed in my backpack. The moment of departure is upon me. Above me is the cold, moist, alpine world of the tundra; below stretches the hot, dry expanse of the desert. Among the trees,

SOUTHWEST CIRCLE QUEST

I stand poised between the two rugged environments which will be my home for the summer and make four vows:

*I vow to live to my highest ideals and follow the voice of my spirit.
*I vow to maintain a state of mindfulness to ensure my safety and enrich my experience.
*I vow to be open to any lessons from the natural world and any people I shall encounter.
*I vow to complete my Southwest Circle Quest and return safely to this mountaintop.

As a constant reminder of my vows, I tie a woven Central American friendship bracelet around my wrist and promise myself not to remove it until my quest is complete. The immortal words of Lao Tze ring in my head: "A journey of a thousand miles begins with one step." Swallowing hard, I take that step.

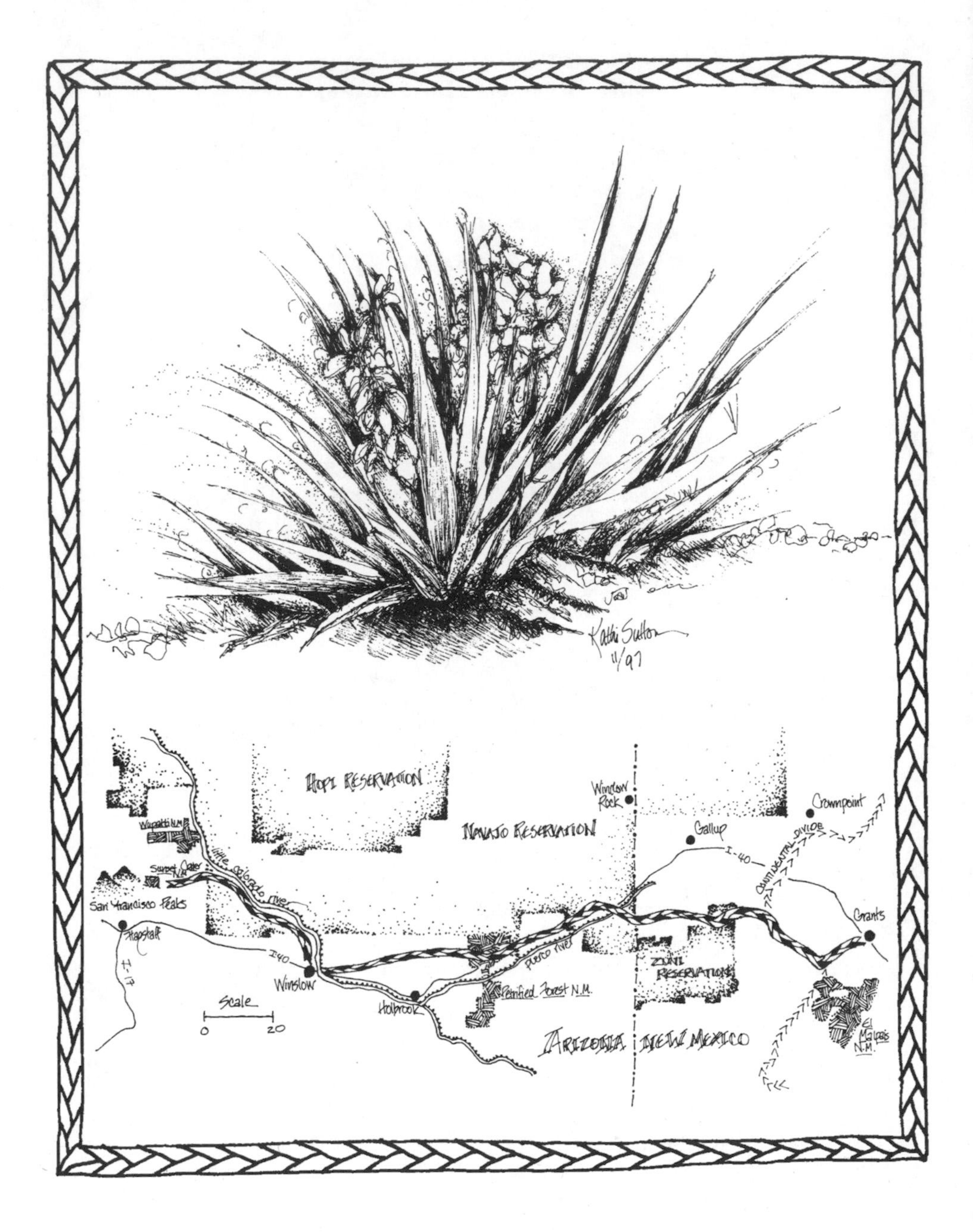
Kathi Sutton
11/97
Hopi Reservation
Navajo Reservation
Window Rock
Crownpoint
Gallup
Wupatki N.M.
Sunset Crater N.M.
little colorado river
I-40
Continental Divide
San Francisco Peaks
Flagstaff
I-17
Winslow
puerco river
Zuni Reservation
Grants
Petrified Forest N.M.
Holbrook
Scale
0
20
Arizona
New Mexico
El Malpais N.M.

EAST
Cowboys and Indians

Go my sons, burn your books,
Buy yourself stout shoes,
Get away to the mountains, the deserts,
And the deepest recesses of the Earth.
In this way and no other will you gain
A true knowledge
Of things and their properties.

Seter Severinus (1571 A.D.)

Day 9, Twelve miles

I dropped off my mountaintop sanctuary yesterday afternoon. After pausing at a small pond in Lockett Meadow to wash off the grime of my ordeal, I work my way around to the eastern side of Sugarloaf Mountain where a gravel operation literally eats away my vision quest hill. I have consecrated this place and the ragged scar is heart-wrenching, like a wound in my own flesh. How many Native Americans have similarly watched helplessly as their ancient holy grounds have been desecrated by pollution and development? Saddened, I hurry on.

Away from the raw sore of the pit, I enter a beautiful, open woodland and follow my compass east. The sun sparkles, the pines are perfume, and now, my spirit soars. After days of sitting, movement feels magically healing. My stride stretches out and I dance down the Yellow Brick Road -- alive, free, healthy, and doing exactly what I want to do!

After a couple hours of easy prancing, I hop a fence and enter Sunset Crater National Monument. The first people I encounter after an intense week of solitude are flabby seniors climbing out of lumbering "recreation" vehicles onto paved campsites. Whoa -- culture shock! I'm still decompressing from my vision quest and small talk with these strangers will only shatter my reverie. I linger just long enough to fill my water bottles at the tap, then camp alone deeper in the forest.

My first full day of walking begins with a stroll through a gorgeous woodland of massive ponderosa pines set amidst more than four hundred symmetrical cinder cones which sprout out of the forest like giant anthills. A blanket of pea-sized black cinders inhibits any undergrowth and each massive pine sports a delicate skirt of buckskin needles. Barren lakes of jagged, petrified lava are the only obstacles to be avoided.

Lunch finds me at a small pass, resting against a ponderosa. Inadvertently, my butt blocks a busy thoroughfare of tiny black ants who quickly decide to investigate the obstacle in their path. All I want is a quick doze in the sun, but a few bites, and I'm in full retreat. Ten of these minuscule tormentors would barely cover my thumbnail, yet they succeed in making me move. My glare softens to a smile as I realize my latest teachers have just found me. Take heart all ye who struggle against the huge obstructions and injustices; I have found you a champion! Your strategy: know where to bite and bring a few friends to help!

After lunch, I crunch, crunch, crunch downhill. Tall ponderosa give way to short piñon and juniper as I leave the national monument and cross onto private land. Ahead, the terrain begins to flatten and the trees thin as I approach the open desert and grasslands of the vast Navajo Indian Reservation stretching to New Mexico. Looking back over my shoulder, the rolling, forested hills and mountains appear so comfortable and familiar. Never before have my backcountry travels taken me onto the plains. Will I find water? Can I navigate? With a curious mixture of eagerness and trepidation, I sally forth onto the prairie.

A dirt track leads me past an unexpected handful of small modern homes. Who lives out here, beyond the reach of electric lines where wells are impossible and the world is so quiet? Hot, tired and still sore from my recent mountaintop "dance marathon," I camp early under the fragrant arms of a juniper. Free of the pack, I'm drawn to explore a house-sized outcrop of lava nearby.

Poking around its base, I casually kick a flat white stone out of the sand and am surprised to find it decorated with a geometric pattern. A pot shard; probably Anasazi, the mysterious people who inhabited much of the Colorado Plateau a thousand years ago. With my eye suddenly trained on flat shapes among the cinders, I quickly gather a big handful of shards -- red, gray, cream, some with delicate black lines, one that fills my palm. I've discovered the occasional Anasazi pot shard near ruins before, but never so many on the surface in the middle of nowhere. The temptation is strong to pocket a piece, but I replace them all. The magic is in the finding, not the keeping. To hold a fragment of Anasazi pottery while alone and miles from civilization is to ponder its maker and his or her life on these desert plains a millennium ago. Bring the shard home to place on the coffee table and it becomes just a piece of dried clay.

Climbing atop the outcrop, I find an ancient wall of volcanic rock encircling the summit. Guess I'm not in the middle of nowhere after all. The Anasazi must have shared my attraction to this promontory. I crouch down, the wall acting as a windbreak as it did for its builders. In the sweet glow of the late afternoon sun, the countryside looks alive. Behind me rise the snow-capped mountains while the Painted Desert ahead is a rainbow of earthtones that goes on forever. What motivated the Ancient Ones (as the Navajo refer to the Anasazi) to sit up here? A collection of crumbling Anasazi pueblos form Wupatki National Monument a dozen miles to the west of here. Was this an outpost to scan for approaching enemies? A lone pronghorn passes close by below, oblivious to my presence. Was this a hunting blind? I spot a modern home not far off. What would my life be like had I grown up with these distant arid horizons and tremendous skyscapes so different from my native New England woods?

The land purrs gently as the wind strokes the bunchgrass. Birds begin their eloquent sunset songs. My earlier foreboding of entering the grasslands vanishes. Atop my volcanic castle, I glimpse the soul of this powerful landscape alive with ancient energy. What better way to experience this new environment than at the speed of the Anasazi -- by foot. I feel welcomed.

Day 10, Nine miles

What an extraordinary day!

I arise with the sun and return to the lava castle to greet the dawn. The cool air is a cacophony of bird song. With my eyes closed, I imagine I'm surrounded by jungle. Like the evening before, I feel completely centered and at peace in this landscape. Perhaps the true function of the lookout is a temple from which to worship the miracle of dawn and dusk.

Returning to camp, I scout a low water tank maintained for cattle -- dry. Guess I'll have to beg some water from the nearby house. Setting off an hour later, I head through the junipers toward the residence and the morning's harmony is shattered by violent shouting. A door slams and tires screech on gravel as a car peels away. The sound of a woman screaming at her kids chases me as I detour around the house back to the dirt track. Hmmm -- I'd rather go thirsty than get tangled in that scene. I'd wager it's been too long since that family has quietly watched the sunrise together from their exceptional backyard. How easy it is to overlook the gifts at our feet.

As I head east toward the Little Colorado River, the junipers finally give way to low clumps of straw-colored bunchgrass in rust brown gravel. I beeline from one low mound to the next, scouting the prairie ahead. Only the occasional scurry of a startled lizard breaks the still, already-hot morning. Unexpectedly, a shack appears near the base of an outcrop. The windows are shattered and furniture lies strewn everywhere, but the basic structure is still solid. After poking through the three room interior, I realize that this is no seasonal cowboy camp, but an abandoned family home. *Newsweek* and *People* magazines from the 1970s cover the plywood floor. A rodent-chewed mattress rests in a small loft. Dusty plates remain stacked in a cupboard. Discarded toys litter one corner and a plastic Big Wheel is parked outside. Another ruin to intrigue me. Who lived here? Why did they pick this isolated spot and how long did they stay? What made them leave? Did they appreciate the subtle beauty here or regard this tough land as an enemy? I walk on, the questions unanswered.

A mile farther I reach the lip of a dramatic bluff. Below stretches a lower desert plain to horizons seventy miles distant. One tiny silver roof gleams in the vastness. With half a quart of water left and at least five miles of hot, shadeless walking to reach the Little Colorado, I wish I hadn't passed up water so hastily. My map reveals that a spring is supposed to be tucked nearby at the base of the bluff. I squint into the glare. Water out there seems an impossibility. Wait, some kind of rusted machinery sags about a half mile away off to the north. Do I use precious energy to check out the tank -- which is probably dry -- or head straight to the river on only two cups of water? The desert sighs, awaiting my decision. I veer left and follow an old cow path toward the tank.

The "spring" is a cesspool of stinking orange liquid ringed with cowshit. A pump and two adjacent tanks are long dead and bone-dry. A second stock pond is pure mud. Yummm! I fill a waterbottle with the murky fluid and attempt to run it through my high-tech filter designed to purify any water. After only two cups of the brew, my filter clogs and the water I do get reeks of cow piss. So much for Plan A! Heading again toward the river, I decide to check on the building which is now en route.

Approaching the cabin on a rutted dirt track, I see no car, yet the place doesn't look abandoned. "Hello?" No answer. The solid door opens easily. At first glance, I figure that the owner must have just stepped out since the interior is so tidy. The single room is furnished with a made-up bed, a wood stove, a refrigerator, a chest of drawers, and a wooden table with chairs. Plastic dishes fill a drying rack set above a sink that drains outside the kitchen window. Then I spy the dozens of plastic milk jugs filled with clear water. Eureka, I'm saved!

Examining the cabin's interior more closely, I realize that nobody's been here for a while. The most recent newspaper dates to last January and a scattering of mouse turds lies near the idle fridge. Surely the door of this cowboy camp has been left unlocked with water inside as a form of frontier hospitality. At least that's how I reckon it, standing there with my throat parched and my tongue hanging out. I ease off my pack, savoring the coolness inside the building. Those exposed miles to the Little Colorado can wait.

As the sun expends its fierce mid-day energy, I relax and ponder the life of my absent host. Unlike the two earlier ruins, this home offers more clues. The homey character of the spread indicates a rustic, yet mannerly existence. Curtains decorate the windows. A framed picture of The Last Supper hangs over the bed. A small medicine cabinet holds shaving cream, Listerine, castor oil, and hair tonic. Nailed to the kitchen counter is a knife rack crafted from a tooled leather belt. A ratty cowboy hat, blue jeans, and a woman's nightie hang on a hook. Outside, a Tonka truck sits abandoned between a weathered dog house and a picnic table.

I like this place -- a sweet, simple homestead. The only clue to the identity of the owner is a custom cowboy boot order from Texas addressed to Barge T. Marcum of Flagstaff. The envelope reveals that I'm not the only visitor taken with this spread. Written on the outside is "Mr Marcum, would you like to rent this place out when you're not using it. Please leave message." Below is a phone number. Before I evict myself from "the Marcum Ranch", I pay for the water I take with a gift of oatmeal and ramen noodles tucked alongside the canned goods in the cupboard.

Another cow trail leads toward the river past Roden Crater, the last of the reddish cinder cones exiled from its peers out here on the plains. At the rickety barbed wire fence that marks the beginning of the Navajo Reservation, I startle a huge bird from the bushes. The golden eagle spreads his tremendous wings and leaps into the air only to crash clumsily into the fence. Scrambling between the wires, the embarrassed raptor hops away, turning to survey me from a safe distance. I see no visible injury and wonder at the significance of meeting this majestic, yet grounded eagle. The collie-sized bird just stares with burning yellow eyes and holds his ground as I ease over the fence and enter the land of the Navajo.

Months earlier, I had written a detailed letter to the Office of Recreation at the Navajo Tribal Headquarters in Window Rock, Arizona, carefully explaining my route and the purpose of my Southwest Circle Quest and asking permission for safe passage. Just before my departure, I received a useless, impersonal packet of tourist information. I decided to forge ahead with my plans without an official permit. While I'm hoping to learn from a culture which maintains close bonds to the natural world, I don't know how an "Anglo" on foot will be received. Nearing the Little Colorado, I stumble upon a flock of sheep and goats grazing among boulders of lava. Dogs charge, then retreat to a modern Navajo home I spot too late just over a ridge. Thus I enter the Navajo Nation in exactly the manner I'd hoped to avoid -- barging unannounced into someone's backyard. Thankfully, nobody appears at the door as I quickly detour widely, my gut knotted. Have I made a foolish mistake in coming here?

A few miles farther, I reach the Little Colorado at a point called The Grand Falls where an ancient tongue of lava once spilled across the river's channel, forcing the water to forge a new path over a sandstone cliff. The falls are several hundred feet across and drop one hundred and thirty feet in massive tiers. But the Little Colorado is a seasonal river, running steadily only during spring runoff and autumn rains with sporadic summer flashfloods scouring the channel. I walk to the lip in anticipation, but the falls are dry. A Navajo man and two boys are fishing in the quiet pools at the base of the cliffs.

I descend a sheep trail to the base of the falls and begin pumping water. Soft footsteps approach across the sandstone and I look up into the face of the Navajo man. His dark eyes are glued to mine, but hold no animosity. With an even tone, he asks, "Where are you coming from?"

"Flagstaff."

The man's eyebrows lift ever so slightly. When I explain that I am on a vision quest to figure out what to do with my life, the forty-year old Indian chuckles, "You look pretty young for that kind of thing!"

We both laugh. My companion sits down and says that he grew up near Grand Falls. Although now a school supervisor in Flagstaff, he returns here on his days off to visit his grandmother and to "get re-centered." The Navajo man gestures toward the rim of the falls and says, "More and more tourists are driving out here these days. When I was young, we never saw any Anglos. Last summer, a bunch of college kids were goofing off near the bottom of the falls and were almost killed when a flash flood came through."

Something in this man's quiet attentive manner allows me to speak freely and soon I'm describing my quest and the motivations behind it. He listens, nods. Sweeping his hand around to indicate the vast desert surrounding us, he says, "The tourists see only a wasteland as they drive through the Reservation. They wonder why we Navajo would want to live in such a place. But this land makes us feel right. I lived in San Francisco for a couple of years, but that place messed up my head. My uncle had to perform a Blessing Way ceremony when I returned so I could get back to normal." .

Now it's my turn to nod in understanding. "I'm also off-balance in the city. Only in the wilderness do I feel centered," I explain.

The two boys bound up to us, but their excitement fades to quiet shyness when they notice the stranger with their father. The man watches his sons race off again and says, "When I was their age, I helped tend my grandmother's two hundred and fifty sheep. We lived in seasonal sheep camps and ate only corn and mutton for weeks. My uncles would wake me up at dawn and make me run across the desert, racing the rising sun. They taught me if I failed, I'd grow up to be a lazy man." He pauses, then looks at me and smiles. "Now the kids think only of TV and microwave ovens."

I ask about the river upstream, my anticipated route between here and Winslow.

"The river stopped flowing only last week so there'll be pools left in the riverbed. I think you should be OK for water. But, you may run into older, traditional Navajo who will not understand why you are on the Reservation. They may call the authorities."

The sinking feeling returns to my belly. Those elders are the very people that I, perhaps naively, am hoping to meet.

The sun is setting and we both realize that we're late for supper. In parting, I ask my new friend the Navajo words for water ("to") and thank you ("a-he-hee") as we stand and shake hands. The Navajo wishes me luck on my long journey and success in my search for answers.

"Thanks. You certainly seem to have balanced the old ways with the new rather well," I exclaim.

The Indian smiles softly and calls to his boys. As he walks away, I realize that this has been my first meaningful conversation with another person in almost two weeks.

Day 11, Fifteen miles

In the morning, I start following the bed of the Little Colorado River upstream. To my delight, the riverbed provides easy walking: a fifty-foot wide carpet of level sand -- sometimes damp, sometimes dry, always firm. Thick stands of tamarisk and the occasional cottonwood tree line the channel with a cool curtain of green. Shallow pools of clear water lie on gouges in the sand on the outside edge of meanders. Perfect timing. Two weeks earlier, I may have ended up like the dead steer still stuck to his belly in what must have been quicksand not long ago. Two weeks from now and this lifeline of ephemeral pools may be gone.

Pleasant miles pass. Cow, bird, and lizard tracks crisscross the sand while I follow a neat line of coyote prints heading upriver. Pumpkin-colored sandstone walls begin to rise on either side until I'm walking down the middle of a one hundred-foot deep canyon. However, when the riverbed begins a series of tortuous meanders, I climb out of the canyon to cut off these detours with a beeline across the desert. This midday stretch in the open proves scorching. The walking itself is easy, following a compass bearing over flat plates of ochre sandstone. Yet the sun feels perched upon my pack as I move like a stubborn ant across a vast, empty frying pan.

Three riders, shimmering in the heat like mirages, appear half a mile ahead. They stop. I stop. I really don't want to be escorted off the Reservation. The riders continue, angling to my left. Sighing in relief, I trudge onward towards the dark band of river vegetation. Shady relief seems imminent until I spy a hogan dead ahead and must detour. Now the emerald cottonwoods are irresistible. Is that another structure ahead? I don't care. Shade and water -- now!

The coral and ramada I pass are empty, but so is the nearby creekbed. Hold on -- a small, damp depression in the sand cradles about four precious gallons of stale water. That's the ticket! I slake my thirst, then wash hair, body and socks using my cooking pot as a ladle. The sun is so intense that my soapy body dries before I can rinse it, but when finished, my contentment is complete -- clean for the first time in half a month. I even feel lighter!

I'm just pulling on my shorts when a Navajo cowboy herding a handful of steers crosses the riverbed a quarter mile downstream. Startled, I slip under the trees. The cowboy, showing no sign of having seen me, continues to the ramada where he rests while I remain hidden in the tamarisk. Feeling like an intruder literally caught with my pants down, I have no desire to make contact and sneak off upstream.

Late in the day, I conclude that Raven has appointed himself my personal guardian on this quest. I first suspected something was afoot the day I left Sugarloaf Mountain. I had been intently reading my letters when two of the ebony birds perched overhead and began squawking loudly at me. Getting up to investigate, I saw that a tremendous squall was bearing down on me and I just had time to set up the tent before it struck without warning. Then, this afternoon, I am stepping onto an innocent-looking sandbar when two ravens again scream at me. I poke my walking stick ahead of me and it sinks to knee depth in the disguised patch of quicksand. I grin up at the glossy black birds. Mission accomplished, they silently take to the wing.

I'm now camped in a jungle of tamarisk. Cows appear and vanish in this tangle, engaged in a bovine version of hide and seek, but I'm too tired to play. My attention is focused on the heaping pot of pasta that simmers noisily at my feet.

What a pleasant sound at the end of a strenuous day!

Day 12, Fifteen miles

Dawn. Already packed and moving down the riverbed as the first rays of light slant in from the east to kiss the ground. Savoring the cool air, I pull dried apricots from my pocket, sucking on them as I walk. Concrete abruptly spans the dry river ahead as I approach the bridge connecting the Reservation hamlets of Leupp and Sunrise, garbage underfoot increasing with every step. Resting beneath the artificial arch, I munch a Sierra cup of granola amidst a sea of broken glass. None of the famed Native American reverence for the land evident here.

Beyond the bridge, the riverbed turns nasty. Silty mud replaces firm sand. I skate unsteadily across puddles of brick-red goo that slops all over my boots. Next, the channel disappears into a tangled jungle of thorny brush. Enough of this! Crashing through the Russian olive trees, I escape the riverbed and start paralleling the channel on the open desert. Nothing improves. The cracked mudpan is spiked with overgrazed bunchgrass that tears mercilessly at my shins. Any hint of wind disappears as the noonday Arizona sun slides to the "Broil" setting. The only movement is the shimmer of the horizon and the plod of my feet switched to automatic. I become Burke and Wells crossing the interior of Australia; Burton and Spekes trudging across Africa in search of the source of the Nile. My mantra become "water, shade, lunch" as I trudge relentlessly toward a distant line of cottonwoods.

This flat, featureless country does nothing for me. The cowshit and garbage baking under a relentless sun holds no hint of the sacred like the junipers and cinders near Sunset Crater. My earlier welcome seems withdrawn. Avoiding all human contact, I've become a fugitive on the run, lost without a passport in a third-world country called the Navajo Reservation. So much for my "intercultural exchange"! And what's going to happen when I leave this paltry river system beyond Winslow?

Maybe I'm just tired and dehydrated. Crossing the Arizona desert in June isn't supposed to be easy. What would a quest be without a little hardship? As Nietzche said, "That which does not destroy me makes me STRONGER!"

Day 13, Twelve miles

A few feet away, the June sun roars and the desert silently screams back. Ironically, I am comfortable, lying tucked in the deep shade in a low, wide crevice of rock just beyond the southern boundary of "The Rez." Stray breezes find me, but the flies do not. Almost done with the first leg of my journey.

Yesterday afternoon, my misery was still blooming. After lunch I continue across the desert next to the strip of impenetrable riparian jungle. An occasional log hogan or low house squats in the distance, but I see nobody. A worn-out Chevy wagon appears ahead. Getting closer, I find that the vehicle is parked on a dirt track which crosses the river channel here. As I turn to follow the road in search of water, a ragged screech from below the riverbank stops me cold. At the same instant, I spot muddy water and the top of black-haired heads. Someone is swimming or bathing here and I'm about to stumble right into the middle of it. Another feminine scream, unintelligible yet severely frightened, shatters the afternoon. Without looking back, I walk/run away as swiftly as possible, my heart thundering in my throat. DAMN! I've come here to learn and appreciate and instead, I intrude and disrupt!

The cicadas echo my frustration with shrieks that shred the afternoon with shrill white noise. I somehow bypass a well indicated on my map. The riverbed is equally barren; a sheet of loose, dry sand devoid of the earlier pools. Down to a quart of warm water and thirsty.

Frustration becomes desperation as dry miles pass. The few depressions I find are slimy mudholes. Finally, at the bottom of an exceptionally deep pocket stands a tiny puddle of lime-green water alive with tadpoles, wasps, and a garter snake. The liquid is too thick with algae to be filtered, so I dig a depression in the mud a few inches away hoping to create a natural strainer. The hole keeps collapsing into thick soup, but I'm patient. Slowly, a lens of murky water forms. Using my Sierra cup with utmost care, I manage to scoop out a filterable quart a few tablespoons at a time. Whew, that was close!

At dusk, I drop my pack into the river of sand and crunch down a dry ramen noodle packet for supper to conserve my shrinking reserve of fluid. As the stars begin to blink on, I slip into a restless sleep, convinced that death by dehydration is probably the result of mental stress over not finding water.

When the stars are blinking off, I'm already moving; using the cool, predawn hours to locate more water. Two dishearteningly dry riverbed miles pass. Then tracks start to appear headed upstream. Damp patches of sand begin to spot the channel. Finally -- a ten foot pool of skanky water. Sure, it has cowshit in it, but at this point, who's fussy? With the solemn thanks of a saved soul, I pump my bottles full.

More sinuous miles lead to another road crossing. A Navajo family drives by in a dusty pickup, tossing hard stares in my direction. The map claims I can follow this track into Winslow where my first cache awaits. With little hesitation, I abandon the river channel and hoof down the road, eager to put the Reservation behind me. I'm ready for the change of pace of a town stop, but yesterday's close call has left me shaken. How will I find water after Winslow when I leave the river channel and strike off cross country?

Day 14, Three miles

The song goes *"Standin on the corner in Winslow, Arizona......"* Well, here I sit. *"Such a fine sight to see...."* Not exactly.

I've entered Winslow to retrieve the first of the twelve supply cache boxes that I hand-delivered to towns and outposts along my route last spring. A typical box contains about fifteen pounds of dried food such as granola, oatmeal, rice, pasta, and trail mix plus film, new maps, and stove fuel. In Winslow, I stashed my box with the folks at the Visitor Center located right off Interstate 40.

I re-enter "civilization" early this morning. The enthusiasm I felt yesterday for a town stop is fading fast as I'm sucked into a swirl of urban colors, sounds, and smells. Exhaust fumes pour down from the stream of vehicles roaring by on the I-40 overpass. A truckstop sign flashes the price of diesel and donuts. I squint at the gleam of chrome and plastic already shimmering in the heat and hurry towards the Visitor Center suddenly eager to get my goods and beat a hasty retreat. After two weeks alone in the wilderness, this blur of "modern life" is too much.

The Visitor Center is closed. Maybe I'm a little early? The sign on the door reads, "Open Monday-Friday, 8-5. Closed Sunday." It's Saturday (I think), so what's the deal? I'd been told that this place stayed open all weekend. Tourists pull up, try the door, puzzle over the sign, drive on as the realization that I may be stuck here for two days condenses in my mind like an ugly, dark cloud. I call the Winslow Police Department and explain my fix. The dispatcher rings the Visitor Center's manager at home -- no answer. "Sorry, try again later," the woman intones. Damn.

I mosey over to the nearby Safeway to pick up fresh food to supplement the stuff in my cache. The supermarket is another jolt to my system; mountains of goodies perused by Navajo and tourists in air conditioned comfort. Munching a heaping salad from the salad bar at a picnic table outside, I finally resign myself to this delay. After all, one goal of this quest is to make the most of what life tosses at me. Time to find out what this Arizona town can teach me.

Winslow is a place where America pauses for gas and a cold drink, then zooms onward to brighter horizons. Once, a thousand years ago, a Hopi pueblo thrived here for generations. The Mormons arrived about a hundred and fifty years ago, building a fort believing that they could tame the erratic Little Colorado River. They didn't last ten years. Eventually the lonely town was reestablished and slowly grew until it peaked in the 1950s as postwar tourists discovered the stunning and sunny Southwest made accessible by Route 66. The Santa Fe Railroad was booming and early commercial airline flights between Chicago and Los Angeles used Winslow as a layover. For a while, a piece of The American Dream shone brightly on the desert plains.

Everything changed when Interstate 40 barreled through in the early 1970s, nicking the north edge of town. Hotels were replaced by truckstops; family restaurants gave way to hamburger joints. The high-speed highway brought with it a new culture -- rootless and road-stoned Interstate America. Down the frenzied four lanes drained the lifeblood and uniqueness of an Arizona town, now just another "Fill'er up" point between Albuquerque and Los Angeles.

I wander through neighborhoods of rundown bungalows to a hot and tired

Main Street. I'm looking for a park, but the only shade is under the old cottonwoods of the Community Medical Center. Already parked under the trees are a couple dozen broken-down Navajo. The ragged men and women gather in small groups, sleeping on bundles or jostling for the bottles making the rounds. They talk and laugh a little in a drunken slur of English and Navajo, but mostly just stare blankly out at the world. I keep moving.

My mind slides into a jumble of confusion, disappointment, and sadness. This first leg through the Reservation has been disillusioning. My plan had been to meet Navajo people in their homeland and learn their point of view directly, not through another book or museum. Yet, on the Reservation, I am an invader continuing an Anglo tradition of intrusion that is five hundred years old. In town, I see dignified Navajo grandmothers bedecked in huge turquoise bracelets and long velour skirts towing gaggles of beautiful, big-eyed children, but these old women wear impassive and undecipherable "town" faces. Their daughters have perms and work as check-out girls, swallowed into mainstream America. The worst are those wasting away in an alcoholic haze; outcasts from both their native traditions and the Anglo world where they've landed. How naive I've been to believe I could tap into the Navajo tradition during my brief passage.

My own culture here is an equal disappointment. Winslow seems a ghost of a town kept alive only by the intravenous feeding of the Interstate. One day among people and I already long for the song of the mockingbird and the prospect of untainted horizons. Yet even the natural world, my ultimate refuge, offers little solace in these parts.

After hours of wandering aimlessly around town engulfed in a blue funk, I stop at the downtown police station and finally receive some good news: the Visitor Center's secretary has been located and I'll be able to pick up my cache today. Excellent! One day in the urban wilds has proved to be more than enough.

Day 15, Fifteen miles

Noon. Alone again amidst the quiet and heat. Well, not quite alone -- cows and flies huddle with me in the paltry shade of a tamarisk. After a strained day in Winslow, I'm back in familiar, if uncomfortable, surroundings.

By the time I've liberated my cache box yesterday, the sun is gone. I decide to stay put and sleep in the shadows of the Visitor Center plaza despite the headlights and neon that compete with the stars. Seems quiet enough here on the edge of town. Yet no sooner have I settled into my bag when a lone figure appears out of nowhere and walks across the courtyard. He continues around the corner, but I'm sure that I've been spotted. Is this a night watchman, a vagrant hitchhiker, or a homeless Navajo?

Before I can react, the figure returns. I lie still, but alert and tense. The interloper enters the shadows and sits on a bench just a few feet away. I continue to feign sleep, but every nerve is wide awake as I watch for any threatening move toward myself or my pack. The stranger makes none, stretching out prone on the bench instead. An uneasy hour passes. As the night grows chilly, my "neighbor" rises with a groan and stumbles over to a nearby dumpster. He returns to the bench with an armload of discarded newspaper and cardboard and rolls himself up in it. Evidently I've been joined by a homeless person seeking the same quiet shadows as myself.

I lie awake, conflicting thoughts swimming through my head. Here I am, comfortable in my two hundred dollar sleeping bag while a few feet away, another human fidgets to readjust a pitiful bed of cardboard. I know all too clearly how the cold nips relentlessly. Hadn't I been naked and unprotected all night just a week ago? Feelings of compassion and service well up. Didn't I vow to live to my highest ideal? Doesn't service mean lending a hand where needed? I remember the space blanket folded beneath me, yet still I hesitate. Also rising within me is the uneasy yet undeniable prejudice I always feel when encountering the ragged homeless of the cities. What if this guy robs me? Will I get my blanket back? Is my spirit being tested?

My higher self eventually wins. I arise, yank the space blanket free, and stand before the prone figure wedged under the bench and enveloped in debris.

"Here brother, use this blanket to keep warm," I say quietly.

"Hey, thanks man," he replies soberly, pulling the blanket into his pitiful shelter.

"Put the silver side next to your body," I advise, sliding back into my sack. Soon I hear snores and I finally drop off as well.

At first light, I'm noisily preparing an extra large serving of hot oatmeal. My huddled companion is still except for an occasional hacking cough.

"Do you want some hot cereal?" I offer.

The stranger pokes his head from the ragged nest and we look at each other for the first time. "Nooooo thanks," sputters the average-looking guy my age.

"You sure?"

"Ya, definitely not!"

I finish breakfast and have just completed packing up when the stranger begins to rouse himself from under the bench.

"I hate to do this," I begin, "but I need my blanket back."

"Oh ya, sure. Here ... and thanks."

The man shakes the sleep from his head, runs a hand through flattened hair, and appraises me through squinted, bloodshot eyes. His sole possessions appear to be four packs of cigarettes and matches.

"Don't I know you?" he asks. "Have you ever been in Hollywood?"

I laugh, any fear of my companion vanishing. In a Hawaiian-style shirt and rumpled slacks he looks more like a rundown used car salesman than the murderous vagrant I'd imagined. My companion explains that he's been in Winslow for three days and declares it "a tough little joint."

"What's your story?" he asks, glancing curiously at my overstuffed backpack.

I tell the abridged version of my tale as the heat is already rising and I'm eager to get underway. We shake hands, wish each other good luck, and walk away in opposite directions. The stranger heads toward the diesel and donuts of the truckstop. I stride into the rising sun and the endless desert plain. And thus, my twenty-four hours of civilization comes to a close.

After less than a mile, I reach the Little Colorado where, ironically, a trickle of water actually flows in the channel. Since my route now leads away from the riverbed, I splash across, worm through the riparian jungle one last time, then set sail on a sandy desert stitched together by delicate wildflowers.

The open space feels wonderful as Winslow recedes behind me. From atop a small rise, I stare back at the San Francisco Peaks anchored sixty miles to the west. Ahead, Cottonwood Wash, the sinuous dry drainage I plan to follow, slithers eastward. Along the length of the wash, my map shows small triangles topped with crosses which indicate wells and windmills spaced at intervals of two to six miles. These artificial water holes are for the cattle that graze this scant prairie, but since my map's about thirty years old, the big question is if these wells are still functional. I can cross this next desert stretch only if the answer is "yes."

I reach the first well by mid-morning and am mightily pleased. Cows surround a muddy stock pond brimming with water. The windmill has been abandoned, but is replaced by a small gas engine which faithfully chugs cold, clear, alkaline water into a trough. No sign of anyone about. I dunk my head, slurping greedily, then stow my customary gallon of water in my pack before continuing along the wash.

The land here is cleaner, less overgrazed than on the Reservation. For once I appreciate the cattle since their wells and stock ponds will make this next leg possible. Cow paths also ease my passage through the shrubs along the meandering washbed. Even the sun is cooperating, hidden behind a high veil of clouds. If this first well is any indication of my water sources ahead, all systems are go!

Day 16, Twelve miles

Oh, how the desert spirits must have laughed at the cocky optimism with which I concluded yesterday's lunchtime entry! They say that it's always darkest before the dawn. Perhaps it's also brightest before the fall. A wiser, humbled pilgrim bearing a few new gray hairs writes today's entry.

The previous afternoon began pleasantly enough. I start up the wash after a midday siesta when yelping explodes from the bushes ahead. A small coyote darts away to my left. From beneath the same bush emerges a tiny coyote pup who fails to spot me at first. He ambles straight towards me, then glances up and freezes twenty-five feet away. We stare at each other wide-eyed. I speak soothingly and advance a few steps. The pup crouches closer to the ground, unsure of the proper response to the upright, humpbacked creature before him.

Finally instinct kicks in and the coyote scoots back to the bush where a den must be hidden. This encounter with wild innocence leaves me glowing.

This joy dims when I close in on the second windmill. The spindly steel tower is standing, but the multibladed wheel overhead is disabled and the trough is dry. A mile farther and I reach what's labeled "Good Well" on the map -- welded shut. The windmill is gone; a huge steel tank rusting nearby booming empty when I rap on it. Another hot mile to "West Well." This one, too, lies in ruins.

By now, my cheer has evaporated and I feel vulnerable and scared. Looking to the empty, distant horizons, I am a speck on an indifferent landscape. Who would know if my lights dimmed and went out on these empty plains? No back-up hogans out here. How far can I walk on a couple quarts of water and will-power? Cottonwood Well lies three miles ahead. Winslow is nearly ten miles behind me. Fighting down panic, I ask my intuition which way to go. Surprisingly, it says to forge ahead.

Soon, a speck appears upon the horizon. At least the tower still stands, but is the finned wheel moving on top? Earnestly praying for water for the second time in a week, I march across the sand. Cow tracks begin to converge in a path toward the tower. Wait, yes, the top is definitely moving. Relief!

What a pretty sight: a rusty tank at the base of the windmill holding water scummed with algae and dead insects. The breeze stirs, the overhead wheel creaks to life, and out from a pipe gushes a steady flow of fresh, cool water. The release from the stranglehold of fear is even more delicious than the first drink and I whoop for joy. Overhead, two ravens echo my excitement with raucous calls. The commotion startles the two dozen cattle who have wandered in for their evening drink only to find a humpbacked apparition dancing crazily around their tank.

I make camp in a nearby dry creekbed and am returning to the tank for cooking water when a pickup abruptly roars up behind me and skids to a stop. Out jump two husky cowpokes looking like a couple of Hoss Cartwrights on wheels. They look as surprised as me.

"Well...we thought you was a wetback," one cowboy says, introducing himself as Scott.

"What you doin' way out here, anyway?" the other man, Billy, asks without any hint of irritation.

I smile weakly and try to explain. Turns out I'm crossing a spread of some four hundred square miles composed of a patchwork of private and federal land. Scott and Billy patrol the ranch in their rig, fixing fence lines, maintaining windmills, and checking on the six hundred head of cattle. These overgrown boys are friendly enough, politely incredulous about my quest and mostly indifferent to the world beyond their home in Jackrabbit, Arizona. With my map spread on the hood of their truck, I learn which wells ahead still produce water and which are dead -- vital information. With our small talk completed, the wranglers get down to the business at hand.

"We aim to get ourselves one of them baby ravens from the nest atop this tower," Scott admits.

"Yup, them crows make fine pets," Billy adds. "You can even teach'm to talk."

While Billy keeps the frantic adult birds at bay with a .22 caliber rifle, Scott lumbers up the frail ladder running up the windmill and heaves himself onto the crowning platform. Immediately, feathers, squawks, birdshit, and hollering begin to rain down from above. Four large fledgling ravens awkwardly launch, but all quickly crash to the ground. Billy grabs one of the helpless birds flapping pathetically around the corral and shoves it into his plastic lunchpail. The hunt is over. While desperate parents direct their remaining young into the cover of the bushes, Billy and Scott return triumphantly to their truck.

Inside, I am screaming in protest against this act of violence. I have always felt a special bond with Raven, particularly during this quest. More than any other creature, Raven embodies the world of spirit that lies beyond our comprehension. Whenever a pair of these glossy knights glide overhead, I greet them with an upraised fist and a greeting of "Brother Raven!" But now, I stand by helpless as one of this brethren is carelessly bound and tossed amidst empty beer bottles in the bed of the pickup. I'm in no position to argue with these guys, but their callous attitude toward their wild neighbors and their apparent blindness to the spirit of the land disgusts and saddens me. As the truck tears off, I'm left alone with the plaintive cries of the surviving ravens. Heartsick, I apologize to the birds for my people's actions and my own inaction.

The day concludes with the finest sunset yet. Flaming clouds flair across the western sky, then fade to maroon and purple. In the half-light of dusk, I notice a plump, cat-sized shadow emerging from the tamarisk near the tent. I approach cautiously, but the animal waddles away in no haste. A porcupine! The large rodents must live in the ribbons of riparian vegetation that lace the desert, yet look so out of place here. Hey, at this point, I'm ready for anything. Waking with a bum beside the Interstate, contemplating my demise during a hot, waterless afternoon, rejoicing in finding an oasis, meeting the local cowboys only to be shocked by their actions, and finally recentering myself with the aid of a sunset and a surprise visit from a forest friend. Who expected such a storm of experiences and emotions on these empty plains? Stretching out on my mattress of sand, I gaze into the depths of the star-spangled sky and wonder how many more surprises await me. Less than a hundred feet away, Coyote calls up to the heavens. I join in with a howl of my own, then roll over and journey into the land of dreams.

Coyote's yipping greeting rouses me at dawn. Before departing the well, I fill my collapsible spare water jug in addition to my usual four quart bottles. This extra eight pound hump of water makes for my heaviest pack ever, but this burden is welcome insurance as the miles unwind beside Cottonwood Wash. The Hopi Buttes, a collection of sheer-sided hills rising five hundred to a thousand feet loom ahead like a softer version of Monument Valley. The wash continues northeast into the Navajo Reservation, but I opt to stay on ranch land for a twelve-mile cross-country trek to LaRoux Wash. Beyond the thickets of riparian vegetation, tufted grass and red sand gives way to bluffs of smooth, naked, rounded earth banded with hues ranging from bone to lavender to brick red. This siltstone gave the Painted Desert its name and has eroded into a badlands maze of ridges and gullies -- an odd, yet gently feminine landscape. One inviting ridge top lures me up and I snake my way to the top of a bluff where a higher broad plain begins.

I am now camped near the edge of the plateau with a churning ocean of pastel earthen waves at my feet. Hundreds of square miles are visible and I see no man-made object, save my own tent. An unbridled wind tries viciously to sweep even this speck of humanity from the plains and several thunderstorms are headed this way to help. The tent is staked down for war, but how exposed I feel. Once inside the bright tube of nylon, my world narrows to the finite, familiar, and comprehensible again. I've come here to embrace the vastness of the desert prairie only to find myself in danger of being engulfed by it.

Day 17, Sixteen miles

Never have I spent so much time on the open plains. Zooming across mile after mile of empty flatlands at seventy miles per hour has always left me unsatisfied and curious. Does anyone else contemplate pulling off to the shoulder of the highway and just walking away from the arrow of asphalt to become a point around which sweeps a boundless world? This prospect must frighten those comfortable only when surrounded by buildings, bright lights, and the hum of humanity. Even people at peace in the depths of a verdant forest or within a cathedral canyon may feel uneasy with the geometric directness of the plains.

This is the simplest of landscapes. There is Earth and there is Sky and there is you. When the vegetation reaches only to your ankles, trails are as meaningless as they are to a sailor. Indeed, you do not hike across the prairie as much as sail across it. The plains here have swells and rolls like mid-ocean waves. Your eye may soon tire of the monotony of the land, but the real show is in the sky. Weather systems are visible a full day before they arrive. Clouds move from the background to center stage. The sky determines the mood of the plains and your mood as well. A world-filling sunset can leave you feeling that all Creation is smiling right at you. But, when the same sky is crashing thunder with a towering black wall of rain marching forth to wash you away, there is no escape. The earth offers no protection and holds you exposed like a sacrifice. Is anyone ever "out there" as much as when alone on the plains?

This morning's stroll is across the huge humpback of Marcou Mesa, a rich grassland best described as high, wide, and lonesome. Embracing my solitude, I revel in the unlimited freedom inspired by the landscape. The sun plays tag with cotton ball clouds while a gentle breeze ripples the range into playful waves. I am Lt. John Dunbar seeking the frontier "before it is all gone." Just give me boots and a star to steer them by!

The sea of grass ends abruptly where cascades of rainbow badlands drop into the LaRoux Wash valley. Mitten Peak, Pilot Rock, and Hennessey Buttes thrust through the plains near the boundary of Petrified Forest National Park. Down I plunge through more weird, sensuous slopes studded with bone-colored chunks of petrified wood. I keep expecting to discover a dinosaur skeleton (or the living, fleshed-out beast!) amidst this prehistoric terrain. After crossing the pavement of Route 77, I walk another mile to a well next to the sandy expanse of LaRoux Wash.

The big, clean iron tank sparkling brimful of clear water is a beautiful sight after a dozen dry miles. I quickly declare it wash day, hop in, and scrub head, body, and clothes. While my clothing flaps dry on a corral rail, I enjoy lunch sitting buck-naked on a capped well pipe feeling carefree as a butterfly. What a glorious gift is water.

An unexpected jeep road in the afternoon leads to a neat ranch tucked between a hillside and the wash. Although the corrals and windmill are still being maintained, the homestead itself is abandoned. I poke around the solid, simple structure: a decor of mouse turds and Hollywood-grade cobwebs, vinyl recliner in the living room, a pair of dusty men's dress shoes in the closet, the kitchen calendar reading December, 1977. Outside, a major storm, my first on the plains, sweeps in from the northwest. I grab a chair and sit protected in the doorway as fat, heavy drops kick up dust, then progress into a steady downpour. As the wind exhales its earthy, moist breath into the house, I smugly savor the security of a solid roof overhead. Perfect timing. Seems someone is definitely watching out for me.

Day 18, Twelve miles

June in the Arizona desert? Yesterday's storm is more typical of the "monsoon" rains that shouldn't arrive here until late July or August. Wet weather continues with a cool morning under pewter clouds splattering wind-whipped drizzle. Dust becomes mud and the plains transformed overnight into a rich emerald carpet resembling the British moorlands more than the Navajo desert. But I ain't complaining -- this damp stuff is a wonderful change.

At mid-morning I huddle under a boulder for a trailmix break out of the blustery weather. A little man waves from a rock face next to my cheek -- a petroglyph! Glancing around the overhang, I find myself surrounded by artwork carved into the stone. Hand and footprints, stylized corn, lizards, spirals, geometric shapes, plus human and animal forms are all chiseled in the black patina known as desert varnish. Once this forsaken alcove hummed with the industrious hammering of the Anasazi. What messages are encrypted here? How long has it been since another person visited this prehistoric bulletin board?

A few miles farther over increasingly broken ground and I'm abruptly overlooking Wildhorse Basin -- a choppy sea of rolling, eroded badlands forming the heart of the Painted Desert and the northern border of Petrified Forest National Park. Another threshold. I feel like a mariner reaching a distant shore across unknown seas. Behind me are the empty plains which I have navigated with luck, wit, and compass. Ahead stands the park's Visitor Center complete with rangers and tourists, ice cream and interpretive signs. Beyond the park I'll need to parallel Interstate 40 for at least two days to find water. The spell of the prairie's solitude will soon be broken; I brace myself for the transition.

A scraggly juniper, my first real tree since Winslow, points the way towards a steady stream of Winnebagos cruising the park's scenic drive. Approaching the fort-like cluster of buildings, I swagger a little, wondering if anyone else ever walked to this outpost of a park? Yet upon entering the Visitor Center abuzz with throngs of tourists fresh off the Interstate, I feel as out of place and confused as a wolf in a Walmart. Instead of mingling, I eat lunch off to the side and watch the steady flow of people streaming between the parking lot, the restaurant, and the Visitor Center. One thought burns forcefully in my brain: So many looking; so few "seeing."

Part of me wants to stand up and holler, "Wake up! Don't worry about another hot dog. The park is out there, not in here! Forget the displays -- go smell a real flower. Put the sky overhead instead of another roof. Get lost! Get filthy! Tremble when the thunder roars. Cry when the sunrise is breathtakingly precious. This place is ALIVE and so are you!" But, I remain silent and feel less kinship with these fellow humans than with the sparrows who hop along my bench, greedily eyeballing my raisins.

A cursory perusal of the Visitor Center ("Don't forget to sign the register!"), a fill-up on water, and I depart this glorified rest area. Time to take my own advice and try something new. I walk only a mile before bivouacking under another juniper. The plan is to eat dinner, watch the sunset, and rest until the stars burst forth when I'll try a night hike for a new perspective on the desert.

Day 19, Seventeen miles

Well...my night hike didn't happen exactly as planned (surprise, surprise!). After a huge sunset dinner, I watch as lightning puts on a great show to the north. The storm migrates south and when the first drops spit from the sky, I reluctantly throw together the tent and dive inside. I intend to wait only until the storm passes, but the patter of rain lulls me to sleep. Sometime after midnight, I awaken and peek outside. Stars decorate clear skies -- time to go!

Groggily, I pack in the dark and start walking east. My route is a service road that runs parallel to I-40. Ribbons of red and white lights a mile to the south delineate the river of ceaseless truck traffic. I clomp down the broken pavement in the chill, moist blackness, glad for the easy footing and distance from rumble and stench of the trucks. All is silent until a false dawn awakens the prairie birds who begin a joyous chorus to the new day. Slowly, a golden light sweeps across the land.

After six miles, I eat breakfast across the crumbling pavement from the ruins of the Painted Desert Trading Post, the faded lettering barely legible on the chipped stucco wall. This confirms my suspicion that I've stumbled onto another relic from America's past -- Route 66, the celebrated highway that once traversed the Southwest on its way from Chicago to Los Angeles. Desperate Midwestern farm families fleeing the Dust Bowl migrated westward to the promised land of California along this road. How many dreams rolled down this narrow ribbon of asphalt? What did those pilgrims think when they reached the bizarre kaleidoscope of the Painted Desert?

The endless flow east and west now speeds a mile south of here along Interstate 40, the highway which replaced this section of Route 66. Today's motorists probably believe those four lanes will be here forever, but who knows? Someday, this thin, tenuous thread across the vast, primal landscape may return to the patient desert like its older cousin.

By mid-morning, I reach Navajo, a wide spot off the interstate which consists of a few government issue houses and trailers surrounding a motel/cafe/gas station/store complex. Everything is shut up and empty. Even the post office has recently abandoned town. One hand-painted sign stuck on a doorknob says it all: "Navajo Closed."

I've wandered into this metropolis only to top off my water bottles. Hunting around for a spigot, I spot an older couple at a tap filling five gallon cans and loading them into a decrepit station wagon. I mosey over. "This water good to drink?" I ask.

"Sure beats the stuff back on our spread," offers the haggard woman. "You hitchin' through?"

As I explain my trip, the grizzled husband scrutinizes my pack and asks suddenly, "You packin' a pistol? I don't go nowheres around here without my .44. They just shot another kid down in Phoenix last night. 'Course, it's different way out here, but we've got lots of mean folks in these parts. Yes, sir," the man mutters as he folds himself back into the car,"...lots of mean folks."

The sun is blazing and while Navajo might not offer much, there is shade handy. I've just retired to a grassy patch with a discarded newspaper when a tall man sporting a uniform and badge strides up. After a quick but puzzled glance around for a car, the security officer pleasantly asks what am I doing here. I launch into another telling of my tale and the guard, Nick, realizing I'm no threat, sits down to enjoy the story. "So, what's the deal with this town?" I finally ask.

"About a year ago, the Bureau of Indian Affairs bought this settlement and some accompanying ranchland as part of a Navajo relocation plan," Nick explains. "Now the tribe is trying to figure out if they're gonna try to revive this place or tear it down and start anew. I run a small security business and the tribe hired me to keep an eye on the place. Pretty easy, but damn boring."

Both starved for talk, our conversation fills out the morning. For eighteen years, Nick worked as an independent logger in Arizona and Colorado.

Watching the industry decline in the late 1980s, he saw the handwriting on the wall and traded his chain saw for a radio and badge in a new career of law enforcement. Getting into a police department proved nearly impossible with one glass eye, so Nick started his own security business. On days off, Nick heads home to Show Low, a small town in the Arizona's White Mountains being overrun by vacation home buyers from Phoenix.

Eventually, Nick glances at his watch and excuses himself to do one of his rounds. I resume reading, but before long, I feel eyes on me. Glancing over the paper, I look into a wrinkled face framed in a snowy Kris Kringle beard and wild, incredulous eyes. The old-timer, caught staring, recovers quickly and stomps right up to violently shake my hand.

"Whitey's the name," the geezer declares. "and Navajo's been my home for twenty years. Seen it all livin' right here. Got a salvage yard down the road a piece. And who the hell might you be?"

For the third time, I explain my presence, then ask Whitey what he'll do now that this is tribal land. Bad idea.

Whitey sucks up his pot belly and unwinds into a non-stop rampage of vindication against the federal government. "Mark my words," Whitey concludes, wagging a grimy finger at me, "the little people aren't gonna take it much longer. Soon the creeks are going to be flowing red just like they warned in the Old Testament!"

I steer the conversation toward the safer subject of the unusually wet, cool weather, but Whitey's eyes again grow fiery as he points to the jet trails overhead. "See them planes up there? That's the government playing God with massive cloud-seeding programs that they don't tell anyone about. Now we got freezing winters in this corner of Arizona like we never had before they started messin' around up there..." Another blizzard of curses upon the federal authorities follows. Finally out of steam, Whitey shuffles off to a vintage pickup and rattles off, still muttering to himself. I glance around, wondering who's next. When Navajo seems like a humming place, I know I've been in the outback too long! Finishing the paper and having exhausted all the social possibilities of town, I continue east.

The double tracks of the Atchison, Topeka, and Santa Fe railroad replace Route 66 as my route. Walking the rails, I feel like a character from a Steinbeck novel. The imagery is strained when a four-locomotive, half-mile long diesel train barrels by at eighty miles per hour. As the rumble and clank of the train fades, I spy an Anasazi pot shard on the railroad bed -- another juxtaposition of the modern and the ancient.

The sun is still high when I veer away from the tracks for a juniper-studded cliff across a pasture. My hip is throbbing and seventeen miles of pounding pavement haven't helped. Swatting at biting flies, I erect the tent only to watch it get blown down moments later by a renegade blast of wind. Irritated, sore, tired, and hot, I wisely ignore the wreckage in favor of a quiet barefoot walk up a soft, smooth wash.

Sensual sand shifts between my toes. The pungent scent of juniper and sage fills the warm breeze tousling my hair. Primrose, globe mallow, and desert marigolds smile at me wherever I look. Ahhh, that's better! The magic hasn't vanished. I needed only to get away from the pavement and train tracks and trailers and people and be still for a moment. Soothed by nature's embrace.

Day 20, Seventeen miles

My second day of roadwalking next to Interstate 40 is coming to a close and not a moment too soon. Today marks the end of my second leg and tonight I sleep less than ten miles short of the New Mexico border.

A humid morning under a hazy sun stirs memories of sticky August days in New England. The first stop is the tiny town of Chambers, another community living parasitically off the interstate. Out of water again, I plop my pack down in front of the Chevron Quikmart. Waterbottles in hand, I ease around back to the men's room -- locked. The blue-haired old lady at the counter inside scowls over her half-frame glasses when I ask for the key. "Bathroom's only for customers," she snaps. Scowling back, I snatch a pint of orange juice from the cooler and dig a couple of singles from the bowels of my pack. The woman slides my change and a key wired to an Arizona license plate across the counter. "Don't make a mess," she growls. This sets the tone for the day.

I crank out hours of easy miles along the frontage road; semis and RVs whiz by on my right, billboards and hardscabble shacks and trailers litter the roadside on my left. Lunchtime finds me outside Sanders at the Ortega Indian Center, a gaudy monstrosity of T-shirts, cheap pottery, rubber tomahawks, and soft-serve ice cream that draws tourists off the Interstate like flies to a roadkill. By mid-afternoon, I reach another tourist trap called Fort Courage. Strolling past the phony log barricade, I enter the trading post and the Navajo woman behind the counter clucks in astonishment. Two months earlier, I had asked her if the trading post would be willing to hold one of my cache boxes. I explained that I'd be walking through later in the summer, and though she'd agreed to help me, her expression had said that I'd never make it. I walk in today all sweaty and tanned and she can't quite believe her eyes.

Now hidden among the junipers less than a mile beyond Fort Courage, I pore over the contents of the cache box like a kid at Christmas, but the sky is competing jealously for my attention. Eastward is the blue-black wall of rain and lightning that violently swept over my camp a half hour ago. Westward, the crystal-clear horizon features a postcard sunset in full glory. Between these extremes, a brilliant double rainbow shimmers -- a sweet gift to redeem this tiresome day of tarmac trudging.

Day 21, Thirteen miles

The good news: made it to New Mexico! The bad news: desperate for water.

After a few more miles on the frontage road this morning, I leave the interstate and its depressing aura and amble south down a dirt road past a scattering of modern Navajo homes -- small, suburban-style houses with outhouses downwind. At a bridge over Whitewater Arroyo, I forsake the road and trek up the sandy creekbed. Everything improves immensely. A trickle of water brightens the bottom of the deeply eroded wash. Bird song replaces the whine of air brakes. Tadpoles wriggle at my feet instead of beer cans. How can so many people never leave the concrete jungle and experience the world beyond the reach of the automobile?

My euphoria is short-lived. The wash grows dry, hot, and filled with foot-dragging deep sand as the afternoon progresses. Where the map indicates a creekside well, I find only a mangled hand pump. Damn -- I was counting on that one.

Now, I'm taking a breather in an abandoned homestead that has been relegated to a hay barn. Sad-faced cows wander listlessly around a corral, but there's no sign of water or people. Reckon I'll just enjoy the deep shade and catch a snooze on the hay bales until the sun calms down. Ahhh, Mother Nature -- forever fickle. No sooner have I returned to your beauty than you burden me with your hardships.

Day 22, Fourteen miles

The afternoon is still stinking hot when I emerge from my long siesta in the barn, but luck is on my side. Two miles farther upstream, a beautiful trickle of water slides delicately down a groove in a slab of bedrock emerging from the river of sand. Whitewater Arroyo becomes a vision of beauty again once there's water swelling my belly and sloshing comfortingly in my pack. When hydrated, I'm a fearless explorer. Dehydrate me, and I revert to a struggling survivalist. Make or break; do or die. Out here, water is everything.

Camp is the finest yet: a sweet alcove carved in a sandstone wall that sweeps skywards from the sunken creekbed. Patrolling my overhang are dozens of screeching, swooping swallows and I smile at their antics. Swallows slicing up the sky, like otters tobogganing through the snow and dolphins dancing in the sea, are teachers that remind me life is meant to be enjoyed, not endured. Twilight fades to evening and the struggles of midday are forgiven and forgotten. As the swallows retire to their miniature mud-daubbed hogans overhead, I can't decide which is more pleasant: the soft cool sand under my liberated feet or the scent of dinner promising of a full belly. At peace at last.

At dawn, I'm walking ten minutes after opening my eyes. For the first blessed hour, I enjoy a delicious coolness, sneaking out of the sun's reach beneath walls and pillars of red, cream, and tan sandstone. Loose Indian ponies prance gracefully out of the wash looking gauzy and dreamlike in the early light. At the base of one particularly beautiful rampart, I pause to examine the stratification of rock art left by those preceding me. The deepest layer is painstakingly pecked human figures and geometric designs chiseled into the wall by the Anasazi while the Vikings were busy sacking Europe. Overlying this layer are settlers names and dates from the first half of this century plus well-drawn horses and a steam locomotive. The top layer is a confusion of shallow scratches and spray paint -- obscenities and lewd cartoons of naked women. What a commentary on the cultures that have lived here: the sacred, the mundane, and the profane!

I emerge from the shallow canyon into a broad, grassy bowl edged with ponderosa pines. An Indian sheepherder tends his flock with dogs who bark cheerfully at my approach.

"Is there a store in Two Wells?" I ask the old man, referring to a dot on my map a couple miles ahead.

The weathered shepherd laughs, "There is nothing there! No store, no homes, no wells. Just a bunch of people playing ball."

Playing ball?

Approaching Two Wells, the glint of steel and chrome glimmering in the grassland catches my eye. Beyond the parked cars, I make out a baseball diamond surrounded by at least a hundred spectators. Everyone is Indian. What are these folks going to think when a skinny belagonna (Navajo term for a white person) lugging a pack walks in from nowhere? Briefly, I contemplate giving the gathering a wide detour, but thirst and curiosity win the day. As I hop the last fence on the edge of a dusty roadway, a bunch of playing kids spot me and race back to the ball field. That's it; I'm committed now.

Families gathered on the tailgates of pickups turn to stare as I try to look casual. My waves, nods, and foolish grin elicit plenty of excited Navajo chatter. I ask a long-haired teenager if I can rest in the shade for a moment and he gives me a poker-faced nod. A Navajo man wearing a US West t-shirt and a smile wanders over and finally breaks the ice.

"Where are you going?" he asks.

"Walking to the Zuñi Mountains, then Grants," I reply, falling back on my short answer. "What's going on here?"

"This is our annual Fastpitch Softball Tournament. Happens every Father's Day weekend. We got about twelve teams this year. Kind of a big deal 'round here," the man explains.

"Do you think it would be alright if I watch for a while?"

"Sure!" the guy laughs. "It's a free country!" I smile back, yet feel completely out of place.

I watch the action out on the diamond, trying to ignore the careful scrutinizing I'm receiving. Closest to me is a family parked beneath a shady ramada of juniper boughs. A young woman from the group asks where I'm from and I leap at this opening. Slowly at first, then with the enthusiasm of a hermit with an audience, I explain my route, my quest and my equipment to the family. Younger kids quickly gather around, looking alternately at my pack, my map, and my face. Behind them, a regal, turquoise-laden grandmother carefully eavesdrops and softly comments to her daughters in Navajo, but will not look in my direction. When I ask the young woman to watch my gear while I get something from the food stand, she grins and says that her family has already taken care of that. Just then, another teenager appears at my elbow with a wonderfully greasy circle of hot fry bread and a Coke. Moments later, an older man comes up with a bucket of cold drinking water to fill my bottles. Graciously accepting my gifts, I take the offered seat on the team bench and start munching. Comments in Navajo still fly around me for a while, but eventually, all attention returns to the game.

On the groomed field, men and boys are enjoying spirited, but light-hearted competition. The spectators are mostly youngsters and womenfolk including plenty of teenage girls cradling babies. Loitering around the front of the pickups are more teenagers indifferent to the game as they listen to rap music from car stereos and keep a wary eye on me. The Zuñi have a separate encampment of trucks beyond the outfield. Players coming in off the field look at me and do a double-take, then spot my backpack and ask where I'm going. The answer is always received with a blank stare.

My team loses 4-2. Without a word, the family packs up and drives off, leaving me suddenly adrift as a new team scoops up the coveted shady seats. As a new game commences, I shoulder my pack and move to a group of cottonwoods about half a mile away.

Well...that was interesting. The gift of food was certainly a pleasant surprise. What was I expecting the Reservation to be like-- a modern version of "Dances with Wolves?" No, but I didn't expected baseball and Coca-Cola either.

Day 23, Thirteen miles

Before me stretches the glistening blue surface of Nutria Reservoir, the first sizable body of water I've seen all summer. Soothed by this extravagance of water, I'm lingering here in the northern corner of the Zuni Reservation for my midday siesta. The scene stirs memories of my New England days: the gentle lap of wavelets on the gravel shore, the squawk of bobbing black coots, a patrol of indigo dragonflies among the dark green bulrushes, the unmistakable coolness of wind off the water ....

After a night near the head of Whitewater Arroyo where chickadees and the swoosh of ponderosa needles sing me an evening lullaby, I hit the blacktop of Route 32 and follow it south against the flow of commuters headed into Gallup. As soon as possible, I swing east again on a dirt road which deteriorate into maze of two-rutters. Repeatedly, I stumble into the front yards of hogans and shacks where the dogs start howling while toddlers and chickens scurry for cover. I duck back into the pines, embarrassed to be intruding again. Finally, another track leads to a height of land where I glimpse my next goal: the Zuni Mountains, an unimpressive forested ridge a day's walk away. Below sits the reservoir and I can't resist its lure.

Across the reservoir, Zuñi teenagers are driving up in faded Cameros and pickups. Rap music pounds across the water as the fishing poles begin to fly. Just another summer day "down at the lake."

Day 24, Thirteen miles

I walk away from my extended siesta at the reservoir into a long, rough afternoon. These midsummer days sometimes seem endless. I arise with the sun and log eight to ten miles in the six hours before lunch. Finding a shady nook to hole up, my two or three hour midday break is filled with eating, writing, and resting. Five hours of daylight still remain, so on I march, gobbling up miles much faster than anticipated. The sacred elements of my quest seem to be slipping to the wayside as my journey has digressed into a repetition of sleep, eat, walk; sleep, eat, walk. My lofty expectations of contemplating and meditating just aren't happening with flies droning in my ears and the sun scrambling my brain. My thoughts cluster on reminiscences of the past or plans for the future. What the hell happened to my vow to remain mindful and to "be here now"?

The open road to the Zuñi hamlet of Nutria is hot, dusty, and deserted. Cutting across a fenced pastureland, my hip pain flares as the low sun slaps my face. Behind me, a bull bellows incessantly. Ahead, a rattlesnake appears suddenly on my path. Enough already! I hobble into a grove of trees, crawl inside my yellow nylon castle to shut out the world, and sulk.

This morning, like all sunny mornings, the world looks like a much finer place. Working my way around a beautiful sandstone ridge, I enter the Cibola National Forest and breathe a deep sigh of relief. Much of the journey preceding this point has been on private land and Indian reservations. Now, with the exception of short stretches, the remainder of the quest will traverse federal public lands. No more days of feeling like a trespasser.

Life continues improving as I gain elevation. A clear, splashing stream dances across a lush meadow where horses snort and stamp before galloping off with flying manes. Bushwhacking up the steep, overgrown slope of the Zuñi Mountains leaves me sucking wind, but after weeks on the desert plains, the forest is exactly where I want to be. When a Forest Service road leads to a small falls cascading into a beautiful pool, my attitude adjustment is complete. New vistas; big trees overhead; cool, pine-scented air, and a genuine swimming hole -- nothing like a hug from Mom Nature to set the world right.

Day 25, Twelve miles

I hunker in my tent, waiting out an imminent midday storm. When the rain comes, some of the drops will trickle down the right side of the tent to begin a long journey to the sea. Gathering in Lilly Canyon, a shallow groove in the western slope of the Zuñi Mountains, this water will rush out of the forest and flow across the plains of the Ramah Indian Reservation to the diminutive Rio Pescado. This tiny creek enters the Zuñi River which, in turn, will drain into the

Little Colorado River. Flowing mostly underground, the water shall cross the Navajo Reservation back to where my journey began. Yet the voyage will be just beginning for these hypothetical drops. Pulled relentlessly by gravity, the water will join the mighty Colorado River as it tears through the Grand Canyon and slides between Arizona and California toward the Sea of Cortez and the Pacific Ocean.

OK, back to the mountains. If the raindrops should happen to land instead on the left side of my tent, they shall begin a completely different, yet equally impressive voyage. First, down a nameless canyon on the east side of the Zuñi Mountains to Bluewater Creek. Across Cibola National Forest to Rio San Jose. Out onto the desert to join the Puerco River which merges with the mighty Rio Grande south of Albuquerque. Across New Mexico, then edging between Texas and Mexico. Around the knees of illegal migrants and into the tropical wetlands near Brownsville. Finally, these raindrops will spill into the Atlantic Ocean at the Gulf of Mexico. Welcome to the legendary Continental Divide!

Reaching this point required gaining more elevation yesterday than in all of the previous three weeks combined. Following a compass bearing, I hump up an old logging road that hasn't seen wheels in a generation that leads to a mountain of weathered boards near a long-forgotten timber mill. I try to picture these quiet woods humming with the bite of axes and rasp of crosscut saws. Did these logging crews speak English, Spanish, Navajo, or Zuñi? Did they live up here in a logging camp or return to valley homes at the end of the day? Were they contemporaries of my grandfather who worked the woods of New England sixty years ago? My thoughts are interrupted when the road quite suddenly arrives on the forested crest of the Zuñi Mountains. According to the map, I've reached the Continental Divide -- yee haa! I camp right there.

The flat-topped 8500 foot ridge that divides the nation's watersheds is unremarkable, but bushwhacking beneath Gambel's oaks and ponderosa pines this morning sure beats struggling across the hot, tawny plains below. The Zuñi Mountains are also called Oso ("Bear" in Spanish) Ridge, but I'm still surprised when I meet a black bear and her cub. Fifty feet apart, we stare at each other in mutual bewilderment until the sow snorts and wheels. Junior scrambles up a pine. Mom stops and grunts what I translate as: "Yo, I said RUN, not climb!" Properly admonished, the cub reverses down the trunk and bumbles after his mother down the Atlantic side. What a treat!

I'm psyched to be strolling along the backbone of the hemisphere, but oddly enough, my endless quest for water continues in this high, cool, green country. All the rainwater rolls away towards the Atlantic or Pacific; none collects on the ridge. My map indicates springs ahead, but this map has broken promises before.

Day 26, Seven miles

The map lies. In my search for the promised spring, I drop off the ridge and nightfall overtakes me high and dry; lost on the mountainside on a maze of cow trails. Once asleep, the frantic search for water continues in my dreams. In the morning, I detour back up and over the divide hunting another phantom spring. Luckily, I stumble upon a seep where a gallon of water is set in a smooth stone basin like a gift from the gods. My thirst quenched, I can also drink in the beauty surrounding me. Wild iris splash blue in emerald pockets of thick grass. Huge yellow swallowtail butterflies flap lazily over the divide. Two elk hustle away after scenting my approach. What an improvement over roadwalking next to the interstate!

A Forest Service road swings up to the divide and, by lunchtime, I'm sitting at the foot of a fire lookout tower perched on a knob of volcanic rock. A figure appears on the metal catwalk surrounding the glass-walled cabin atop the tower.

"Mind if I check out the view from up there?" I inquire, squinting skyward.

"Nope, come on up." replies a blond man my age. Thus begins my afternoon with Allen, Cibola National Forest Fire Lookout Ranger.

After a week of solitude, I quickly find myself blabbering like a filibustering Congressman. Allen listens with interest as I explain my route, describe what I've seen, and ponder what lies before me. We break for lunch, then it's Allen's turn. A native of Truth or Consequences, NM, he studies range management at the state university in Las Cruces and works for the Forest Service during the summers. Although Allen would rather be out fighting fires like he did last summer, he seems quite content serving as the relief Lookout Ranger rotating between three fire towers in the area. As the afternoon winds down, our conversation ranges from puma sightings to philosophy until our tongues are worn out and we're content to sit silently in this magnificent perch and marvel at the 360-degree northern New Mexican vista. My gaze keeps returning to the northeast where 11,300-foot Mount Taylor dominates the horizon. Only the periodic crackle of the two-way radio disturbs the quiet grandeur.

At 4:30 pm, Allen locks up the tower's cabin and heads home to Grants, NM. I linger on the catwalk, enjoying my first lazy day since Winslow. What a job -- an endless cycle of sunrises and sunsets, thunderstorms and star-spangled nights overlooking vast tracts of wilderness. Definitely not for everyone, but you wouldn't find me complaining.

Day 27, Twenty-four miles

Today marks the completion of the third leg and the first quarter of my Southwest Circle Quest. I have reached the southeastern extreme of my grand circle and will begin veering north toward Colorado. Finally, I racked up my biggest mileage day yet. Welcome to the Summer Solstice.

After a windy, chilly night camped at the foot of the tower, I climb to the catwalk in the pink of the predawn. I sing up the sun from behind a shoulder of Mount Taylor and watch it begin the longest journey of the year. Following this simple ceremony, I hurry down a gravel Forest Service road beneath shady pines, heading out of the high country toward Grants and my next cache box.

By lunchtime, I realize that town is within reach today if I push it. That would make my third leg completed in seven days instead of the anticipated ten. A guilty voice inside my head nags, "Slow down; do fewer miles. Contemplate more and make this a spiritual as well as physical experience." This familiar refrain has plagued me for a week now. However, when I resume walking, I ask myself if a preconceived notion of this quest is determining my actions and expectations? Maybe this is the wrong time to be "inside my head" when the lessons of the natural world are all around me. If I want to focus on thoughts and meditation, I should find a beautiful, remote spot and just stay put.

But, a major part of this quest is about movement, completing the circle, exploring the region where I want to settle. There's a time for contemplation and a time for action. And my search for enlightenment and inner peace? Clearly, this process must be a life-long adventure of which this summer is only a small part. "Being here now" doesn't mean that I must live like a prayerful pilgrim all the time. I should go with the natural flow -- walk as much or as little as my body desires and take a rest day when I need one, not when my schedule calls for one. Hey, I'm out here to dance, not march! Lingering doubts about betraying my quest disappear as this new understanding becomes crystallized. A great weight lifts from my soul. Striding toward Grants with renewed vigor, I decide to make this solstice day my longest day as well.

Hours later, I pull into the downtown Grants Visitor Center hot, sweaty, and exhausted, but proud of my twenty-four mile day. After packing up my retrieved cache, I duck into a supermarket for fresh supplies. Sitting outside the store munching chips and salsa dinner, I'm joined by a group of Hispanic kids in Little League uniforms enjoying their victory ice cream cones. We talk and laugh as the sun finally heads for bed. I follow suit and camp in a quiet arroyo on the edge of town.

Now I lie in the darkness enjoying the afterglow of a long day, a good meal, and a new outlook. Beyond the glow of my flashlight, the celestial blanket of ancient stars looks as dazzling as if I'm looking upon the beauty of the heavens for the first time. In these changing and uncertain times, how comforting to realize no matter how much we screw up our precious planet, the stars will remain forever untouched. On they will shine, as they did for the Anasazi and their ancestors; as they shall for me and my descendants. Is there anything you can trust as much as a constellation?

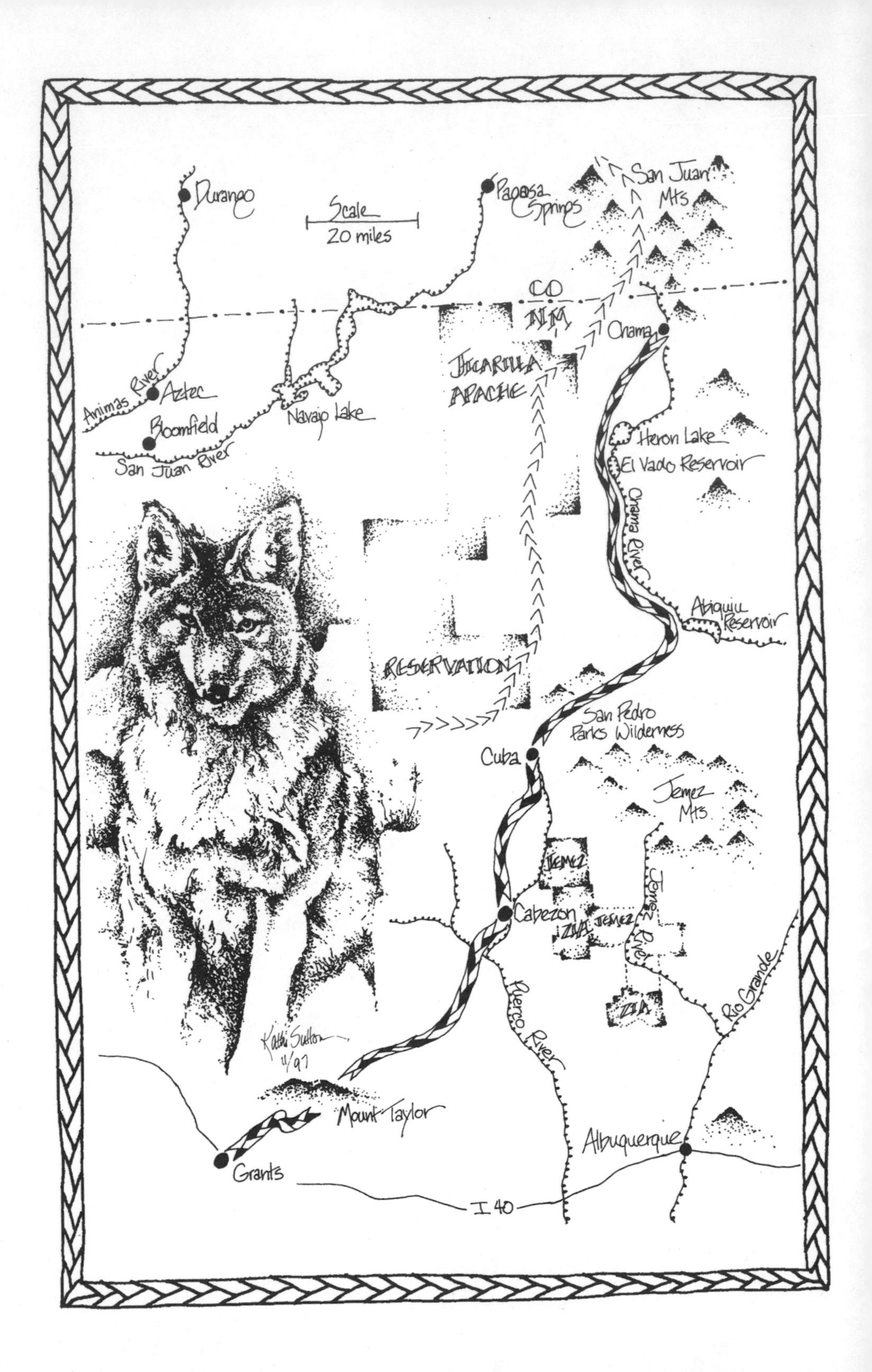
Durango
Scale
20 miles
Pagosa Springs
San Juan Mts
CO
NM
Chama
Jicarilla Apache
Reservation
Animas River
Aztec
Bloomfield
Navajo Lake
San Juan River
Heron Lake
El Vado Reservoir
Chama River
Abiquiu Reservoir
San Pedro Parks Wilderness
Cuba
Jemez Mts
Jemez
Jemez River
Cabezon
Zia
Puerco River
Rio Grande
Kathi Sutton 11/97
Mount Taylor
Grants
Albuquerque
I 40

NORTHEAST
Big Sky Country

One of the best paying professions is getting ahold of pieces of country in your mind, learning their smells and moods, sorting out the pieces of the view, deciding what grows there and there and why, how many steps that hill will take, where that creek winds, and where it meets the other one below, what elevation treeline is now, whether you can walk this reef at low tide or have to climb around, which contour lines on the map mean better cliffs or mountains. This is the best kind of ownership, and the most permanent.

It feels good to say "I know the Sierra" or "I know Point Reyes." But of course you don't -- what you know better is yourself and Point Reyes and the Sierra have helped.

Terry and Renny Russell
On The Loose

Day 28, Sixteen miles
282 Miles Total

The fourth leg begins with a walk up Route 547, heading north out of Grants toward Mount Taylor. The last vestige of urbanization before I reenter Cibola National Forest is a huge state prison complex. A few strolling prisoners in the exercise yard wave to me from behind three impenetrable fences of barbed wire. I wave back, the contrast between our worlds frightening. While I have the rest of the summer and the whole world at my feet, the only contact these guys have with the outdoors is a small walkway of fenced-in concrete. Freedom is truly my greatest possession.

Climbing into the foothills of the volcano, I take a breather at Lobo Canyon Campground, a shabby collection of picnic tables beside a thread of flowing water. Gathered near the only car in the place is a group of black-haired teenagers talking and laughing much too loudly. I turn to leave, but they spot me.

"Hey dude, come on over. We're having a party!" one kid in a heavy-metal band t-shirt beckons. Warily, I approach the raucous mob.

The group is a bunch of kids from the nearby Laguna Pueblo Reservation. Although it can't be later than 10 am, two of the guys are falling down drunk. Congenial hosts nevertheless, one of the young ladies offers me a beer and vodka. I settle for OJ on the rocks. As I field the usual barrage of questions, the teenagers seem both interested and impressed, particularly when I describe the walk as a vision quest. For a while, we talk and joke and take each other's picture. When I ask what they do back home, one guy giggles and hoists his bottle, "More partying, dude!"

Shouldering my pack to leave, the group hands me a quart of icy orange juice from their cooler and wishes me luck with a blessing. Fifty yards away and out of sight of my companions, I suddenly remember that I haven't pumped any water yet. Kneeling next to the stream, I fill my bottles and eavesdrop on the loud party continuing behind me. After discussing "that walking dude," the conversation reverts to its original topic; bitching and moaning about their lives back home. Every other word is a profanity as they trade stories of their woes. How sad to see the joy of life extinguished so early. Trapped in despair and a lack of direction, these teenagers seem as imprisoned as the inmates down the road.

My dirt road winds up onto Horace Mesa, tugging me forward toward the coolness promised by a return to the high country. Mountain euphoria grabs me upon reaching a verdant stand of aspen that shimmers and twinkles in a delicious breeze. Desert-weary senses are spellbound and my thoughts fly ahead to the weeks I'll spend in the alpine zone of Colorado. Perhaps Abby is right; the mountains are the place to be!

Late in the afternoon, I leave the road for my first officially designated foot trail after almost three hundred miles of hiking. A few steep miles farther and I plop down near a gorgeous spring. After climbing thirty-five hundred feet over sixteen miles lugging a sixty pound pack, I'm whipped. But camped now near 10,000 feet on this sacred mountain, it was worth every step.

Day 29, No forward miles

To the Navajo people, Mount Taylor is Tsah Dzil or the Turquoise Mountain -- the Sacred Peak of the South. Mount Taylor is also a holy mountain to the numerous Pueblo tribes in the nearby Rio Grande valley. Rising alone from the desert like the San Francisco Peaks, this massif is undeniably a place of power. Wandering around the upper slope's rich forests today, I've come to appreciate and understand the spiritual energy of this peak. Mount Taylor has become and shall always be a sacred mountain to me as well.

I decide upon awakening to make this a layover day. During breakfast, I tell myself to be mindful. No burning sun to race, no miles to put in my wake -- just quality time with this special place. With only a light daypack, I set off to explore the neighborhood. Quickly clearing treeline above an aspen grove, I peer south to the low ridge of the Zuñi Mountains and can sense the Painted Desert looming just beyond the distant horizon. How far I've come to stand here!

Ambling back into the emerald ocean of aspens, I lie down in the sun-dappled grove and literally hug Mother Earth. Like a man entranced, I nibble on a dandelion leaf, sample the perfume from a carpet of wildflowers, climb a spruce. Why this euphoria? Is it the contrast to the starkness of the desert? Am I touching deep memories of childhood romps through the lush forests of New England? The morning spins by like an enchanted dream. The only moment of melancholy comes when I realize how much Abby would love it here. Sometimes, the months and miles between us seem interminable.

Back at camp, I begin a ritual which has occupied my thoughts since my arrival up here. I have decided to mark special landmarks along my route with a gift, a simple offering expressing my thanks to the land which is teaching me so much this summer. First, I fashion two hoops from green aspen limbs. To the smaller hoop I lash a cross of twigs, then lace this hoop into the center of the larger circle, creating a symbol of my Southwest Circle Quest. The smaller hoop represents my route around the Four Corners while the larger circle symbolizes the region of the Rocky Mountains and the Colorado Plateau which shall be my homeland. I complete the offering by adding a downy grouse feather to Mount Taylor's location along the inner hoop. Pleased with my efforts, I set the gift aside for tomorrow's mountaintop dedication. Now I bask in the rare luxury of a campfire, mesmerized by the dancing flames that chase away the sharp chill of the alpine air -- a perfect ending to a superb day.

Day 30, Thirteen miles

After fragrant, fluffy hunks of bannock bread for breakfast, I start switchbacking up to Mount Taylor's summit. Ascending slowly with a sense of respect, my eyes remain focused on the path just before me. Never have I approached a mountain summit with such concentrated reverence, yet it feels so right. Hindu and Buddhist pilgrims will spend weeks prostrating themselves around their sacred Mount Kailas in the Himalayas. I, too, have become a pilgrim.

Within a dozen yards of the rock pile marking the summit, I ease off my pack and dedicate my gift with a simple prayer. Placing the offering at the base of a boulder, I slowly raise my eyes for the first time and drink in the quarter of New Mexico that lies visible below me. Albuquerque is a brown smudge below the Sandia Mountains seventy miles to the east. Far to the northeast are the jagged, snow-patched peaks of the Sangre de Cristo range that loom above Santa Fe and Taos. Looking north and east, I stare into the unknown terrain that awaits me -- a broad forested plateau that sinks into the desert only to rise again in the hazy Jemez Mountains. Whooping for joy as the world falls away in all directions, I feel truly blessed.

Nestled inside the summit cairn is a logbook signed by hundreds of previous visitors. This peak has attracted a remarkable cross section of people: locals, east coast folks, and foreigners; Anglos, Hispanics, and Native Americans; families, couples, and individuals. Nearly everyone who has stood here has found it to be a profoundly emotional experience. Praises for the beauty abound and many write of feeling centered and rebalanced. After my name, I add: "Long Live the Sacred Summits of the World!"

A trail winds down through a thick stand of spruce where a few ancient snowbanks surprise me. A lower second summit bristles with radio towers -- offensive technological intrusions on this sacred mountain -- but I detour up the service road to the tower in hopes of meeting an "old friend." Sure enough, Allen pokes his head from the fire tower and tosses me a grin. A quick chat fills in the details since our afternoon together at the Oso Ridge lookout. Borrowing Allen's powerful binoculars, I glass my route ahead. The Colorado Rockies are still invisible below the horizon, but I feel my internal compass shift to the north where the high country beckons.

Day 31, Seventeen miles

Rolling off the backside of Mount Taylor on a Forest Service road yesterday takes me down through a delightful patchwork of open, grassy parks and thick, fragrant spruce and fir forests. The road levels off at 7,000 feet atop Mesa Chivato where game trails lead to the evening's destination -- Llanito Frio tanks. My map indicates two small lakes here; I find dry lake beds with tiny ponds on their centers. No problem -- a mere gallon or two suits my needs just fine.

The end of these long June days often finds me bedding down with the sun. I am just unrolling my sleeping bag within the tent when the sound of splashing startles me. Peeking past the tent flap, I spot a female elk sipping from the pond only fifty feet away. Sensing my presence, she prances away on stiff legs. Two young bull elk with budding summer antlers ignore their nervous companion and trot up to the water. I sit motionless, the tent forming an excellent blind. More elk emerge from the forest's edge. One crazed bull starts bucking and spinning like a rodeo bronc in a futile attempt to dislodge a deer fly. Illuminating this tranquil scene are the long, golden rays of the setting sun which melts into a spectacular vermilion explosion at dusk. I am spellbound, the words to a Navajo prayer flashing in my mind:

Beauty before me, I walk
Beauty behind me, I walk
Beauty above me, I walk
Beauty below me, I walk
Surrounded by beauty, I walk

In the morning, I drop out of the forest onto an open plain studded with small hills or "cerros." Ahead, a swirl of dust dims the morning sun and out of the brown cloud emerges an impressive herd of fifty or sixty elk. Majestic bulls lead the parade with a few deep-throated bugles while the cow elk call to their gangling calves with strange, whale-like moans. Standing there breathing the musky animal scent, I am transported back ten thousand years to when this entire continent was alive with vast herds. My walking stick becomes a spear staff and I am a Pleistocene hunter tracking game for my people. The elk melt into the scattering of juniper, but their voices continue to echo over the grassland and energize my step.

¿Habla Espanol? My map is awash in Spanish place names such as the "Nuesta Senora de la Luz de las Lagunitas" land grant just to the east. A dirt track leads past Laguna Cuatas, Laguna Bonito, and Laguna Grande -- small natural lakes that are nearly dry. The Southwest was Mexican territory much longer than it has been a part of the United States. Anglos remain a minority in most of northern New Mexico. I'm back in cattle country, hopping fences and stumbling across remote seasonal cowboy camps. Some of the camps appear to have once been year-round ranches. How long ago did these families move into town, forsaking a life in the outback? People come, people go; the land remains.

Day 32, Nineteen miles

Two days ago I was flying high and cool at over 11,000 feet. Well, the honeymoon is over. I'm down to 6,000 feet, my lowest elevation in New Mexico, and back in the sizzling skillet of the desert.

After yesterday's siesta, I continue across the high plains where each step envelops me in a continuous whirling cloud of grasshoppers. Just call me Antonio Chavez, famed grasshopper shepherd of northwest New Mexico! Actually, that's not a bad idea. There's probably more protein per square mile in the form of grasshoppers than beef out here. 'Course, getting your brand on the little buggers could be tricky ....

My bottles and my throat are rattling dry when I reach Laguna Piedra. The shallow depression holds water, but it's the color of strong coffee and doesn't smell anywhere near as appetizing. Iodine tablets and boiling are my only hope of purification. Dreaming longingly of the crystalline springs back on Mount Taylor, I'm back to depending on diluted cow piss for survival.

By late afternoon, the spring in my step is ancient history after seventeen dusty miles and I drag myself back up into the trees on autopilot. Fresh bear tracks in the road dust give me a temporary shot of adrenaline, but my shoulders throb long after I've dumped my load under a ponderosa. The magic of the last few days is fading fast.

The next morning's challenge is navigating a flat, tree-covered mesa with a map that delights in being wrong. Turnoffs from the road appear unexpectedly or fail to materialize when anticipated. Finally, I dig out my compass, take my best shot at a bearing, and start crashing through the underbrush. It's amazing the audacity with which I now forsake roads and plunge cross-country into unknown terrain. Yet I always seem eventually to get where I'm headed. No doubt my guardian spirit has mastered the compass too!

Another large herd of elk sucking water from a pond makes over a hundred and fifty elk I've encountered in this National Forest with only a handful of cattle mixed in. What a refreshing change from the majority of the west where the

Cow is King, roaming from canyon bottoms to mountain meadows spewing their obnoxious pies throughout nearly every acre of public land. I'll take elk pellets underfoot any day. A few miles farther, I come to the abrupt edge of the mesa. Below stretches broken sandstone desert studded with black volcanic outcrops, a tawny land shimmering with heat. Drawing in one last lungful of pine-scented air, I descend almost two thousand feet to the banks of the Rio Puerco -- back to the land of cactus and cottonwoods. I'm pushing hard through this section because I can see the Jemez Mountains before me and the desert just can't compete with the high country in midsummer.

Day 33, Twenty miles

According to Navajo mythology, Changing Woman (Mother Earth) gave birth to two children who became the famed War Twin Heroes. The twins left their mother in a quest to seek their father, the Sun. The Sun, after testing the children to insure that they were indeed his offspring, gave them names: Monster Slayer and Born of Water. In this long-ago time, the world was plagued by terrible monsters including an ogre called Big Giant who resided on top of the Mountain of the South (Mount Taylor). Together with their father, the War Twin Heroes traveled to the Mountain of the South and, in a tremendous battle with lightning bolts that split the peak into two summits, the Big Giant was defeated. His blood flowed south and dried in the desert (the El Malpais lava field). The War Twin Heroes took the giant's severed head and threw it far to the north. Here it rests to this day, rising sixteen hundred feet above the Rio Puerco -- a massive, sheer-sided lava butte known as El Cabezon. Alternatively, the modern mythology of science explains El Cabezon as the exposed core of an ancient volcano. Take your pick.

Lying naked in the four-inch depths of the Rio Puerco while gazing at the black battlement towering a few miles away, I prefer the Navajo legend. This region is not just a collection of postcard vistas and geological wonders. Unlike more developed regions of the United States, the Southwest remains vibrantly animated in the mythic and spiritual as well as the physical realm. Local mythology takes on new relevance as I move through this landscape that is literally legendary. Alone in my wandering, I am tuned into the voice of the land like never before.

My muddy midday siesta extends to late afternoon until, with a glance at the map and the sinking sun, I realize that I'll have to hustle to reach the remote village of Cabezon. After a difficult trailess passage, I spy a distant gathering of mud and stone buildings gilded gold by the setting sun like Coronado's El Dorado. A little closer and I realize that many of the adobe dwelling lie in ruins. Does anyone live here?

A primitive road heading into Cabezon is fenced off with a huge sign stating "Private Property -- No Trespassing. You will be fined $500." Hmmm ... I'm counting on Cabezon as an important water stop before plunging into the desert beyond. Quickly, I conclude that since: a) I'm curious about this place; b) I don't have $500 to my name anyway and; c) I'm damn tired of almost dying of thirst in the desert, the choice is clear. I hop the fence and enter Cabezon.

The village looks like the set of a Hollywood western. Tumbleweeds roll down empty, dusty streets. Sagging adobes slowly return to the earth while weathered window frames stare blankly back at me. I expect Clint Eastwood, shooting irons drawn, to step from behind some ramshackle barn any second. The classic New Mexican adobe church complete with picturesque graveyard out back is filled with bailed hay. Nearby, a scattering of modern farm machines indicates that someone still inhabits this ghost town. I mosey on.

At the far end of town, a beat-up pickup is parked beside a well-maintained house. An enormous pig sits in front of the stoop, obviously on guard duty. Dropping my pack with a thump, I utter a tentative "Hello?"

A slight Hispanic woman appears timidly at the door. "Lupe, shoo!" she commands the pig who's trapped her behind the screen door. The giant swine stumbles to its feet and makes a grunting, waddling retreat.

"Ahhh ... Ma'am, could I bother you for some water?" I ask, hoping I don't look too scary.

The woman disappears into the house and quickly reappears with a long-handled metal ladle brimful. "Thanks, but actually, I need about a gallon." I smile. When the woman returns with a full bucket, I try to explain myself between long drafts of the cold, clear water. "So, what happened to this town?" I finally ask.

The woman folds her thin arms across her print dress and declares, "Cabezon used to be a nice little place when I was growing up here, but the war changed everything. All the men went to Albuquerque to work in the factories. After a while, the wives and children left for the city too. I moved out in 1966. Cabezon was abandoned until my husband and I and a few other families came back to the old places to start ranching again. We like .... " the woman stops abruptly at the clatter of hooves rising behind me.

I turn to face a straight-backed old man on horseback pushing a small herd of Herefords ahead of him. A trio of mangy mutts trots at his horse's heels. While his wife speaks to him in rapid Spanish, the man's dark, weathered face stares silently down at me. I search for hints of anger or resentment, remembering the big sign, but the cowboy's stony visage reveals nothing. Finally, he speaks, "Where did you come from?"

"Flagstaff, Arizona," I reply.

The man looks at my pack and walking stick and finally smiles, "You have done well to come this far."

I dig out my map and begin asking about routes and water sources between here and the town of Cuba, my next cache stop. The rancher leans out from his saddle, peers ruefully at my map, and screws up his face. "Just follow me up to that ridge," he says impatiently. "I'll show you where you want to go." Grabbing my pack and giving the woman a nod of thanks, I obey.

An odd, dusty procession snakes up the hill: an old cowboy, a tired hiker, and a string of hounds dragging their tongues. On the ridgetop above Cabezon, the rider reins to a stop and asks my name. I learn that his is Lucero. Pointing to a pass between two low buttes on the northern horizon, Lucero advises, "Go to that notch and you will find the old post road to Cuba. You should find water in the cattle tanks along the way. It's a ways, but I guess you can handle it," he adds with a wink. For a few minutes, we are quiet as the last rays of the day does its magic on the sandstone desert. When I thank Lucero, he reaches down from his mount and shakes my hand. Another smile tells me that I've earned his respect. Wheeling his big bay, Lucero slowly leads his patient dogs back down the hill where supper is doubtlessly waiting. El Cabezon glows like a golden tombstone above its namesake village.

Cooking dinner under a nearby juniper, I watch as a luminous full moon slips magically out of the eastern horizon. One moon ago, I sat in a circle of stone anxiously awaiting the first night of my vision quest. How far I've come in so many ways since then.

This morning, when the dawn is a red smudge, I awaken. When the sky blossoms with the majesty of a Bierstadt painting, I am moving. When the first rays of sunlight catch me in Arroyo Chavez, I'm enjoying breakfast with several miles already in my wake. Back to the rhythm of the desert. Carved sandstone outcrops lining the arroyo whet my appetite for Utah's canyon country and I imagine myself stumbling across an unknown Anasazi ruin tucked in an alcove. This fantasy isn't too far-fetched since one of the largest centers of Anasazi culture, Chaco Canyon, is but a few day's walk west of here.

I strike a track -- Lucero's post road -- which leads me to the pass between Cerro Colorado and Dead Man's Peak. The Jemez Mountains to the north look invitingly cool and close, but for now, I'm stuck in a slow rotation around a scraggly juniper spending the intolerably long midday hours avoiding ants, flies and "el sol." Tomorrow I'll invade Cuba (New Mexico, that is), get resupplied, then head for the mountains. One more desert day ....

Day 34, Fourteen miles

When am I going to learn? I left my siesta yesterday thinking that I had an easy stroll to Cuba and the high country beyond. But the desert wasn't finished with me yet! Time for a review of that favorite lesson of mine: "It ain't over 'til it's over!"

As the two ruts of a road continued north past full cattle tanks, I foolishly ignored Desert Hiking Rule #1: Always top off your bottles at any opportunity. I figure the tanks ahead will be just as full, so why lug the extra weight? You can guess the rest. As soon as I need water, it is impossible to find. Tanks continue to abound, but now they are filled with only tumbleweeds. A spring that Lucero mentioned somehow escapes my scrutiny. Three cow camps I investigate offer nothing. Not a single pickup cruises by all day. I walk on and on, believing that the next tank will surely be my redemption, yet I find only more disappointment and thirst. Calling it quits at dusk, dinner is two old crumbling tortillas and a hunk of dried-up cheese since there is no water to boil for pasta. To make matters worse, the sleep I'm hoping will send me into a peaceful oblivion is as elusive as the water.

Ragged and desperate by morning, I abandon the post road and begin following another track downhill towards the Rio Puerco and the state highway. After only a few minutes, a rancher drives up ("You walked here from Flagstaff ... Frijole!") and I bum a quart of water. With this, I make it to the river -- saved again.

The eleven-mile road walk to Cuba next to heavy traffic should have been tiresome, but once rehydrated, I cruise; singing songs, slapping at flies, and shouting at the prairie dogs. It's not even noon when I arrive at the small logging and farming community with fourteen miles already under my belt.

The rest of the day is a lazy exploration of the amenities of Cuba. The nurses of the women's health clinic where I deposited my cache box months earlier are surprised and pleased to see me, having debated only yesterday if I'd ever make it. After a visit to the market, I sit in the shade, gobbling down bananas and taking the pulse of Cuba. The population seems about 40% Native American, 40% Hispanic, and 20% gringo. Beat-up pickups -- the official vehicle of New Mexico -- parade through town. Logging trucks rumble down Main Street with loads of fresh pine for the mill. Not a bad little place; even has a movie house open almost every Friday and Saturday night!

I've completed a third of my odyssey twelve days ahead of schedule. Thank goodness the desert plains are in my wake. Although I've been occasionally surprised by their beauty, I'm reminded of a Mark Twain quote: "I'm glad I did it, partially to have done it, and chiefly because I won't have to do it again!" Ahead lie the high mountains and the redrock canyons -- my two wilderness passions. Feeling good, feeling strong, feeling proud!

Day 35, Eleven miles

The fifth leg of the Southwest Circle Quest begins with a three thousand-foot climb to the cool, lush forests of the San Pedro Parks Wilderness Area in the northern Jemez Mountains. A country road becomes an overgrown wagon track that fades away as I struggle to find a good route up the slope. Finally, I opt to tramp straight up the mountainside, smashing through brambles and undergrowth. "Trails? Trails? We don't need no stinkin' trails!" I mutter in my best tough hombre accent as I swim into another nasty thicket of oak and locust. Elk paths eventually lead the way onto the high escarpment cloaked in aspen, fir, and spruce. Catching my breath, I gaze over the tan desert to El Cabezon with Mount Taylor barely visible on the southern horizon, then plunge into the dark, wet woods.

Suddenly surrounded by the lushest forest I've seen since Washington's

Cascade Range, I shift gears and begin strolling slowly and mindfully. Stately grandfather trees rise above fern gardens crisscrossed with downed timber. Deep elk hoof prints punctuate the rich, black mud beside precious streamlets. Following a compass bearing through dark, hallowed groves, I eventually emerge into a strip of grassy valley divided by a gurgling creek. A signpost points the way down the Anastacio Trail and I take it, following the boot prints of another hiker for the first time on this journey.

Now camped in a gentle rain under a canopy of spruce, it's hard to believe that I was frantic with thirst in the sagebrush only two days ago. Could this all be a dream? Will I wake up sweltering under a cactus? Guess I'll take another layover day up here and find out!

Day 36, No forward miles

What an ideal day to spend at 10,000 feet! After a solid sleep snuggled deep in my bag against the cold night, I luxuriate over a hot bannock bread breakfast. Low clouds shred through the treetops, filling the world with dripping moisture. Crystalline creeks snake brimful across meadows of wildflowers bound by groves of aspen and spruce. A heavy, loamy perfume drifts in a gentle breeze which tosses harmless puffball clouds overhead. Is this really New Mexico? This flat-topped island-in-the-sky plateau acts like a giant sponge, gathering snow and rain, then releasing it slowly and steadily to the parched deserts below. Ecology becomes more than just an academic concept as I move from desert to mountain ecosystems and back again. Everything is truly connected and this land is surely alive.

I encounter a number of other forest visitors while enjoying a layover day of happy rambles, but two meetings result in new insights on people and wilderness. The first conversation is with the first fellow backpacker I've met since the quest began. The hiker, a teacher on the reservation, explains that he comes up here often to camp and fish and escape the heat in this high country oasis. "It's as close to heaven as anywhere I know," he cheerfully proclaims. As we talk, I sense we share a similar love and commitment to wild places. My new friend's tone is reverent when he describes other designated wilderness areas in New Mexico which he has visited. We part, each aglow with the quiet joy of meeting a kindred wilderness spirit.

Later in the afternoon, I spot several folks on horseback leading about sixty head of cattle into a meadow of knee-high grass rippling in windblown waves. Inwardly, I groan. There's been blissfully little indication of cows up here and now the spell is broken. Eventually, I catch up to the trio of Hispanic riders where they have stopped to fish a beaver pond. An older man sits on a log by himself, watching a man and woman in their twenties trying hard to hoodwink a couple of trout.

"Bringing your cattle up?" I ask the older fellow in a neutral tone.

"Yup, the rangers wanted us to wait until July 1st, but we convinced them to let us up here early since today's Saturday and I gotta be back in Albuquerque by Monday," the rancher explains.

"Don't you live down below in Cuba?" I exclaim.

"My family still has a ranch in the valley where my niece and nephew live," he says, nodding toward the anglers. "My great-grandfather started that ranch and we've been using this mountain for summer pasture for a hundred and fifty years -- long before it became part of the Santa Fe National Forest. I work in Albuquerque, but get back here as often as I can. You been hiking up here long?"

"Nope, just arrived yesterday."

"I first came up here as a boy about forty years go," the rancher reminisces. "In those days, we hardly ever saw anyone else up here -- never anybody on foot. Now there's hikers all over the place and I get flak from people who don't like seeing my cows in 'their' wilderness."

"Could the Forest Service revoke your grazing permit?"

"No," he scowls. "But they can raise the grazing fees to the point where I can't afford to ranch anymore. Hell, everything's changing. Albuquerque is getting full of Easterners who don't understand our lives. Those people want every place to be their own private playground. They don't have much tolerance for people who have to make a living from the land."

Behind us, the horses stamp impatiently. I look into the rancher's leathery face and realize that although his love for these mountains may be different than the earlier backpacker's devotion, it is just as strong.

Eating my pasta dinner back at camp, I digest the day's encounters. I have always been in favor of halting public lands grazing in order to better protect wildlife habitat and riparian ecosystems. Like most western backpackers, I'm sick of sidestepping cow pies on every hike. But the "enemy" here isn't some easily-hated greedy corporation raping the environment for profit, but rural families following a traditional way of life. All across Arizona and New Mexico, I've seen where people have been forced to leave their remote homes and rural roots for work in the cities where they become urbanized, pasteurized, and homogenized. Surely, the solution can't be forcing all the traditional rural land users out of business and into Albuquerque, Phoenix, and Denver. The future of the backcountry must be more than well-to-do backpackers with their Gore-Tex and freeze-dried food umbilical cords tied to an urban existence. Can't we protect Mother Earth without forcing people from their homelands? My thoughts swirl like the swift trout stream at my feet.

Day 37, Eighteen miles

This day which began with a frosty dawn under a lichen-covered Douglas fir now ends with a torrid sunset camped under a stunted juniper. Back to the desert again.

Departing the San Pedro Parks Wilderness is like leaving a cathedral. I savor the dew drenching my boots, the happy dance of the sparkling creeks, the mosaic of emerald foliage against a flawless cobalt sky. From the eastern edge of the dome, Rito de Oso (Bear Creek) leads me into a thick, primal forest where mud and wildflowers mingle underfoot. If parachuted blindfolded onto the mountainside, I would have sworn I was back in New Hampshire. Across the Wilderness Area boundary, my foot trail becomes a Forest Service road. The aspens linger behind as the spruce are replaced by pines.

After lunch, an inexplicable feeling of weakness and general malaise forces me to stop walking. I lie down in the shade and consider the symptoms: low energy, nausea, gurgling stomach, explosive farts that reek like a dead dog in the summer sun. Hmmm, sounds like a classic case of giardia. Maybe all those microscopic nasties in the mucky cattle ponds I've been slurping have finally caught up with me despite the iodine and boiling. It's a frightening prospect with two-thirds of my quest remaining. Feeling suddenly alone and vulnerable, I dig out a possible remedy from my first aid kit -- an herbal tincture of Echinacea designed to strengthen the immune system. Forcing myself upright, I swallow a double dose of the foul concoction, then collapse back onto the pine needles. After a nap, the gurgling and wrenching pain in my gut subsides and I weakly resume walking.

Maybe it's my enfeebled pace or just the fact that I'm a backpacker walking these remote dirt roads, but vehicles stop four different times and offer me a lift. One pale green Forest Service rig hauling four older Hispanic gentlemen pulls up and everyone stares at me slack-jawed. "Are you lost or what?" the driver demands. Nobody can believe that a lone gringo would be walking these back roads voluntarily.

The heat and dust pick up predictably as I descend into the scrub oak and juniper. With the striking red sandstone cliffs of the Rio Chama canyon ahead, I'm cruising along until the track dumps me unexpectedly into someone's junk-filled backyard. Cursing the government map makers once again, I backtrack, detour, and wind up reaching Route 96 at the tiny hamlet of Arroyo des Agua. The elderly couple from whom I beg some water declare that they have never seen the likes of me in their town before. Brace yourself, New Mexico...I'm here!

Day 38, Fifteen miles

I sit on a sandy beach beside my first real river of the quest. Small rapids chatter upstream and down, but before me, the Rio Chama runs silent and deep. Moments ago, I clambered out of the water after a delightful swim and the waning sun now massages my naked back like a lover. A cricket fiddling a sunset song accompanies the rustle of riverside willows as the water becomes a pool of molten bronze. I've entered another official wilderness area, a sanctuary vastly different from the one I just left, but the effect is the same: I've come home!

Today began as magically as it now ends. Sometime before sunrise, I'm awakened by the sound of a lyrical Spanish folk song being sung by an unseen stranger strolling down the nearby highway under a bright moon. This surprise serenade seems like a magical dream and the magic lingers into a clear, sharp dawn alive with the undeniable promise of a fine day. Perhaps the lack of distress from my guts is reason enough for celebration. A coyote howls his greeting to the morning from a near ridgetop and I joyously howl right back.

A few miles down Route 96, I enter another village named, appropriately, Coyote. Sitting on a storefront bench munching granola, I watch this classic northern New Mexican town wake up. Coyote holds maybe a hundred residents; ninety-five of whom I'd wager speak Spanish as their first language. There's nothing extraneous or pretentious about this place -- simple, well-maintained adobe and wooden homes scattered around an elementary school, a post office, a medical clinic, and a weaving shop. The hub of the village is the rambling Coyote Country Store where you can purchase gasoline, crushed ice, chicken feed, a head of cabbage, a hammer, live bait, Jello, a new faucet, a wood stove damper, or a fresh steak. When the store opens, I'm welcomed inside and choose none of the above items, settling instead for a half-dozen bananas, an orange, and a fistful of free pecan cookies next to the free coffee. What a swell place!

My next stop is the biggest employer in town -- the local National Forest ranger station. From Ranger Ed, the recreation specialist (and apparently one of the few gringos living in the valley), I learn that the nearby Rio Chama has recently been awarded Wild and Scenic status.

"Will I be able to wade across it?" I inquire.

"During spring runoff, you'd probably get swept away, maybe run over by a raft," Ed frowns. "Now you should be OK -- just pick your crossing carefully."

A few more pavement miles, then I'm back in familiar turf -- striding down empty dirt roads all alone. Alone, that is, except for magnificent storm clouds, another coyote, a squadron of deer flies, the piercing cry of a red-tailed hawk, soaring sandstone cliffs of ocher and cream, plus enough fresh air for a lifetime! This is Georgia O'Keefe country. Her famous home, the Ghost Ranch, is only a few miles east of here. I'm surrounded by the stark, haunting landscapes that decorated her canvases and understand how this beautiful valley filled the artist with inspiration.

When I reach the Rio Chama in early afternoon, my first reaction is dismay and betrayal. "Ed, what the hell were you thinking?" I stammer aloud, staring across the seventy-foot expanse of deep, quiet water. Fortunately, this "river" is actually the narrow backwaters at the tail of Abiquiu Reservoir where the Rio Chama has been rudely damned as it emerges from a deep canyon. I head upstream and soon reach the river proper.

The sun lingers now only on the pine-studded canyon walls overhead and I can't remember a finer end-of-the-day afterglow. The universe smiles unabashedly. Has a river ever brought me such joy? Maybe I'm not so much a desert rat as a canyon coyote since the combination of naked, vertical rock and living water hold such appeal over the arid plains I traversed.

Day 39, Ten miles

Scanning the map in the morning, I notice the symbol for a church deep within the canyon. A church in the middle of nowhere? I cross the Rio Chama on a Forest Service bridge, continue upriver on a dirt track and, sure enough, reach a gate and a hand painted sign announcing "The Church of the Desert Benedictine Monastery." Since "Visitors Welcome" is also written on the sign, I enter.

From the moment I lean my pack and walking stick against the earthen walls of the guest house, I know I've arrived someplace special. There's nobody about, but a small gift shop beckons and I duck into the low, thick doorway. Inside, simple wooden furnishings are arranged to display Christian books and pamphlets plus a collection of candles, cards, crucifixes, and other religious objects lovingly handmade by community members. The aroma of pine and incense fills the room and the aura of peace and mindfulness is palpable. No shopkeeper is necessary as money is simply left in a collection basket near the door.

From a brochure I learn that the monastery was started in this beautiful and isolated canyon in 1964 by Father Aelred Wall. Now it's a self-sufficient community of a dozen resident monks who create a small income by offering week-long retreats to paying visitors. Famed Christian philosopher Thomas Merton once spent a number of months in residence here.

Still alone, I wander up a gravel path to the three-story adobe and timber chapel which forms the centerpiece of the community. The structure is a pleasing combination of classic New Mexican and contemporary designs featuring local materials and large glass windows. The simple elegance continues inside where heavy wooden benches surround a central altar covered with a square of crimson cloth and a hand-carved cross. Like simple churches everywhere, the love, care, and devotion of its congregation seems to emanate from the walls. Back outside the chapel, I'm greeted by an older man in a slate-blue smock, canvas pants, and sandals who introduces himself as Brother Christopher.

"Your community is very beautiful and so peaceful," I admire.

Brother Christopher smiles gently and says, "Please join our midday service. It will begin in a just few minutes. You are also welcome at the community meal afterwards."

Back inside the chapel, five monks in matching smocks and jeans stand together on one side while I join an equal number of guests sitting across from them. Led by Brother Christopher, we sing a series of Benedictine psalms or chants which roll and echo beautifully within the large, open space. Little did I realize that I'd be going to church when I got up this morning!

After the twenty-minute service, I follow everyone into a more private section of the compound. My unexpected presence at the long, dark table of oiled wood elicits only serene smiles from the faces around me. After more prayers and songs, everyone takes pewter plates into the kitchen and we help ourselves to steamed vegetables, hunks of homemade bread, a large scoop of bean and potato casserole, and a serving of hot apple crisp. My eyeballs are practically drooping at the sight of my first home-cooked meal in a month and a half. Easy, big guy, I chide myself. Let's accept this hospitality with a little dignity. The food tastes as good as it looks and smells, and I don't hesitate to join the others when they return to the kitchen for seconds. We eat in silence and complete the meal with a bowed prayer toward a painting of the order's founder, St Benedict.

As everyone files out of the dining room, an Asian man my age approaches and introduces himself as Brother Rafaelito from the Phillipines.

"Brother Christopher tells me that you are on a pilgrimage," the monk begins.

"Well ... " I chuckle. "It's more of a vision quest."

"Please, tell me more," requests Brother Rafaelito as he ushers me into the library. We talk for over an hour. The young monk is spending a year in residence at the Church in the Desert before returning home to continue his training in the Phillipines. Comparing and contrasting our spiritual journeys, we realize that although our paths are vastly different, our goals are quite similar. We also agree that our current monastic lifestyles of isolation and introspection are primarily a means of stepping back to center, strengthen, and prepare ourselves for a greater task that lies ahead in society.

"There is a Hindu parable that is popular in my country." Brother Rafaelito explained. "Long ago, the ancient gods decided that they must hide the secret of life from humans so that people would not think themselves equal to the gods. The deities knew that mankind would always be searching for this secret of life, so they decided to hide it where nobody would ever think to look...in our hearts. The gods knew that we are usually too busy to stop and examine what we carry within ourselves."

Now, as I sit outside the guesthouse, I realize that visiting this monastic community doesn't seem much like a random accident anymore. I've been thinking about my life beyond this quest and the idea of joining a close-knit, spiritually-oriented community set in the wilderness has frequently surfaced. And here it is! No, I'm not ready to trade my hiking shorts for a smock and my boots for sandals, but living communally with like-minded people on a common plot of land may be somewhere in my future. Today has also been a strong reminder of my vow to live to my highest ideals. I've been too caught up in the pains and pleasures of the flesh and deaf to the demands of the spirit lately. I give thanks for the inspiration of others who are "voices crying in the wilderness for a vision." My search may be lonely, but I'm never alone.

Day 40, Fifteen miles

Beyond the monastery, Rio Chama canyon narrows dramatically. Pushing farther upstream late yesterday, I snake slowly through a tangle of trees and undergrowth on game trails and cattle paths. The sheer sandstone walls and the winding river remind me of Zion National Park with a mosaic of ecosystems clustered together: open woodlands of spruce leading into thickets of desert willow, sage flats running up against lichen-covered talus slopes. When I bed down in a riverside clearing with a rafter's fire ring, I realize that this is my first night in a "real" campsite. Bats begin working the twilight as I cook dinner and relax into the serenity.

I awake to an amazing juxtaposition of bird song as a canyon wren's lilting scale of notes is punctuating the chatter of a chickadee -- desert and mountain denizens together in this glorious canyon. Bobcat, beaver, and raccoon tracks decorate mud banks as I continue upriver. Cliffs springing from the water's edge make route-finding increasingly difficult until I'm forced to ford back and forth across the waist-deep river. Ahead, the tight canyon looks even more rugged, so when a trail appears leading to the canyon's rim, I take it.

By late morning, I'm bushwhacking back down to the river searching for a dot on my map labeled "Ward Ranch Hot Spring." I'd read at the Coyote Ranger Station that the Ward family dipped their sheep in the hot mineral water to kill parasites -- probably not a bad idea for this hombre! Alas, my hopes for a good soak are dashed when I reach the crumbling ruins of the riverside ranch house. The small hot spring nearby is a soup of lukewarm water and orange algae. Bath day will just have to wait.

Over lunch sitting in the doorway of the weathered wooden structure, I imagine Mrs. Ward washing dishes in the tin sink, watching the river flow by as she carefully stacks clean plates in the cupboard that now hangs half torn away from the wall. In another doorway, notches in the jamb record the growth of her children over the years. In the living room, the interior walls are gone, revealing an insulating layer of newspapers. For the next few hours, I read the crumbling slices of yellowed newsprint dating to 1928, losing myself in this inadvertent time capsule. I'm transported back to the days when a new three-quarter ton Chrysler truck cost $895 and two dozen pencils were yours for a dollar. Jack Dempsey had just lost the heavyweight boxing title to Gene Tunney because he'd married a movie starlet, gone soft, and "lost his killer instinct." That upshot in baseball, Babe Ruth, had the nerve to ask for a salary of $150,000 a year and it looked like those damned Yankees might give it to him! When sixty-three year old news holds your attention, you know you're out of touch.

A quick dip in the Rio Chama brings me back to the present. Three sweaty, twisting miles out of the canyon and across sagebrush flats lead to the El Vado dam and reservoir, a clot in the river created in 1935. One last look into the wilderness down canyon, then I march back into civilization for drinking water at Zeke's Lakeside Inn -- a rundown resort catering to the weekend party crowd whose idea of a good time is racing their roaring motorboats in mindless circles on the stagnant lake. The adjacent state park is not much better as I'm forced to brush aside broken glass and rusted cans to clear a space for my tent. Ugh!

What a contrast with yesterday evening. Downstream, the Rio Chama runs wild through an untrammeled wilderness. Here, the river has been transformed into a flooded playground of noise, speed, and garbage. I fear neither the canyon wren nor the chickadee will serenade me awake tomorrow.

Day 41, Twenty-three miles

My mood yesterday evening improves when dusk settles on the lake. Speedboats return to their docks and the great expanse of water grows still and calms my emotions. While wolfing down a pot of rice, my head shoots up at the crack of an explosion. The sky overhead is shattered by green, pink, and blue light -- fireworks! Eventually, the horizon becomes a colorful war zone and I deduce that it's America's birthday. Mother Nature joins the celebration with a distant display of lightning in the north. Overhead, the stars out dazzle everything else.

Up early, I motor north to another reservoir and state park, but this time, I'm pleasantly surprised. Heron Lake sparkles turquoise and tranquil through the pines. Graceful sailboats threading between islands are a welcome change after El Vado's noisy outboards. I can't resist a swim before lunch. Paddling out into deep water, I dive, float, and frolic like an otter escaped from a zoo -- what a treat! Just as solitude creates an appreciation for the company of others, only a desert rat truly understands the miracle of abundant water.

Feeling cool and refreshed doesn't last long as I bushwhack up a steep, wooded hill beyond the reservoir. Dripping once more, this time in sweat, I pause on the ridgetop to catch my breath, only to have it swept away again by the sight before me. Looming jagged and snowy and enticingly close to the north are the South San Juan Mountains -- the beginning of the Colorado Rockies. How often during the last forty days have I dreamed of reaching this high, cool, alpine world. At last, my goal is within sight!

More miles roll by as I tromp across ranch lands full of rich grass, brimming water ponds, legions of cattle, and nary a soul. With only cows for company, I find myself chatting, yelling, or cooing to the blank-eyed beasts.

"OK, everybody up!" I shout merrily to a bevy of Herefords lying peacefully on my track. "It's time for your aerobics!" With widening eyes and audible groans, the bovines stumble to their feet, perplexed by the humpbacked, stick-waving apparition coming up fast.

"Good afternoon, ladies," I bellow. "I'm your new fitness trainer and I can see that you've all been neglecting your Stairmaster workouts. How's about we begin with a light jog OVER THERE!" In response to my frantic arm-waving, the bewildered heifers turn and stampede away in a rumble of hooves and dust. I grin with diabolical delight.

When the twenty-mile mark is in my wake, it's my turn to be dusty and befuddled. A few hours short of my next resupply in the town of Chama, I bed down with unseen elk bugling and nighthawks singing and dancing overhead, happy to be falling asleep within sight of snowcapped mountains.

Day 42, Fourteen miles

If I were to live anywhere in New Mexico, I would probably choose the village of Chama. Known primarily as the southern terminus of the Cumbres and Toltec Narrow Gauge Railroad, this small town of a thousand souls is fronted with beautiful pine forests and redrock canyons, yet backed by some of the finest untrampled Rocky Mountain high country anywhere. "Chama ain't heaven," locals say, "but you can see it from here!"

I arrive in town by late morning, barely escaping alive from hordes of mosquitoes and deer flies which chase me from the boggy pasturelands. Abby and I have passed through Chama several times and we've always stopped for an authentic northern New Mexican meal at Viva Vera's Mexican Kitchen. Weeks ago, I decided I would celebrate my arrival at the foot of the Rockies with a restaurant meal in Chama. Now, I'm nearly tripping on my lathered tongue as I slough off my pack and walk through Vera's door. As my eyes adjust to the dark interior, I suck in the heady aroma of spice and grease and nearly keel over. Seated at a back table beneath the huge, smiling studio portrait of Vera, I devour one meal, rest a spell, then order another entree.

When my waitress brings the additional plates of streaming grub, she remarks, "Are you sure you can finish all this?"

"Listen, I walked five hundred miles for this meal and I'm hungry in places I didn't even know existed!" I declare.

After hearing more of my tale, the waitress clucks in astonishment and says, "Too bad Vera isn't here to meet you." She flips over the bill, "Here, write Vera a note. She'll be so pleased!"

Engorged and satiated, I waddle the last mile into the center of Chama. In search of information about the mountains ahead, I duck into the only outdoor gear store I can find: The Double Hackle Tackle Shop. Surrounded by an orderly array of fly fishing equipment stands a lean older gent with the air of a retired college professor. I ask which is the best way to get from Chama up to the Continental Divide and the kindly face gives me an appraising look, then squints down at my map spread on his counter. His finger traces a route up an unmarked path known locally as the Crack in the Rock Trail. The grandfatherly man begins describing his years of hiking and fishing in the mountains. His eyes gleam as he remembers flower-filled meadows and crystalline tarns and creeks.

"You know," he says wistfully. "I've always dreamed of packing up a burro and spending an entire summer up there -- just exploring and fishing and living." The man frowns and looks down at his hands. "Of course, I'm too old for that now."

I describe my summer's journey and the fisherman listens carefully, perhaps recalling his own backcountry adventures years ago. We chat awhile longer and when I turn to leave, he adds, "About seven or eight years ago, I left a little food and supplies -- candy bars and such -- cached in a tin can wedged in a spruce at the head of that Crack in the Rock Trail. Figured I'd use it next time I got up there. Well, I never did make it back," he sighs, "and now I probably never will. I don't know if it's still up there, but if you find it, you're welcome to it ."

Nodding my thanks, I step outside and realize that this wistful old man has offered me a lesson along with the trail information -- don't grow old having failed to live all your dreams. Carpe diem -- Seize the Day!

I pick up my resupply box from the drugstore and repack in the vacant lobby of the neighboring post office. In the trash can, I notice a discarded cardboard box like mine and the name on it rings a bell -- the Continental Divide hiker whose entry I read atop Mount Taylor. Guess I'm not the only crazy walker roaming through these parts.

I'm now camped a few miles from town next to the clear, mountain version of my old pal, the Rio Chama. But excitement over my imminent arrival in Colorado and the Rockies is tempered by a grave discovery moments ago. I had noticed a spot of delamination in the heel of one of my boots yesterday, so I picked up a syringe of epoxy in town today. As I completed my repairs, I checked the toes of the boots, and to my horror, discover that the soles are separating from the uppers in a BIG way. A knot has settled uncomfortably in my gut. I've applied the rest of the epoxy, but it looks doubtful. Are these boots going to survive the mountains? What does this mean for the rest of my trip?

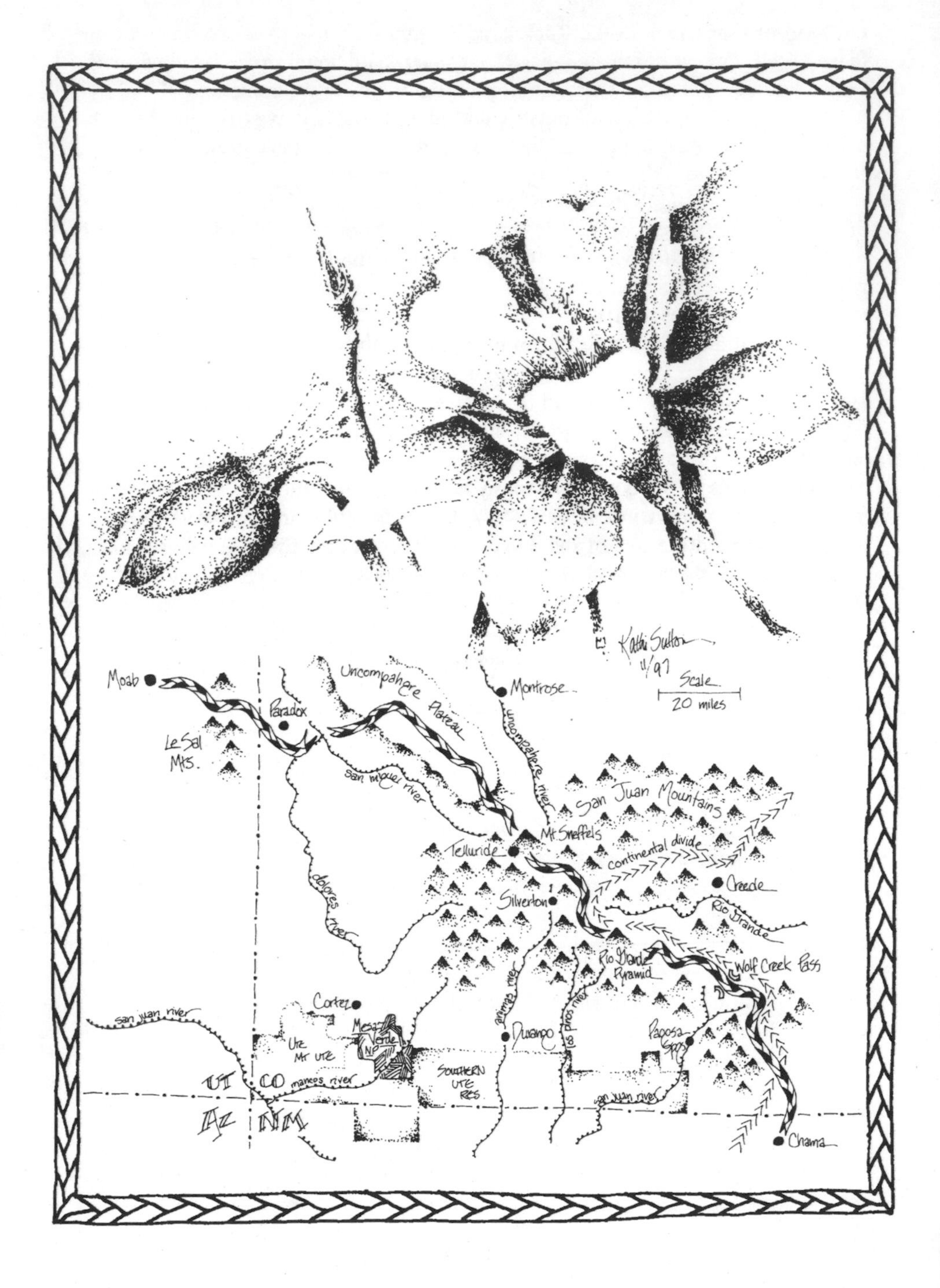
Kathi Sutton
11/97
Scale
20 miles
Moab
Paradox
Uncompahere Plateau
Le Sal
Mts.
Montrose
uncompahere river
san miguel river
San Juan Mountains
Mt Sneffels
Telluride
continental divide
Creede
Silverton
dolores river
Rio Grande
Rio Grande
Pyramid
Wolf Creek Pass
Cortez
Mesa Verde
NP
Ute
Mt Ute
animas river
Durango
los pinos river
Pagosa
Spgs
san juan river
SOUTHERN
UTE
RES.
UT
CO
mancos river
AZ
NM
san juan river
Chama

NORTHWEST
Crest of a Continent

Climb the mountains and get their good tidings.
Nature's peace will flow into you as sunshine
flows into trees. The winds will blow their
freshness into you, and storms their energy,
while cares will drop off like autumn leaves.

John Muir
My First Summer in the Sierras

Day 43, Sixteen miles
494 miles total

After a handful of morning miles, my boot soles are already coming unglued. Out comes the small stash of duct tape, that all-purpose fixer that I'm carrying for such emergencies. But even as I wrap my boot toes with the metallic gray strips, I realize that this solution is temporary at best.

Life improves as I follow the shrinking Rio Chama towards its birthplace in the impressive wall of mountains dead ahead. Soon, a nondescript sign along the gravel Forest Service road announces that I've entered Colorado. Pulling into a primitive campground, I wander over to a trio of rangers saddling their horses and ask if they have any duct tape to spare (my stash is woefully inadequate for the task at hand and I'll need a mess of the stuff to get me to Pagosa Springs). No luck, but one ranger suggests I try asking the large group camped nearby.

The campsite is a jumble of baggage, backpacks, and boys. I wade into the chaos of equipment and locate one of the leaders, a scruffy guy in his late twenties sporting muddy gaiters over his hiking boots and the "hat head" hairdo formed by a week in the backcountry. I learn that the group is a mobile summer camp called Prairie Trek that just finished a multi-day hike in the South San Juans and is headed into the urban wilds of Santa Fe and Taos. An explanation of my current plight leads into a description of my entire trek and the circle of wide-eyed young faces around me expands and grows silent. The leader grins in appreciation and tells me of the three weeks he spent alone on The Long Trail in Vermont when he was seventeen. The young man sends one of his charges scurrying to fetch the duct tape, another to fill my water bottles, and tossing me a knowing grin, disappears into the commissary truck. Moments later, he reemerges lugging two apples, four packages of granola bars, and a couple "lines" of Fig Newtons. "Here," he says with a wink. "I bet you could use this too!"

Walking away from the hubris, I think back on my three summers as an

Outward Bound instructor and smile. Ahhh yes ... leading a gang of neophytes into the backcountry, worrying about everyone else and dealing with a million details all at once -- been there, done that! Might even do it again someday.

But for now, it's up, up, and away! The dirt road peters out to a trail threading through a gorgeous mountain vale. Thick forests of aspen and spruce cloak high, tundra-topped ridges rising on either side of the valley. On my left, Chama Falls, a striking, Yosemite-sized cascade, drops hundreds of feet from an unseen lake -- the source of the Rio Chama. Beyond an old sheepherder's cabin, I step off the trail and, following the elderly fisherman's directions, bushwhack toward a pair of smaller falls at the end of the valley.

The Crack in the Rock route turns out to be an elk trail with a pitch severe enough to send mountain goats to the coronary unit. The switchbacking path through the scree appears to lead me straight to an unscalable cliff, but true to its name, a faint trail sneaks through a hidden slot in the wall. From the clifftop, I lean on my staff and savor a last view of the upper Chama valley before entering the dark, damp, pungent wonderland of huge, virgin spruce that leads to the tundra.

I'm now camped a few feet from an aged snowbank near my first highland tarn. Dipping Lake doesn't appeal for a dip as light drizzle and a sharp wind turns my breath into puffs of steamy vapor. Beneath a craggy ridge, a marmot, golden as a lion, whistles a welcome and dives into lichen-encrusted rocks. Hot, dusty deserts seem far away as I bed down in this world of rock and ice. My trek through the Rocky Mountain has begun.

Day 44, Ten miles

Bundled up in more layers than I've worn since Sugarloaf Mountain, I face a cold, overcast morning. A light rain keeps me tentbound through breakfast, but when a rainbow arcs across clearing skies, I'm trundling up a trail above treeline towards the Continental Divide. Time to check on the Pacific side of things! I grunt up a snowfield to the beckoning crest.

The view from the ridge is breathtaking. Beneath foaming clouds streaming overhead close enough to touch, row upon jagged row of soaring peaks and alpine ridges spread west and north to the horizon. The San Juan Mountains, Colorado's greatest convolution of high country, glow in the morning light. Ten thousand square miles of alpine terrain -- an area larger than my native state of New Hampshire -- lies before me in a pair of protected wilderness areas. Eastward, the broad San Luis valley is split by a silver thread of the fledgling Rio Grande. Beyond, the Sangre de Cristo range rockets skyward, blocking my view of the Great Plains still farther east. Spanning the full width of the Colorado Rockies, I spy both Blanco Peak and Hesperus Peak, the sacred eastern and northern cornerstones of the Navajo world. Never have I gazed upon such a magnificence of mountains!

Without warning, an intense wave of emotion washes over me and I weep uncontrollable tears of joy and thankfulness. It's love at first sight and my heart burns with the sudden, yet undeniable epiphany that these peaks must someday become my homeland. Other places have called to me, but never like this. How long have I waited for this feeling in my soul? Alone on the windswept crest of the continent, I cry, laugh, dance, and cry again.

When the emotional hurricane subsides, I continue along the knobby backbone of the nation, amazed at the beauty. Clean, icy water flows everywhere. Forested plateaus scored by deep stream valleys sweep away from this twelve thousand-foot high corridor of rolling tundra. Large glaciated lakes and innumerable tarns grace alpine grasslands splotched with lingering snowfields like a string of azure jewels on a mosaic of emerald and ivory velvet.

And the wildflowers! Two dozen varieties of hardy alpine blossoms paint the tundra in pink, purple, white, lavender, yellow, and crimson. My favorite are the clusters of thumbnail-sized flowers of bright blue surrounding yellow centers. Lacking any sort of field guide, I dub these beauties "Bright Eyes" as they bring to mind Abby's smiling face and her passion for wildflowers. Abby's post at the Alpine Visitor Center of Rocky Mountain National Park is only a mile away from the Continental Divide and somehow I feel as if this thin, imaginary line is a telegraph wire connecting our souls. Is she receiving any of my intoxicating happiness right now? If not for this heavy pack, I'd be prancing and dancing down this trail like a demented Julie Andrews!

In my exuberance, I fail to notice the storm clouds forming overhead until the first ominous rumble of thunder. Remembering how this paradise turns deadly when afternoon electrical storms roll in, I drop off the divide to treeline. One storm, then another, blow in just to the north during the final three-mile pull to Blue Lake. The popular lake is already crowded with campers, so I move to a nearby pond and erect the tent just as the third storm makes a direct hit. My sparkling Eden has turned cold and wet, but that's just part of the admission price. I'm still as content as a cat on a warm lap. Bravo for the mighty San Juans!

Day 45, No forward miles

Whoa, I forgot how chilly it gets up here, even in July. Sleeping in extra clothing barely did the trick. Of course, I've already broken Rule #1 of camping above 11,000 feet: bring your sweetie to cuddle!

Basking in the warmth of the morning sun, I declare a layover and decide to dayhike to the summit of nearby Conejos Peak. Heads poke from neighboring tents when I tromp by, looking like groggy bears emerging from hibernation. Near Glacier Lake, where a ten-foot thick snowbank lingers on a north-facing slope, I spy a tiny fawn only a few yards away, huddled protectively under a dwarf willow. Elk and deer hoof prints and droppings are everywhere. Bold sparrows explore the lichen-covered cairns leading me up the easy, grassy dome.

By midmorning, I'm atop the 13,172-foot summit of Conejos, absorbed by one of my favorite activities -- sorting out the landscape with my map and visible landmarks. Few things are more gratifying to a hardcore geography junkie like me than a good hit of map-reading atop a high mountain on a clear day! After lunch, I'm snoozing like a marmot on the sunny slope until a distant growl of thunder wrecks my nap. The rest of the afternoon is a race with storm clouds back to camp.

Trouble in Paradise. I'm sitting next to my front yard pond pumping drinking water through my filter when the devil's winged horde descends upon me like a thousand swarming vampires. One slap leaves six or seven blood-splattered mosquito carcasses on my calf. RETREAT! Only the wind on an exposed ridge above camp brings relief from the insects. My failing boots are another nagging worry. All my elaborate spider webs of duct tape eventually disintegrate. Today I tried a simpler set-up using parachute cord and this rig should get me to the next town stop. But are they repairable? I need good boots -- this is no place to lose my sole!

Day 46, Fourteen miles.

What a day! I can honestly say that today has been the finest stretch of walking on my quest. In fact, I'm hard pressed to remember a more impressive day anywhere. And tonight, at 12,300 feet, I shall sleep higher than ever before.

After sunset last night, the temperature plummets, sending the blood-sucking swarms into a stupor. I stroll down to the lake and wind up at the fire of two local guys spending their annual retreat in the mountains. We sip tea, eat cookies, and gawk at the explosion of stars plastered overhead. Heading back to my tent, I spurn the kindly offer of a flashlight ("Naw, it's just over the hill") -- and proceed to stumble around lost in the darkness for twenty minutes.

The dawn is as clear as the choir of coyote voices which awaken me. Beyond Blue Lake, the actual divide is an untraversable jagged ridge, so I roller coaster around massive basins; diving into the forest, then climbing mercilessly back to the tundra. When the trail disappears completely beneath a steep snowfield, I stare down the icy pitch and swear softly. An imaginary headline flashes through my brain: "Unfortunate Hiker Found Mangled at Bottom of Deadly San Juan Snowfield!" Tentatively, I step out onto the steeply angled snow. The surface is firm, but not glazed. Keeping my weight on my heels and using my walking stick as a brake and rudder, I start sliding/skiing downhill like a toddler on the bunny slope. As my confidence grows, fear becomes exhilaration. By the time I reach the bottom, I'm already eager for the next snowfield. Fortunately, my parachute cord boot repair system works like a charm. Yippee -- glissading in July!

My surroundings continue to dazzle. Dramatic crags splashed with sparkling snowfields are connected to emerald meadows and robust conifer forests by lacy networks of cascading meltwater. A kaleidoscope of wildflowers cluster in gardens so thick that I dare not step off the trail. The cerulean sky above is as clear and bright as the dancing creeks. I am weak with delight.

By the time I'm climbing out of Adam's Fork of the Conejos River, I'm also weak with exhaustion. Miles at this altitude are twice as demanding as those below. A treeless bench of ponds and pikas below Summit Peak is too inviting to pass by and now I'm camped in a slice of heaven. I surely hope this ain't all a dream that I'll wake up from back in Winslow!

Day 47, Fourteen miles

When dawn is but a promise in the east, I crawl from my frost-encrusted tent, wriggle into every stitch of clothing I have, grab a camera, waterbottle, and a handful of dried fruit, and strike off for a sunrise ascent of Summit Peak. A coyote, shaggy as an arctic wolf, surprises me at 13,000 feet as the first arrows of golden light strike the mountaintop. Coyote, Raven and Swallow have become my totem animals on this quest. Like myself, these creatures are found from the highest mountaintops to the deepest canyons throughout the Southwest. I feel a deepening brotherhood with these fellow nomads of the wilderness, their presence offering me friendship and inspiration wherever I roam. With companions like these, who can feel lonely?

On top at 13,272 feet, I'm perched at the highest point in the southern San Juans. Squatting out of the biting wind, I eat dried apricots and watch the newborn sun flood the ocean of crags before me. A handful of 14,000-foot peaks stand head and shoulders above their comrades while, to the south, the bluish dome of the San Pedro Parks Wilderness rises out of the dusty, flat basin of Chaco Wash and the San Juan River. So much seen; so far still to go.

I zip back to camp via the express route -- an exhilarating and dangerous glissade down a frozen couloir. The trail remains above 12,000 feet as it contours around two more peaks. A small herd of elk prance from the Atlantic to the Pacific drainage at the foot of Montezuma Peak. Next along the ridge, Long Trek Mountain, is only a shade under 13,000 feet tall, but with a name like that, how could I resist a quick pilgrimage to the top? The summit cairn is a pitiful affair, so I construct a decent three-foot high rock pile and start a summit log proclaiming this peak to be the patron mountain to all Continental Divide Trail hikers and the rest of us "long trekkers." Hmmm, maybe I could be the Forest Service's "Official Inspector of Summit Cairns and Editor-in-Chief of Peak Logbooks." Now there's a career I could handle!

The spell which has held me bewitched over the last four days is broken when I cross the official wilderness boundary and immediately hit a two-rut dirt bike trail littered with cigarette butts gouging its way over the divide. At Elwood pass, a gravel road from the east deadends. I stare glumly at a knot of parked cars and the scars of past logging and mining. When the trail drops off the tundra and into the trees, a sense of melancholy grabs me. Oddly enough, I would have waxed poetic about this spruce forest a week ago, but the beautiful trek across an alpine wonderland has spoiled me. Imagine being denied ice cream for years. Suddenly you get all the Ben and Jerry's you can eat. When you're served Hood ice cream after that, who wouldn't complain a little?

The afternoon sours further when blustery hailstorms descend and the trail loses itself in ragged clearcuts. Now a cold rain drums on my tent pitched in the forested saddle of Silver Pass. Tomorrow, I'll hit the highway at Wolf Creek Pass and hitch down to Pagosa Springs for my resupply and boot repairs. Maybe I'll even take in a few "flatlander" luxuries before returning to the pass to tackle another leg along the Continental Divide.

Day 48, Ten miles

I crank out fast morning miles to reach Route 160 and Wolf Creek Pass, tromping past hibernating chair lifts of a ski area and dropping a quick thousand feet in switchbacks. Abruptly, I step from the trees into a swarm of tourists snapping pictures of each other astride the Continental Divide. More culture shock. Another backpacker stands across the highway trying to bum a ride toward Pagosa Springs. Could this be the mystery hiker whose tracks I've followed since Blue Lake? I amble over to find out, but before I can even introduce myself, a van pulls up beside us offering a ride and we both hop in.

Next thing I know, I'm whizzing down the mountainside at 60 mph, sipping a soda, listening to music, and hoping the middle-aged Missouri couple in front aren't noticing the ripe body odors blossoming from their backseat. The other hiker sits beside me -- a tall, baby-faced young man with gentle smile, a soft voice and golden dreadlocks. We take turns telling our tales. The other hiker, AJ, has just completed an eleven-day trek on the Continental Divide Trail from his home in Telluride. This is exactly my next leg and I'm alive with questions. Soon we are chatting and laughing like long-lost buddies and the driver can't quite figure it all out. "You mean you guys aren't hiking together?" he asks, shooting us glances over his shoulder. We giggle and wag our filthy heads.

I jump out when we arrive in Pagosa Springs and head straight to the boot repair shop. The prognosis is as expected; the boots can be fixed, but I will have to stay off them for at least twenty-four hours to allow the glue to properly cure. Since the boots are my only footwear, I duck into the nearby Methodist Thrift Shop and emerge sporting a pair of two dollar used leather sandals on my blindingly white feet.

Next stop is the Rolling Pin Bakery where the sight and smell of delectable cookies and pastries leave me dizzy. I purchase and inhale a few sweet rolls, then head to the ranger station next door for trail information while leaving my backpack stashed on the bakery's porch. An hour later, I'm back at the bakery, hoisting my pack and wondering vaguely where I'll camp tonight when the door flies open behind me.

"Hey, wait! Are you Brett LeCompte?" a female voice hollers.

I spin around to face an unknown blond woman in her forties and slowly nod.

The woman grins, then chuckles at the confusion written across my face. "Don't worry," she assures me. "We're friends. Can my husband and I buy you lunch?" And thus, I am introduced to Barb and Don Rosner.

Turns out that the Rosners are old buddies with my friends Kitty and Brian Benzar who live in neighboring Durango, Colorado. The Rosners have just left the Benzar's home this morning after a week's visit. Since Kitty knew I'm scheduled to reach Pagosa Springs soon, she gave the Rosners a bag of treats to drop off at the visitor center where she knew my resupply box is stashed. Don and Barb, passing through town, completed their mission and stopped at the bakery for lunch. When Don walked by my unattended pack on the porch, he had joked that maybe it was mine. When they later spotted me through the window leaving with the pack, Barb decided to find out. Et voila!

Despite the unusual introductions, I feel an immediate kinship with the Rosners. Between bites of my chicken sandwich, the story of my Southwest Circle Quest spills out. Don explains how he and Barbara have been on a sort of quest themselves since they sold their home and computer business in Phoenix two years ago, bought a fancy RV, and set off to explore America. After a final winter holed up in Talkeetna, Alaska, the Rosners are back in the Southwest searching for a new place to set down roots. Like me, this part of Colorado calls out to them. On we talk like old friends until I abruptly realize we are alone in the restaurant with the waitress sweeping up.

When the Rosners learn about my boots and my need to stay in town for a couple of nights, they quickly invite me to stay with them in their mobile home. I gleefully accept their offer, happy at this unexpected turn of events. A couple of hours later, I'm sitting down to a huge heaping of Barb's savory home-cooking in the Rosners bus-sized home on wheels. My hair is still damp from my first hot shower in almost two months. The Rosners accept me like a long-lost son as we gab and laugh like a reunited family and I can't stop grinning.

How starved I've been for real human contact! Stories have poured out of me in an unstoppable flood. Tonight I give thanks for the many gifts of kindness bestowed upon me by strangers during my quest.

Day 49, No forward miles

In the morning, I return to Pagosa Springs with the Rosners for a day of separate errands. Don and Barb strike off to haunt the real estate offices while I loiter around town -- browsing the bookstores, mailing postcards to let people know I'm still alive and kicking, checking out the famous hot springs ("the Largest and Hottest in the World!"), and catching up on the latest National Geographics in the library. Reading my favorite magazine, I have to laugh. One minute, all I can think about is settling down and creating a home for myself and Abby. Yet, hand me an engrossing article about Patagonia, Tibet, or any other far-flung locale, and I'm ready to pack my bags and wing away. Sometimes I feel as flighty as a pigeon!

In the afternoon, I'm all business. First, fresh food for the next leg plus a leafy lunch salad from the supermarket. Next, I head to the visitor center and retrieve my cache box. Finally, I reclaim my boots from the repair shop. My soles seem resurrected and ready to tackle the heavenly high country again.

When Don and Barb pick me up at the town green, they wear the weary look of frustrated house-hunters. Parked at a campground on the San Juan River, Barb whips up another culinary masterpiece (anything beyond boiled grain or pasta seems positively epicurean to me these days!), while Don and I walk his two Airedales, Rocky and Anna. Another stimulating conversation over tea ends this mellow day. It is hard to believe that I met these fine people just yesterday. As someone once said: "You will know a true friend better after ten minutes than you will know an acquaintance after a lifetime."

Day 50, Ten miles

This morning I'm up early, eager to start my end to end traverse of the Weminuche -- Colorado's largest designated wilderness area. My plan is to hitch back to Wolf Creek Pass, but over breakfast Don announces that he and Barb are eastbound and can drop me off. A few hours later, we step out of the RV into the crystalline, rarefied air of the 10,800-foot pass. How can I thank these fine people who have given me so much with their gifts of food, shelter, comfort, and company? The new book I bought them yesterday hardly suffices, so I try to squeeze my thanks into them with bear hugs. Stepping off the pavement with a final wave, I slip into the trees and begin a hundred miles of Colorado's finest.

I feel great: clean clothes and hair, full tanks of fluid and fuel, rejuvenated mind, body, and soles! When I climb above treeline and stride along the rocky ridge of the divide, my pleasure is complete. Ahhh, back among the marmots and the Bright Eyes. Did you guys miss me?

This close to a major trailhead, I meet a variety of hikers: three gawky lads with excited tales of the fishing in the lakes ahead, a couple from Santa Fe hobbling out on blistered feet, a doctor vacationing from his post on the Navajo Reservation. My favorite encounter is with a covey of fluffy ptarmigan chicks. I would have walked right by these camouflaged balls of downy feathers if one hadn't accidentally tumbled from under a rock and onto the trail -- two ounces of pure innocence.

The afternoon clouds have gathered when I pitch my tent near Archuleta Lake, but out in the clear water, the trout are jumping and without hesitation, I join them. Yeeeow, that's cold! Pulling on layers over my bluish gooseflesh, I promise myself to slow down, climb more peaks, shiver in more lakes, and drink more wildflower perfume on this leg. The journey, not the destination, is my true goal.

Day 51, Ten miles

Nobody stirs in the other tents around Archuleta Lake as I quietly climb out of the basin at first light. Don't those folks know that dawn is one of the best shows up here? No matter -- I'll enjoy it for them. Remembering yesterday's vow, I ditch my pack and scramble with breakfast up the boulder-strewn shoulder of 12,800-foot Mount Hope. Over granola, I gaze contentedly at past and future mountains until an arrow of melancholy skewers my heart. How I'd love to be sharing these summits with Abby! I miss my best friend.

The trail clings to the crest of the Continental Divide, heading north toward Sawtooth Mountain where a herd of twenty elk explode up one side of the ridge, then gallop down the other side. The trail cuts west and climbs to nearly 13,000 feet. The view is awesome, but so are the black clouds spitting lightning and blowing my way. This exposed ridge is a prime lightning target and I'd rather not be the bullseye since my CPR self-rescue skills aren't really up to snuff!

Chased by thunder, I drop sharply off the firing line on a convenient side trail. Up goes the tent and I crouch inside only to watch the storm dissipate and the sun reappear. Ahhh, the fickleness of mountain weather!

Day 52, Twelve miles

The pikas, usually invisible squeaks emanating from the talus piles, are unusually conspicuous as I huff back up to the Continental Divide Trail. These fist-sized, furry-faced dynamos are always good for a laugh with their skittering antics. The twenty elk who shared their basin with me last night are quietly grazing below. Rocks clatter above and I look up into the delicate face of a mule deer daintily picking her way down my trail. She looks thoroughly lost and confused in the scree at 13,000 feet.

A little ways along the ridge, I spot another hiker coming my way. After the customary preliminaries, I ask if he's passed my mystery Continental Divide hiker. "Nope, haven't seen'm." Then the backpacker adds, "but I did meet some folks who met a guy on the fiftieth day of his trip who says he's walked from Flagstaff." I laugh and beam, proud to be on the "trail telegraph."

At Piedra Pass, I pause where two small ponds sit a hundred yards apart yet drain into different oceans. The morning has spun by with pitifully little progress along my map. Ten miles up here leaves me as exhausted as eighteen miles down below. The trail remains empty as Palomino Mountain rolls by and I wonder if it's always so quiet. The other end of the Weminuche is said to be more popular. Brian, my buddy from Wyoming, is working for Colorado Outward Bound School trips somewhere in these mountains right now. Wouldn't it be a kick to meet up with him. I could tell his students a story or two!

The sky turns nasty again by lunchtime. Vague booms of distant thunder become nearby crashes. I tuck under the protective cover of a spruce grove and brace myself for the brunt of the storm. Crackling bolts lick the ridge where I just strolled. Thunder rips the air, its rolling echo forming a continuous roar. I'm hoping the system will move out as quickly as it enveloped me, but the clouds just swirl and darken. Feeling like a helpless pawn before an angry Zeus, I cower beneath the trees.

The storm eases and the sky lightens a little. Cautiously, I continue within the protection of the forest until the trail wriggles out on another section of exposed ridge. I hesitate, juggling the odds of more lightning, but eager to reach my planned campsite several miles farther. Convinced the weather ahead is indeed improving, I start along the rocky crest. Suddenly, a jagged shaft of white-hot electricity smashes into the ridge less than a mile ahead. OK, Zeus -- that message was loud and clear! Backtracking, I abandon the ridge and crash down a steep elk trail. Five hundred feet lower in thick timber, I crawl into my nylon home, drenched and wide-eyed.

The thunder has quieted, but a cold, steady rain pours down. Every paradise has its serpent and in the mountains, it's the erratic and often dangerous weather. I'd hoped to be farther along, but I guess today's lesson is "go with the flow."

Day 53, Thirteen miles

Today has been a day of superlatives to match the one a week ago in the South San Juans. The weather was as wonderful as it was rotten yesterday. I enjoyed incredible hiking, stupendous wildflowers, beautiful lakes and creeks, a circus of marmots and pikas providing non-stop entertainment, and a flurry of interesting human encounters. To literally top it off, I'm now camped on an awesome lookout at a shade under 13,000 feet. Now if only that storm vaguely blowing in my direction will just veer ever so slightly and avoid striking me dead, I'll give this day an A+!

After slumbering like a hunk of granite, I bushwhack straight back up to the divide -- a grueling grunt that makes a Stairmaster workout look like a nap in the sun. Once I'm cruising on the ridgetop, it's clear that I did the smart thing yesterday afternoon; the long, exposed crest, so pleasant under today's bright sky, would have been deadly in yesterday's storm.

The long list of characters destined to cross my path today begin to appear. Everyone has a story about yesterday's storm. First, a couple from England also crossing the Weminuche Wilderness, but heading north to south ("You've got a bloody nice piece of hiking ahead, mate!") Next, I overtake two middle-aged high school teachers from Washington. Finally, I pass a church group of geezers and teens from Dallas strung out along a mile of trail. The trail's social possibilities seem exhausted until I top a ridge and stumble into a mob of *nineteen* backpackers on a snack break. Whoa, when did the tundra get so crowded? Up here, I don't even stick out like I did back in New Mexico and Arizona -- just one of the many grungy, happy souls with his home on his back and his head in the clouds.

I mingle, sampling trail mixes and exchanging pleasantries at this impromptu alpine cocktail party. When I learn that this gang is going my way, I ease back into the harness, eager to put some distance between me and the crowd. Five attractive women, apparently a separate party, also disengage from the rest of the group and start down the trail just before me. Hmmm...nice timing! I follow these lovelies from Boulder like an overgrown puppy, chatting away and enjoying the view until the ladies pull over to scan for elk with binoculars. On down I pound, descending through spruce and fir to the wide notch of Squaw Pass.

Plopping down for lunch, I hear hooves on talus and look up to see Davy Crockett approaching. The bearded, buckskin-clad horseman, accompanied by his wife and three loaded pack horses, rides up and hollers, "Howdy, partner! That was a helluva storm yesterday, wasn't it? I usually don't come up here until later in autumn during elk season. Ya know -- hauling gear in and out for those Texas hunters. Ya camping here tonight?"

"Nope, but I just passed over a dozen backpackers who are," I explain.

Crockett lets loose a long, low whistle and swivels in his saddle. "Hear that, honey? Maybe we'd best keep riding for a piece." With a dip of their broad cowboy hats, the couple wheel and start plodding up the trail, looking every bit a vision from a century ago.

My last encounter is another solo hiker bound from Lake City to Wolf Creek Pass. After hearing my quest route, the balding backpacker smiles appreciatively. "I used to do that sort of thing myself. Hiked the John Muir Trail three times. I toyed with the idea of tackling the whole Pacific Crest Trail. But, I got married, had a kid ..." The hiker sighs. "Now I'm lucky to get away for just this five-day trip."

The last few miles between Squaw Pass and Squaw Lake are glorious as the trail weaves in and out of beautiful basins beneath a sawtoothed skyline. I had planned to camp near the lake, but the view from a nearby whalebacked ridge is so captivating that I've decided to sleep on top. It's risky to camp here so high and exposed, but tomorrow's sunrise from here will be worth it.

Day 54, Ten miles

STUPID! How could I be such a bonehead? Maybe the 40,000-volt jolt to my noggin that I narrowly avoided last night is what I need to knock some sense into it.

After writing yesterday's entry, I cook dinner and make a final weather reconnaissance before turning in. The western horizon is a boiling black mass, yet it seems to be blowing safely away to the north. Of more concern is the smaller storm heading my way that's dropping not only a dark veil of rain, but also an occasional brilliant bolt. A hollow feeling creeps into my belly as I review my situation: camped at 13,000 feet on a bald dome (Zeus' altar?) ringed by treacherous cliffs, light failing fast, lightning apparently approaching on the frigid wind. I crawl into the tent, opting to chance the storm over probable hypothermia and perhaps a nasty tumble in a hasty retreat in the dark. Listening to the thump of my heart punctuating lightning flashes, I alternately curse and pray, scared as a lost child. But, wait -- where's the thunder? I peak out the tentflap, expecting to find Death bearing down, but the storm is actually miles away, backlighting distant peaks. As if in answer to my prayers, the storm has swerved and I'm out of danger.

When dawn appears, the sky is overcast. The photo for which I risked my life never even materializes. Some of the teachings from the natural world are candy-coated and easy to swallow, but others, like last night's, are being branded into me with a hot iron. Actually, I'm lucky that this lesson was accomplished with just a good scare. Properly humbled, I break camp and descend from (newly dubbed) Second Chance Mountain. All morning, the elk and pikas and ptarmigans flee at my approach as if embarrassed to associate with such a knucklehead. Even the trail hides for a spell, forcing me to barge through thickets of chest-high willows.

Weminuche Pass is the lowest point along the Continental Divide in the San Juans: broad, boggy, buggy, and uninspiring. A man-made ditch tinkers with the plumbing, diverting Colorado River-bound water down into the Rio Grande watershed. The only redeeming feature of the pass is the excellent view of Rio Grande Pyramid, a rocky pinnacle looming four miles to the west. This dramatic peak has been a local landmark since Ute hunting bands roamed this range. An early government geographic survey team made the first recorded ascent of Rio Grande Pyramid in 1874. My plan is to make the latest recorded ascent tomorrow.

The Rincon La Vaca drainage leads the way toward the peak. Three elderly women in their sixties are camped just off the trail. Way to go, ladies. I hope I'll be returning to these mountains until my wheelchair rusts away! A little farther, a nest of teenagers with packs is sprawled by a cabin-sized boulder. Two leaders are preparing a big lunch for everyone with no help from their sulking brood. I learn only that this group is neither Outward Bound nor Prairie Trek, but another outfit based out of Creede, Colorado before the pregnant clouds overhead give birth to a vicious hailstorm. This stirs the kids into action -- up goes a patched tarp that barely shelters the huddling bodies. I shuffle into my raingear, squat on my heels under the dense cover of a nearby conifer, and hunker.

For an hour, we're pinned down by the hail, rain, and a several close lightning strikes, but in contrast to the previous night, I'm relaxed being out of the line of fire. The splash and gurgle of a stream at my feet seems to neutralize the raging of the storm. Wolfing down trailmix like popcorn at a new movie also helps. When the system slides east, the teenagers emerge from beneath the tarp like baby spiders spewing from their egg case. As they gawk at what appears to be a fresh dusting of snow (actually hail) frosting the jagged skylines, I disappear like a ghost into white mists surging uphill in the wake of the storm.

I'm now camped right at the foot of Rio Grande Pyramid on a bench of verdant tundra and volcanic scree fields infested with pikas and marmots. Try to recall the sound of your bathtub rubber duckie -- now you know the call of the pika. Think back to the lifeguard's shrill whistle when he caught you goofing off in the community pool -- that would be the marmots. Everyone's out enjoying the late afternoon sunshine after the storm. What a ruckus!

Boot update: it looks like my soles are destined to be eternally damned. That's right -- they're coming unstuck again. A new and improved parachute cord system is back in place around the toes. Time for new boots when I reach Telluride.

Day 55, Seven miles

When John Muir first submitted his writings of his life in the Sierras for publication, one editor was impressed, yet reputedly complained that every other word was "glorious." After this extraordinary day, I'm afraid this entry may suffer from the same malady. Bear with me.

I rouse myself at dawn and organize a daypack for climbing the fifteen hundred-foot rock pile before me. After an hour of stumbling up loose scree, I'm halfway up, sucking down thin air and dried apples as the sun kisses the apex of the spire. The final seven hundred feet appeared to be a technical climb from a distance, but turn out to be a straightforward scramble. Reaching the summit cairn rewards me with the finest vista of the quest. The sawtoothed spires of the Needles and Grenadier Ranges a dozen miles to the west are as rugged and wild as any I've set eyes on. Clear and sharp as Eden, they seem to glow with an inner holy light. Pristine creek valleys below form green fingers reaching towards the headwaters of the mighty Rio Grande. Behind me, Weminuche Pass is submerged in a shadowy lake of swirling mist with the faint silhouettes of the South San Juans rippling along the eastern horizon. The sky is flawless; the air is calm and warm. Every direction begs for my attention as I stand bedazzled atop the world muttering, "Glorious, glorious!"

Reaching this peak is particularly special to me. Standing atop the 13,821-foot summit, I'm higher than ever before. Since I'm about midway through the sixth leg of my thirteen leg journey, Rio Grande Pyramid is also the halfway point of my Southwest Circle Quest. Finally, this peak affords the grandest overall view of the mountains which I intend to call home. Raven, Swallow, and Coyote, my three totems, have each made an appearance this morning to join my celebration. It was worth a week of rain and lightning storms to be up here on this glorious morning. Whoooooeee -- I'm as happy as a hawk!

A priceless, magical hour flies by. When the first puffy clouds begin forming above the Needles Range, I reluctantly start down. The descent is as enjoyable as the climb without all the oxygen debt. Far below, a colorful line of ants -- the group from Creede -- is just reaching the talus slopes on a parallel route. I wave and give them the thumbs-up signal, glad to have had the peak to myself. Some grand moments are not meant to be shared.

Once packed and rolling, I examine my next destination: La Ventana (The Window). A huge gap in a jagged rib extending off Rio Grande Pyramid, this unique feature resembles a battle-blasted breach in the castle wall of some alpine Titan. The main trail contours around the mountain's shoulder, but I huff up a demanding elk trail, determined to explore this famed attraction.

The wind barrels through the hundred-foot gap as if the mountain is drawing in breath. Chinese Taoists describe an energy called chi that flows through pathways in the Earth to focal points such as mountaintops. Braced in the throat of the wind between towering ribs of stone, I cannot deny the forces flowing through this spot, permeating my being. Unfortunately, this chi doesn't improve my judgment one whit. Instead of an easy retreat back down the way I came, I boldly pass through La Ventana and wind up traversing a treacherously steep scree slope, almost taking a nasty tumble. Back down on the Continental Divide Trail, my tail is tucked between my legs once again.

After lunch, the landscape undergoes a subtle change of character. A plethora of large lakes and smaller ponds lie scooped in a bedrock of granite which replaces the porous volcanic rock through which I've been tramping. The sheer towers of the Mount Oso range ahead looks more like the Sierra Nevada than the southern San Juans. The daily thunderboomers, however, are unchanged, swooping in and skipping out. Under a pelting hail, I climb another pass, but upon top, sunshine bursts forth and I feel like Moses looking into the Promised Land. Ahead in an dramatic cathedral of cliffs and peaks lies the archetypal alpine lake -- a liquid sapphire sparkling in the rain-freshened air. Enraptured, I am floating down an intoxicating meadow toward this glorious Nirvana when a sudden turn of events sends me crashing rudely back to earth.

My footing feels funny. Glancing down at my boot, I'm stricken with horror ... my left heel is flapping loose. The damage is much worse than before and, in an instant, I know that these boots aren't going to make it to Telluride. As this realization sinks home, I groan in despair, then plop down and yank out my map. One side trail off the divide leaves this basin and heads out to Vallecito Lake, a trailhead near Durango. Hmmm ... Durango? Looks like I could make it out in one long day. There's several outdoor supply stores in town and I could stay with my friends, Kitty and Brian. Another glance at the map, then my boots, and the choice is clear: tomorrow, I'm outta here! Still chewing on this new plan, I carefully hobble down to Rock Lake and set up residence in Shangri-la.

Now darkness has fallen and the pasta is simmering. I've expanded my parachute cord system to stabilize the backs of my dying soles and, with little luck, they'll make it one more day. I can't believe I have to leave this beautiful place. How will this new twist affect my quest? Too soon to tell. Time to roll with the punches.

Day 56, Eighteen miles

As I write this dawn entry, black night is slowly resolving itself into shapes and colors while a gentle choir of birds warms up nearby. After living outside continuously for two months, this scene is familiar. Yet this morning, I lie in a soft bed, write by an electric lamp, and view the day's awakening through an open window. Ready or not, I'm back in what most people erroneously call "The Real World."

The proceeding night on the tundra was a chilly one. I am burrowing into my down cocoon after supper when a loud snort explodes just outside my tent. Moments later, frantic hooves pound away. The elk soon return and I lie still in my bag and listen to their grazing just outside my door, wondering what they think of the bright yellow nylon boulder that mysteriously appeared on their dinner table.

When the spires above me are bathed in a rosy hue, I'm packing the dew-drenched tent -- no time to dry now. I have miles to go before I sleep. Farewell, Rock Lake ... I shall return. Treading carefully on my battered boots, I start my long retreat to civilization.

The gorge of Rock Creek is a miniature Yosemite Valley. Grassy meadows sliced by a tumbling stream curve upward to borders of thick spruce. Magnificent granite cliffs, domes, and pinnacles soar higher still, forming a grand corridor striped with cascades fluttering down from unseen tarns. And then, beside the trail, a dead elk swarming with maggots -- beauty and death side by side.

Turning left into the immense Vallecito Creek valley, I move like a determined ant beneath the formidable wall of the Needles Range rising four thousand unassailable feet above me. The wildflower gardens, the patches of snow, and the expansive vistas disappear in my wake, but new delights await me in the lower elevations. Deciduous trees reappear. Gem-like strawberries and hammerheaded grasshoppers peek from the tall, thick grass. A balmy breeze swirls the heady fragrance of green profundity. Hey, it's summer down here! I'd almost forgotten what July normally feels like.

Biting flies and the need to make miles keep me moving steadily down the eroded horse trail until I finally succumb to the unaccustomed heat and the siren song of the luscious creek. One sandy spot near some glassy pools is just too sweet to pass by. I strip and dive into the icy water. After drifting with the current awhile, I haul my shivering, naked body onto a sunny boulder and stretch out like a seal, then notice a string of horsepackers plodding by less than a dozen feet away. I throw in the only thing handy -- a foolish grin--and wave.

Five miles farther and I'm smelling the campground at the trailhead before I can see it: barbecues, wood smoke, bug spray -- the aroma of car campers. One hour and a jeep ride later, I'm fighting culture shock amidst a clot of tourists swarming in downtown Durango on a Friday afternoon. Calling the Benzars from a pay phone, I hear the shock in Kitty's voice when she realizes that it's me. "No ... I'm OK," I explain. "It's my boots that are injured." After listening to a quick rundown of my situation, Kitty promises to pick me up within an hour.

I try my luck at the outdoor gear stores while I wait. Another repair job is out of the question, but I'm hoping to convince the salespeople that these relatively new boots are defective and that I deserve a free replacement pair. Two stores listen to my woeful tale, yet can promise nothing until they talk to their distributors on Monday morning. Nobody has my size (13) in stock anyway, so I'm looking at a 2nd day air delivery after that. It all boils down to at least four days in Durango.

Kitty and Brian's smiling faces are a great relief as they whisk me away from the din of downtown to their comfortable country home in the aspens. The Benzars are graciously serving as my emergency contact throughout the quest. They are also holding onto trip slides coming from the lab where I've been sending exposed rolls of film. After dinner, I tell the story of meeting Don and Barb in Pagosa Springs and try to answer their questions about the last two months, then glance through a few boxes of the slides. Images from Sugarloaf Mountain and the Navajo Reservation stir up powerful memories of my journey's beginning. Finally, I retire to the guest bedroom, exhausted but unable to sleep; my mind still swirling from the rapid transitions of the day. For better or worse, my Southwest Circle Quest is getting a temporary mid-trip suspension.

Day 61, No forward miles

Five days have passed since I emerged from the wilderness into the comforts of the Benzar's home. The Southwest Circle Quest has already begun to feel like ancient history as I peruse trip slides from the depths of an easy chair while grabbing yet another handful of potato chips. With the edge removed from my daily existence, the days have blurred together. To the twin temptresses of Comfort and Ease, I must now say, "Thanks, I enjoyed my visit and appreciated your company, but it's time for me to go home." And home to the wild country is where I'm ready to go.

Earlier in the week, when I returned to downtown Durango, my hope of wrangling a free pair of replacement Asolo boots was quickly shot down. I settle for new Danner boots, but a pair my size must be shipped from Portland, Oregon. More waiting. Returning to the sanctuary of Kitty and Brian's place, I resume the two activities which filled my weekend -- eating and reading.

Back in the men's room of the Pagosa Springs laundromat, my first full-length glimpse of my naked body in seven weeks had resulted in a slack-jawed double take. Below were my tanned, well muscled thighs atop a pair of calves grown so huge that they had become heifers! This much I'd been able to see all along. It was my torso, or more specifically the lack thereof, that shocked me. On my snowy-white chest, the pectoral muscles (not much to brag about on a good day) had been replaced by a protruding rack of ribs. Hey, who's that refugee in the mirror wearing my mug?

The Benzar's bathroom scale reveals the ugly truth -- my six foot, four inch frame carries a mere hundred and fifty pounds. Somewhere between Flagstaff and Durango, fifteen pounds of yours truly has evaporated! At this rate, there's gonna be holes in my shadow before I get back to Flagstaff! At least this explains my manic hunger on the trail.

Time to fatten up. Using this golden opportunity in civilization, I upgrade my normal "see-food" diet into "The Southwest Circle Quest Seek-food Health Plan." Three servings of breakfast lead smoothly into an afternoon of lunches. Kitty creates a series of scrumptious dinners which I guarantee never reach leftover status. Thankfully, the Benzars are busy and don't observe the carnage that I inflict on their cupboards. Little do they realize that the containers on their shelves are just empty decoys to cover my tracks! I chow big time without reserve or guilt and my body responds. Over five days, I regain twelve pounds.

The other activity that fills my "time off" satisfies a hunger even greater than my gut's -- the hunger of my mind. I made a vow not to take any books on my quest in order to focus on the "here and now," yet literary celibacy has proven surprisingly difficult. During town stops, I've gravitated towards words: bookstores, used books, and libraries. Now with access to the Benzar's excellent library, I feed my brain as eagerly as my belly.

Music is another simple, yet glorious pleasure. With everything from classical instrumental pieces to foot-stomping bluegrass and rock and roll, I drink deeply from the Benzar's CD collection and quench a powerful thirst.

Another quest vow was to restrict all incoming news from family and friends -- no phone calls, just occasional outgoing postcards to let people know I'm OK. But since this vow has been largely negated by my time in Durango, I decide to call Abby. Our hour and a half conversation flies by, but I would trade all the time on the phone for a minute in Abby's arms.

Now that my mid-quest "vacation" is drawing to a close, I can honestly say that I'm glad it occurred. As I suspected, my time in Durango became more than just a chance to get new boots. My depleted body was restocked and my starving brain was satisfied. Now I can enter the second half of my quest invigorated and free of the distraction of unsatisfied hungers. These last few days have also taught me about my needs and desires, both real and imagined. One thing is clear -- no amount of food or music or comfort can substitute for the freedom and happiness I feel in the wilderness. Before me lie more mountains followed by the beauty and challenge of Utah's redrock country. I am ready.

Day 62, Fourteen miles

Moon Lake encircles the peninsula of granite where I sit. A stout breeze swooshes through the scattering of stunted spruce which grow in defiance of treeline. From an rock outcrop, a golden marmot sits upon his throne and makes regal proclamations that continue to sound more like an irate lifeguard. Welcome back to the tundra!

My return to this world began last evening after picking up my new boots and enjoying a farewell dinner with Kitty and Brian. With sunset approaching, the Benzars drive me to a trailhead near Vallecito Reservoir where I can camp and get an early start in the morning. As with the Rosners, I know that I owe Kitty and Brian a huge debt of gratitude that my parting bear hugs can scarcely begin to repay. Watching the taillights of their truck bump away into the half-light of dusk, I again savor the gift of good friends.

My path back to Rock Lake and the Continental Divide is up the Los Pinos River, one drainage east of my escape route down Vallecito Creek. The first people I meet are four hikers who take turns helping a dazed and ashen-faced teenage boy stumbling out to the trailhead. A little farther, I meet the rest of his group breaking camp and learn the boy was vomiting and suffering from a raging headache through the night. The leaders suspect altitude sickness although they only made it to 10,000 feet. Either way, it's a powerful reminder that these mountains don't take kindly to mistakes. Nobody's going to be around to help me if I screw up. Mindfulness remains my best defense.

I swing north, following a smaller drainage up to Emerald Lake. Beyond the expansive lake, the trees thin, the valley narrows, and the climbing begins in earnest. Dark clouds gather to rumble on the tundra, but the hail and lightning pass and the sun is shining when I reach Moon Lake at 11,500 feet.

The local marmots soon emerge to check out the newcomer setting up his home at their lakeside resort. One stout fellow pads royally atop my ground cloth spread out in the sun to dry, and after a careful sniffing, proceeds to delicately lick its coated surface. Another marmot studiously ignores me while busily digging an addition to his subterranean bungalow, dirt spraying everywhere. Yet another of the buck-toothed rodents silently waddles up while I'm writing to steal a whiff and lick of my outstretched bare feet. Marmots, also called mountain woodchucks or whistle pigs, are the undisputed clowns of the tundra, lolling away their lives munching wildflowers and basking on scree slopes. I have no doubt they are actually overweight, long-haired hippy otters who have retired to the mountains. Who can be lonely with these fuzzballs for company?

Tonight, the full moon will rise for the third time on my journey. The last full moon loomed above the dusty, desert ghost town of Cabezon where I marveled at the events of that first month. Now my experiences have doubled and my trek is only half completed. What a magnificent summer!

Day 63, Five miles

Señor Coyote awakens me with an echoing howl at dawn. I unzip the tent, wincing at the rush of cold air in my face. Above me, the crags glow with ethereal light in a robin-egg blue sky begging for a peak ascent. I am only too happy to oblige. At 13,684 feet, Mount Oso, the crown point in this knot of granite, seems the obvious choice.

Bidding my marmot buddies farewell -- the sluggards are still asleep in their dens -- I hike to the pass separating Moon Lake from the Rock Lake basin, then bushwhack to the foot of the nearby massif with just my daypack. The north side of Mount Oso is mostly a sheer cliff, but one section looks broken and manageable. Standing beneath the towering wall, I crane my head back and scout my intended route. Still not sure if it goes clear to the top, but feeling adventurous and lucky, I begin scrambling upwards.

Although not a true "rock jock," I have always enjoyed climbing. Knowing this, Abby made me promise to keep my primate instincts in check while alone out here this summer. I had agreed. Scrambling is one thing, but solo technical climbing can be as foolhardy as a midnight stroll around Central Park. Unfortunately, life is rarely that clearcut. Halfway up the north face of Mount Oso, I cross that subtle line from scrambling to climbing. Just this next little section and the angle will ease off, I assure myself. Yet the climbing continues. I remember the stricken lad's face from yesterday, but at this point, downclimbing seems even more risky than moving up. Keeping my cool, I complete the ascent to the summit ridge without incident. Whew, I ain't going down *that* way!

The view from the patio-sized rock pile of a summit is everything I'd hoped. The Needles Range with its 14,000 foot peaks seems close enough to touch across the deep groove of Vallecito Creek. Inaccessible azure tarns not even drawn on my map lie below jagged ridges. I'm already planning future expeditions here as I sign the nearly empty summit register and descend the mountain via a thousand feet of ankle-wrenching talus. Safely back to my backpack, the glow of accomplishment outshines the sting of the stupidity of the climb. Nothing ventured, nothing gained, I argue pompously with my guilty conscience. You're just a lucky bastard, it yells back.

At Rock Lake, I'm back on my quest route. The basin is still enchanting, but I keep moving over "Dying Boot" Pass until I'm back on the Atlantic side on the continent. Oddly, the fluffy clouds of lunchtime soon evaporate rather than build and the rest of the afternoon is unusually clear and scorching. Whipped by the rapid return to altitude, the morning's peak ascent and the pounding sun, I camp early beneath the prow of Mount Nebo. Later, from a box seat in this grand stadium of snow, rocks, and flowers, I watch the sinking sun paint the world golden, then peach, and finally burgundy with velvet alpenglow. Happily drowning in a sea of beauty once again.

Boot update: Yowza! Considering these puppies were still in their box forty-eight hours ago, my feet are pretty happy. A few hot spots; nothing major. The smooth uppers are already battle-scarred from this morning's punishing scree, but what a relief to have footwear I can trust.

Day 64, Eight miles

I begin the day slowly, savoring a pot of hot oatmeal as the sun burns the frost off my tent. An image from the night before lingers in my head, but is it dream or reality? I remember standing outside, taking a leak under a moon so bright that I'm squinting. Without warning, a large, noiseless shadow dive-bombs my head, wheels, and dives again. I duck, throwing up my hands to ward off the attacker, but the ghost owl vanishes without a trace. I'm alone again, shorts down, amidst silvery mountains. Eerie!

The trail yo-yos up over the divide, down Nebo Creek, up the headwaters of Vallecito Creek, then back over the divide at Hunchback Pass. As I stop to gobble trail mix, twelve human silhouettes appear five hundred feet above me on the crest of a trailless ridge. The air is calm enough for me to hear their whistles and hoots of disbelief as they examine the treacherous scree slope they must descend. One voice hollers, "Holy shit, we gotta go down this crap?"

Even from a distance, I know I'm watching an Outward Bound patrol in action. Ten people with matching packs begin descending with the unsure tentativeness of alpine neophytes followed by two more figures hanging back and moving with visibly more ease. Students and instructors. I listen to the banter and jokes ("Hey, wanna hear a Brooklyn yodel? YO, YO, YO!") and remember similar days on the Appalachian Trail in Maine a decade ago when I was first the worried student, and later, the confident instructor. Good memories. Unfortunately, mi amigo, Brian, isn't among this group.

The trail temporarily dips outside the wilderness boundary and I tromp up a jeep road to an old miner's cabin on Kite Lake. Across the water, a yellowish tailings pile fans out below a small tunnel opening at the base of a cliff. The Northwest has its clearcuts; Colorado has its mining scars. Although hardrock mining put Colorado on the map a century ago, most mines are abandoned and now, instead of silver, lead or gold, the tunnels produce a dangerous brew of tainted groundwater. Several stream beds near the lake are tinted an unnatural rust and it's sad to discover that we've fouled the nest even up here.

The trail swings up to the divide again and I gladly reenter the Weminuche where another incredible vista lightens my heart. To the south and west rise the Grenadier Range, a tangle of vertical rock towers where technical mountaineers spend weeks dangling off crags with imposing names like Wham Ridge, The Guardian, and Storm King Peak. No dangling for me today. I head north where the divide widens to a gently rolling carpet of inviting green tundra. Storm clouds gather back on schedule after yesterday's hiatus. Determined not to be suckered into another beautiful, but exposed campsite, I drop off the divide to Highland Mary Lakes, a place whose name is a perfect fit. The scudding clouds scraping over ridges of glaciated stone and the blustery winds whipping the lead-gray lakes into whitecaps form a scene straight from Scotland. I wouldn't be surprised if the local marmots play bagpipes!

Day 65, Fourteen miles

Clear skies in the morning transport me out of Scotland and back to the Rockies where Mama Marmot and her four youngsters defrost on a nearby rockheap -- no bagpipes visible. A mile down the trail, I miss a turnoff and descend considerably before realizing my error. Since the cardinal sin of backpacking is losing elevation unnecessarily, I'm obliged to grumble all the way back up to the divide. The correct trail isn't much better, quickly petering out to leave me bushwhacking to a jeep road. The official wilderness area ends here at Stony Pass, and as at Elwood Pass in the South San Juans, I'm jarred by human intrusions after weeks of pristine wildness. Little do I realize that the jeep track is only the beginning.

A few miles farther along the divide and I reach the point where I must part company with the mythic line that splits the hemisphere from Alaska to Tierre del Fuego. The Continental Divide Trail has been my home since I left New Mexico nearly three weeks ago and I'm reluctant to leave, but the divide swings sharply eastward and I'm headed northwest. The 1800-mile long Rio Grande starts right here at the muddy puddles at my feet. Good-bye, Great Divide! Adios, Rio Grande! Thanks for the glorious ride.

Descending toward the Animas River, I hear bleating and spy an army of five hundred sheep storming their way up the mountainside. The "hoofed locusts", as John Muir aptly called them, move like a single, multi-limbed, bawling monster invading the tundra. Down I go, parting the woolly waves with a shake of my staff like Moses. In their wake, the absence of wildflowers is conspicuous among the trampled grasses. Fresh pellets glisten underfoot and the air reeks of sheep shit and wet wool. It's bad enough that the cows own the deserts. Isn't anyplace safe from getting munched?

The trail becomes an old mining road and I coast, stretching my legs as I drop nearly three thousand feet to the banks of the Animas River. A gravel road parallels the river and I follow it upstream. The valley and the riverbed has a washed out, abused look. Dirt bikes, Broncos, and 4-Runners roar by, enveloping me in clouds of dust. Old mining debris rusts everywhere. My map promises a ghost town called Eureka, but all I find is an encampment of RVs next to the concrete and iron roots of an abandoned mill. After weeks among pristine lakes and virgin meadows of wildflowers. I see only scars on Mother Earth. Why would anyone want to camp in this ugliness?

I escape the Animas Valley and its vehicles by following a steep track up Eureka Gulch, but the ghosts of the mining era continue to haunt me: tailings piles, dilapidated shacks, dark holes gouged in the mountainside beneath crumbling wooden headworks. I climb back up to the tundra with Eureka Creek a steady, soft cascade of white silk beside me, but rusting pipes and rotting timbers strewn in the creekbed tarnish this beauty.

My plan is to camp just under the next pass beside Emma Lake. Nearing the end of the road, I see that mining has scarred the land nearly to the mountaintops. I walk the last few steps to the lip of the alpine basin, then stop cold in my tracks. The lake is gone! The bastards just drained it away. Instead of turquoise water, I'm gawking at a series of gaping holes surrounded by tailings and rusting junk.

This is the last straw. These mountains have been violated. I have been violated. How can we tear the guts out of a mountain like this? Why must we destroy everything we touch? Heartsick, bitter, and exhausted, I retreat to a small patch of green amidst the ruin. Even the marmots clowning around my camp offer little cheer. I wish I could apologize to them. Tonight, I am ashamed of being a human.

Day 66, Twelve miles

Above the grave of Emma Lake, I stand at an unnamed pass, peer into the next drainage, and take stock of the alpine landscape ahead. This triangle of mountains between the towns of Silverton, Ouray, and Telluride was the heart of mining activity in Southwest Colorado. Most of the mines closed during the 1970s and the 1980s, but resourceful locals have found new gold in the deep pockets of Texas tourists and other visitors. Four-wheeling is the name of the game now. The wide valley before me is laced with a network of jeep roads that snake up each mountainside and penetrate nearly every watershed. A whining herd of fire engine-red jeeps bounces out of the spruce heading toward an abandoned mine shaft. Another jeep track begins at my feet and I start clomping down it, already missing the trails of the Weminuche Wilderness. Welcome to the motorized mountains!

The first people I meet in Ross Basin aren't tourists, but miners -- a pair of hardhatted roughnecks tinkering with new-looking equipment near a partially collapsed mine opening.

"Are you reopening this one?" I ask.

One man takes a long drag on a butt of a cigarette and flicks it away. "Nope," he exhales. "We're closin' her up tight. Just ain't profitable to work these little mines anymore. The money's in reclamation and clean-up work now."

"Good deal!" I smile, happy to find someone cleaning up a mess instead of creating a new one.

Farther down, a giant white snake writhing its way up an opposing mountainside catches my attention: more sheep, hundreds of them head to tail bound for alpine meadows. Just then a border collie trots up the road towards me followed by a copper-skinned man on horseback.

"Howdy," I greet the rider.

His dark face bursts into a silly grin. "Hello," he replies amicably, but with a thick accent.

"Where are you headed?"

The man scowls for a moment at my question, then the dazzling smile reappears. "Sheep!" he states triumphantly, jerking his thumb toward the woolly snake.

"OK...how many do you have over there?" I ask, speaking slowly.

The man shakes his head from side to side. "Bye-bye!" he says brightly, apparently exhausting his repertoire of English. With a sharp whistle to the collie, the shepherd spurs his horse and continues uphill with a little wave. I'd been told that the big sheep ranches around here import shepherds all the way from Peru to work the high country. I wonder how these mountains compare to his native Andes.

On the Continental Divide Trail I traveled along the moderately rolling spine of the mountains. Now I'm cutting across the grain of this rugged terrain -- grinding down thirteen hundred feet into Ross Basin, grunting a thousand feet to the rust-colored slopes of Red Mountain, dropping a vertical half mile to Red Mountain Creek. Kinda tough even for a mountain goat like me! Jeeps, fat-tired three-wheelers, and off-road motorcycles rumble by in smelly, noisy packs. Occasionally one of the drivers stops to ask directions or exchange pleasantries with the hump-backed, two-legged curiosity that he has nearly run down. Then, mirrored sunglasses back in place, he's off in a spray of gravel and a cloud of exhaust in search of another grade to conquer. At times, I wonder if I've stumbled into some hideous Disneyland ride ("TEST yourself and your MEAN MACHINE against THUNDER MOUNTAIN! Get your tickets NOW!") Where's the sweeping silence of the wilderness?

Late in the morning, I reach Route 550 and take my first step on asphalt since Wolf Creek Pass. Unfortunately, no convenient trail beckons just across the roadway and I begin a four-mile, two thousand-foot hump up paved switchbacks to Red Mountain Pass. No pikas and alpine forget-me-nots for company here as I hike beside crawling Winnebagoes and 18-wheelers reeking of frying brakes. Mines are everywhere, including the sprawling tin sheds of the huge, still-active Idarado complex. Ugh!

Atop Red Mountain Pass, I slump against the big informative plaque in a pulloff, weary inside and out from the jeeps, the pavement, and the accumulation of steep miles. As I pull out the fixings for a long-overdue lunch, an aged pale green RV sputters the last few feet up the steep pass and sighs into the pulloff. "We're spending our children's inheritance!" the bumpersticker proudly proclaims. The aluminum door on the side creaks open and out sloughs a pastel geezer armed with a whirring video camera. The old man records a thirty-second panorama, then huffs toward me and the sign. I'm hoping that he's coming over to toss me a bag of pretzels or something, but instead he asks me to move my pack out of the way. I comply with the retiree's wishes, then watch bemused as the old fella trains his camera on the nondescript sign for several long minutes, reading every word aloud for the microphone (presumably for the benefit of his blind relatives in Peoria). A shrill woman's voice calls out from the motorized behemoth. Ignoring his wife, the senior pans his lens in my direction, capturing me midbite on a carrot. "And here's a hiker ... " he drones, "... enjoying his lunch after a walk in the mountains." Before I can do anything obscene, the geezer snaps off his electronic eye, gives me a perfunctory smile, and shuffles back to his rig. Get me outta here!

My plan is to follow jeep roads to Black Bear Pass and camp above Telluride, but I zig when I should have zagged and wind up one basin too far south. Above treeline near Bullion King Lake, I meet another jeeper who explains how he uses his jeep to get into the high country so he can trek around on foot. As we talk about the mountains, my attitude toward him and his comrades softens a bit. OK, maybe jeeping isn't what John Muir had in mind when he said: "Go to the mountains and get their good tidings", but I'll take a jeep over a mining truck up here any day. Attitude is everything. Are the mountains enjoyed in their own right or are they just a backdrop for power-crazed entertainment -- contemplating or conquering?

Boot update -- PAIN! The honeymoon is over -- I want my old Asolos back. The unpadded collar of the new Danner boots is cutting into my ankle tendon in a big way. I've tried athletic tape, moleskin, and Second Skin, all to no avail. Today I resorted to stuffing a folded bandana in the top of my boot -- crude, but effective. Either my feet or these damn boots better break in real soon!

Day 67, Seven miles

After a nasty scramble over a headwall of treacherous scree to get back on course, I drop a whooping forty-five hundred feet and arrive in the Telluride valley by lunch. To enter Telluride from the mountains is to stroll back through the history of this famous town. The first structures I encounter are the hulking remains of an ore processing plant. Once, Telluride was one of the busiest mining towns in Colorado. Millions of dollars worth of gold and silver ore poured out of the three hundred and fifty miles of mining tunnels that were chipped and blasted into the surrounding mountains. Butch Cassidy was inspired by all this wealth to pull his first bank heist here in 1889. The mines eventually went bust and the boom town of Telluride became a virtual ghost town. The lime-green settling ponds and ominous pile of tailings just above town are all that's left of this era.

The next zone I reach is the mobile homes and funky, broken down houses which recall the 1960s and '70s when back-to-the-earth hippies rediscovered and revitalized Telluride. A downhill ski resort and a growing tourist industry turned Telluride into a thriving community of urban escapees seeking an "alternative lifestyle" by the early '80s.

Finally, I walk into downtown Telluride where brightly painted Victorians compete for a chunk of hillside with fancy "trophy" homes built of glass and stained wood. This scenic alpine valley has been discovered by the "Lifestyle of the Rich and Famous" crowd. Telluride is now known for its ungodly high real estate prices and as the festival capital of the Rockies, hosting not only world-class bluegrass and jazz festivals, but also events featuring movies, mountain bikes, mushrooms, wine, hot-air balloons, and "ideas."

Resting on a sidewalk bench, I watch the kaleidoscope of humanity hurrying between dozens of ritzy shops and boutiques. High heels and Hollywood cowboys are as common as dreadlocks and dirty jeans. The bejeweled and the bohemian chase their dreams in a town surrounded by such fantastic beauty that anything seems possible. What a difference from Winslow and Cuba!

After lunch, I stash my pack in a handy bookstore and attend to business. I learn from a mechanic in a mountain bike tour shop that AJ, the hiker I met at Wolf Creek Pass, is off on another adventure -- rock climbing in Wyoming and Montana. With my remaining thirteen dollars, I carefully buy the fresh food for the next leg to Moab, Utah (where a money order from Abby awaits me). Late in the afternoon, I snag my resupply box from the natural foods store that's been holding it. I ask the bearded fellow behind the counter if he can suggest a good place to camp. He mentions the town park, but that costs money and I'm as penniless as a pauper now. The clerk thinks a minute more, tugging at his chin, then says, "I know of a cabin, a hut really, that a buddy of mine built on Forest Service land on the hillside above town. He was trying to escape the hellish rental rates. The rangers eventually discovered his place and kicked him out, but I think the hut is still there."

The young man draws me a quick map on a scrap of paper and I'm delighted to learn that the shelter is along my proposed route out of town. Thanking my friend for the tip, I struggle into my bulging pack and head out of town under rainy skies.

The hidden structure built right into the hillside of aspens is a dream come true. Actually an open-sided lean-to, the ten-foot by six-foot log hut is an ideal one-person hobbit home with a bed on one side facing a row of shelves and a built-in table. A small wood stove once stood in between. After sweeping away a few mouse turds, I lie on the bunk and listen to the gentle patter of steady rain on the solid roof. Seven legs down, six to go.

Day 68, Ten miles

Little did I realize as I lingered at the lean-to this morning that I was in for one of the toughest hiking days of my life. Add to this late start a three-quarter of a mile of elevation gain, a major wrong turn, raw weather, a sixty-five pound pack, and a long, trailless stumble across loose scree at the end of the day, and you'll understand why I barely have enough energy left to write.

Back at daybreak, overcast skies and a gentle rain tapping a lullaby on the tin roof keeps me lounging in camp much later than usual. I decide to create another two hoop gift of thanks like the one I left on Mount Taylor. This offering is destined for the summit of Mount Sneffels, one of Colorado's famed fifty-four peaks above 14,000 feet. One last hurrah before leaving the Rockies. The sacred gift slowly takes shape in my hands as I work mindfully. To the completed hoops I add a marmot jawbone to mark my progress along my circular route.

Braving a cold drizzle, I move up an abandoned mining road through thick timber. The rain tapers off when I break treeline. The roadbed disappears under the scree, but I forge ahead, scrambling straight up to the jagged skyline. Atop the ridge, my thighs are screaming and my lungs are on fire, but I've reclaimed all of the forty-five hundred feet of elevation that I lost yesterday.

A faint foot trail drops through the talus into a new basin where a pile of weathered timbers lies next to a mine. Twenty minutes and a thousand feet later, I'm sitting on a spool of cable near the mine resting when I notice the top of the Telluride Ski Area visible ahead over a ridge. Holy screw-ups, Batman! That's not possible unless .... Whipping out my map, I see I've dropped into the wrong basin and am heading back to Telluride. Sorry -- been there, done that! Groaning with resignation, I turn around and huff back up what I've just descended.

The correct path is no more than a goat trail, but soon I can spot the craggy top of Mount Sneffels tearing at the bellies of low storm clouds. Any hint of a trail vanishes and I endure hours of crunching and grinding down and across more screefields. Rock, rock, and more rock, each one eager to turn underfoot and mangle my tired ankles.

Yankee Boy Basin is the most rugged country I've traversed all summer. Ringing the basin are scowling, serrated pinnacles with large lakes of thick, dirty snow still pooled on the north-facing slopes. When I finally plop my pack on a patch of flat tundra at the foot of Mount Sneffels, the setting sun is transforming the broiling thunderheads to the east into colossal balls of flame. Yet, I'm just too tired to gawk, struggling to remain conscious through dinner and this entry. A pooped pup tonight.

Day 69, Ten miles

Poking my head out the tentflap at first light, I hope to find clearing weather, but get slapped with a faceful of thick, damp mist. Well, it can only get better, I kid myself, rolling over for a little more shuteye. For once, I'm right. An hour later, the sun is burning through the clouds and I'm off and rolling with a daypack.

The 14,150 foot summit of Mount Sneffels is a fifteen hundred foot scramble above my camp. The peak is readily accessible -- most people four-wheel drive to within two miles of the base -- and it's a popular goal for "Fourteeners" junkies. Even so, I'm still surprised by the wide swath on the lower slope where countless boots have eroded down to gravel. The last several hundred feet are a hand and foot ascent up a boulder-strewn couloir. After one final pitch, I clamber up on the living room-sized summit block and reach the highest point of the summer.

A family of three are already on top and we share an orange and snap pictures of each other. The low, dark clouds finish their morning coffee break and hurry back on duty, convincing my companions to start down. Once alone, I pull out my gift to the mountain and tuck it in a protected niche with prayers of thanks. Then, despite the angry sky closing in, I try to soak in the view.

Weeks ago, I stood on Conejos' peak and looked across the San Juans from their southeastern edge. Now I stand atop the crowning point of the western end of this glorious wilderness of peaks and can scarcely believe I've traversed its length. Rio Grande Pyramid stabs the sky far to the east. To the northwest, crags ease to foothills, forested mesas, and open grasslands and I peer into my future where my next goal, the wooded ridge of the Uncompaghre Plateau, lies low and massive. Through the thickening clouds, I strain to catch glimpses of the distant profile of the La Sal Mountains across the border in Utah. This next leg is the longest and I wonder if even the enormous food bag stuffed in my pack will see me through to Moab.

My worries become more immediate when hail starts rattling on my hat. I'm just shouldering my daypack when the panting, flushed faces of another party pop into view. During my descent, I pass at least twenty people (and two dogs) as the mountain socks in. Smiling smugly, this earlybird knows he'll be among the few graced with any view today.

The showers come and go as I break camp and escape Yankee Boy Basin via Blue Lakes Pass. Beyond the pass, I enter the Mount Sneffels Wilderness Area and the change is immediate -- no jeep roads, no mining scars, fewer people. Zig-zagging down toward gorgeous Blue Lakes and acutely aware that this is my last stroll on Colorado's alpine tundra, I fawn over the gardens of wildflowers, wondering when I'll see these new friends again. These past weeks above treeline have been such a highlight. Can I really be saying goodbye?

At this point, the mountain gods notice that I'm having trouble leaving their inspiring realm so, with a nod to Thor, they decide to prod me along. The bruised sky splits open, dumping the heaviest, coldest downpour of the summer as thunder rocks the basin. Crouching under a scanty overhang, I toss down trailmix, but become steadily more and more soaked and hypothermic. Suddenly, the warm, dry deserts ahead seem sort of ... appealing! "Alright, ye gods," I shout into the wind. "You win; I'm leaving your dark, stormy kingdom -- for now!" One last look at the misty heights, then I jog down into the trees, desperate to get warm.

Forty minutes later when I'm engulfed by a lush forest of spruce and fir, Thor lays down his hammer, satisfied. The sun bursts free, releasing the pungent aroma of wet humus and ferns. The trail contours along the base of the Sneffels Range, but becomes indistinct just as I walk off the edge of my map. I hop a fence, hit a dusty road, and find myself surrounded by my old adversaries, the beefy bovines. What a transition: marmot pellets to cow pies in an afternoon!

Now tucked in a beautiful aspen grove overlooking a rolling pasture, I close my eyes and mentally return to the lush tundra, the snowy crags, the dancing wildflowers. But when a cow starts bawling at the setting sun, reality becomes perfectly clear -- my Rocky Mountain adventure is over. Utah -- here I come!

Day 70, Twenty-four miles

The day which completes ten weeks on my quest begins with coyote songs and elk bugles. The morning is a confused stroll on dirt roads through a charming mixture of aspen groves and open pastures framed by the Sneffels Range. A track finally leads out to Route 62 and after a six mile hump on the asphalt to reach Dallas Divide, I'm back on track.

Sprinkles begin dotting the pavement as lunchtime approaches. "A little shelter would be nice right about now" I wish aloud. Like magic, an abandoned shack appears next to the road. Whoa -- maybe I'm on to something here! Squeezing my eyes shut and holding out my hands, I shout up to the sky, "Thanks -- now I'd like a cheeseburger and a big ol' plate of French fries." Only more raindrops appear in my palms. Oh well.

The shack is dirt-floored and filthy, but I'm dry for lunch. Stacked in the corner are piles of disintegrating magazines: *LIFE, Saturday Evening Post, Modern Home,* and a Montgomery Ward catalog -- all dating from 1958-60. I roll some slices of jack cheese into a tortilla and flip through the crumbling pages for a glimpse of America just before I was born. Neither the different styles nor the ridiculous prices capture my attention as much as the attitudes and outlooks of the advertisements. One power company asks you to check off all the electrical appliances you own from their outrageously long list so you can rate your "electrical standard of living." The message is clear: the more electricity you manage to consume, the better off your life will be! Another ad for the "Pure Oil Company" boasts of constructing a new road into virgin Venezulan rainforest ("where few people live") to explore for oil and open the area to new settlers and cattle ranchers -- sowing the seeds of rainforest destruction. I find myself laughing at the apparent naiveté of the period, then wonder which "obvious truths" I believe today will be the bitter jokes of the next generation.

The rain has moved on by the time I abandon the shack, ditch the pavement, and turn north on more dirt roads winding up to a rolling, open grassland. This high expanse reminds me of Wyoming and soon I'm trucking along, whistling cowboy tunes, and wishing for a horse. I picture a sweet cabin tucked under the open aspens that edge these meadows, Abby and me together on a porch swing, a couple of dogs chasing each other though a carpet of golden leaves .... someday.

Reaching the base of the Uncompaghre Plateau, I hop a fence and wade into the thigh-deep grass of a horse pasture in search of a flat camping spot. Another sodden storm drives me prematurely into the tent and washes out the sunset. What happened to sunny Colorado?

Day 71, Nineteen miles

There is nothing like awakening to a crisp, porcelain-blue sky to cure the tent potato I've become. The entire day is a monotonously beautiful stroll down a Forest Service road along the top of the Uncompaghre Plateau, a broadbacked ridge cloaked in blond aspen and dark spruce above fairy forests of ferns. A pickup spins by, driver waving, as the scent of freshly-cut firewood wafts in the truck's wake. Sure, the ubiquitous cattle are here as well as an occasional clearcut, but with a sweet sun on my back and a cool breeze in my face, I can think of nothing finer than this pleasant amble through the woods.

Lunch finds me seated in the cab of a log skidder parked in the ruinous clearing it created. Nobody's about -- it's Sunday, I think -- and I'm not sure why I've chosen to eat within the greasy confines of this beast of pitted steel and grimy cables. Is it the dark thrill of the forbidden or the desire to "know thine enemy," this ultimate ORV? Suddenly, I'm five years old again, remembering eagerly scrambling into the driver's seats of huge, shiny yellow tractors, backhoes, and bulldozers on display at the county fair. I look down at my father's smile and my mother's frown as I gleefully pull levers, yank handles, and make engine noises. What a thrill it was to be at the heart of something so massive and powerful. Perhaps some boys simply never outgrow this stage, instead they become the grown men who are more enchanted with their roaring machines than the quiet forest they grind beneath them.

Late in the afternoon, I detour into a small campground to fill my bottles at a spring. A tremendous racket rises behind me and three trail bikers roar up. A powerfully-built, silver-haired biker in his forties walks over for some water and says, "Looks like you're out for a ramble. Pretty good one too, by the size of your pack."

"Yeah, it started last May and won't end until sometime in September."

"Good Lord -- guess you like to walk! Where ya headed?"

I outline my travels to the motorcyclist and he smiles and nods in appreciation. When I'm finished, he tugs off his leather gauntlet and offers me his hand.

"I'm Mike," he says. "Ever been on the Uncompaghre before?"

"Nope."

"Well, if you use any of the trails up here, you can thank me and my buddies for keeping them clear."

When I raise my eyebrows incredulously, Mike pulls out a map of the plateau produced by his chapter of the Motorcycle Trailrider Association and traces all the single track trails that his club have adopted to maintain. We ease over to Mike's trail bike -- a lightweight assembly of steel, chrome, and plastic atop knobby tires -- and Mike shows me how he carries a small chain saw to remove blowdowns. "The rangers around here are usually too busy to do trailwork and you hikers aren't gonna lug a saw around," Mike explains.

"Don't you guys tear up the trail pretty bad on those things?" I protest.

"Horses are worse," Mike counters. "Smart riders stay off the trails up here in the spring when they're soft and muddy. You know, a lot of environmentalists like to lump us trail bikers with the loggers, but I love these woods as much as you do. There's nothing finer than seeing elk and deer up here. Caught a glimpse of a mountain lion once." Noticing my smirk, Mike adds, "Listen, I used to be a backpacker; bagged a lot of fourteeners in my day. Then my knees gave out and I got into jeeping and eventually discovered trail riding. Keeps me out in the woods all summer. I think there's room up here for everybody." I nod slowly, not sure if I agree. Mike's made his point, but his rig still makes a helluva racket in the woods.

I bed down near the high point of the plateau where a dozen radio towers rise spindly and silver above the treetops. Once again, the temptation of mischief gets the upper hand and soon I'm a hundred and fifty feet off the deck, clinging white-knuckled to the top rungs of the tallest tower. The highest object for thirty miles in every direction, I'm royally rewarded with a magnificent sunset panorama of western Colorado and eastern Utah. My gaze strays to the northeast, to distant peaks visible beyond the Elk Mountains not far from Abby's summer home. This is the closest I'll get to her in the course of my walk and a familiar longing swirls inside me. Carefully descending, I add this plateau to the long list of places to return to with my sweetheart. That shall have to suffice for now.

Day 72, Twenty-two miles

Back at dawn, I awoke cold and dewy under a spruce at 10,000 feet. Now at dusk, I'm bedding down under a piñon pine beneath a faded red sandstone cliff where the heat of a sage-scented afternoon lingers past sunset. The theme of today has been ecological transition and my mind frantically tries to catch up with the changes my feet have created.

At first light, I veer west off the ridgetop road and start a gradual descent from the top of the Uncompaghre Plateau to the valley of the San Miguel River. Throughout the day, I move from one community of trees to the next. The dark, moist, balsam-scented richness of the spruce forest becomes a woodland of sunny, twinkling aspens. Ferns and lupine disappear as the soils dry out and short, gnarled Gambel oaks replace the elegant stand of aspen. Outcrops of sandstone begin peeking through the vegetation. Tall, somber ponderosa pines line the track along the rim of Tabeguache Canyon, a massive groove scoring the flank of the plateau. When the rutted road levels off on Pinto Mesa, I'm back among my old desert pals: Piñon, Juniper, and Sagebrush. Howdy partners -- ain't seen your scruffy hides since Chama Canyon back in New Mexico!

My return to the desert is complete when I drop a thousand feet beside sheer cliffs of burnished sandstone to Tabeguache Creek. Staking my tent to a fine chunk of riverside property next to the sweetest of desert streams, I kick off my boots, sink my toes into the deliciously warm, clean sand and release a sigh a deep contentment. Ambling for weeks in the alpine zone, I'd almost forgotten the pleasures of the desert. But with a tapestry of chiseled sandstone behind me, a warm creek embroidered with watercress and cattails before me, and a symphony of crickets filling the air with summery music, I can't imagine wanting to be anywhere else.

Day 73, Ten miles

The pale flicker of a candle illuminates the pages of my journal as I write nestled in my sleeping bag. My belly is happily distended by three cups of cooked bulgar, cheese, and rehydrated veggies. Stars are appearing in droves as the cinnabar glow to the west settles into darkness. A peaceful end to what has been one of the most stressful days of the quest.

Sleeping like a babe in my cradle of sand next to the happy gurgle of Tabeguache Creek, I awaken to yet another overcast morning. Instead of taking the hint, I roll out of the tent and start downstream. My map shows a trail winding down the canyon, but the faint path is overgrown with stiff oak saplings and every step is a struggle. The beautiful walls beg for admiration, but all my concentration is directed towards making headway. After a couple of tough miles, the showers begin. The stew of pewter-gray clouds overhead isn't the "take no prisoners" thunderstorm variety of high country afternoons. No, this insidious low-pressure system looks like it has nothing better to do than rain on my parade. Somewhere up there, Thor and Zeus are pointing down at me and snickering.

As my thrash through the oak thickets continues, I feel like Dorothy lost in the Tinman's evil forest of apple-chucking trees. Every branch gouges my body; every bough snatches at my pack; each root entangles my feet. The sopping vegetation has drenched my poor excuse of a rain anorak and I'm soaked to the skin. Where are those ruby slippers to spirit me out of this jungle?

The rain pours down with a vengeance. I crunch ahead like a frustrated robot, lost in misery. The shivering begins. The only shelter is a shallow scoop in the bedrock up the mouth of a sidecanyon. Squeezing into the meager overhang, I hunch in my niche like a cornered animal and watch the drips creep ever closer to my face.

An hour passes. Only peals of thunder break the monotony. My bag of trailmix becomes a security blanket; each mouthful of nuts and raisins is a pacifier keeping despair at bay. I had been anticipating a hot, sunny day to wash some clothes and clean my odorous body. Well, I'm getting my bath alright! I haven't been this wet, cold, and uncomfortable all summer. I survive weeks in the arctic environment of the alpine tundra only to perish of hypothermia in the desert. What the hell is it with this wacky weather?

Daydreams of screwing this quest nonsense and hitching to the nearest video arcade are becoming disturbingly real when the sky finally lightens and the rain starts to taper. I ease off the ledge and am stretching my cramped legs when the sound of rushing water appears out of nowhere. The sidecanyon is filling with foaming muddy water -- flash flood! Fortunately, the slurry is only about a foot deep and poses no danger. But what of Tabegauche Creek? I run out to the main canyon, expecting a raging torrent, but find that the stream has only risen a little and turned muddy. Shouldering my dripping pack, I move on.

The trail improves, but not much; I'm still whacking a lot of bush. The canyon walls are lower here, so I decide to escape the riparian maze by climbing out. On the final leap across the creek, I miss and fall in to my knees. Between mumbled curses, a nursery rhyme pops into my head: When she was good, she was very, very good; but when she was bad, she was horrid. No doubt the author had ol' Mother Nature in mind!

I forge straight up the side of the canyon, overcoming an "exciting" twenty-foot rock-climbing pitch near the top. Free at last, I pick my way over slickrock between junipers and cactus, paralleling the canyon down to pasturelands. The sun makes a blazing return just before setting behind the looming silhouette of the La Sal mountains. Dinner goes a long way toward returning my composure, and once fed, warm, and dry, the ordeals of the day seem like someone else's nightmare. Never a dull moment ....

Day 74, Twenty miles

Tabeguache Creek completes its voyage off the Uncompaghre Plateau by dashing through a pipe beneath Route 141 just before merging with the San Miguel River. I follow the creek, then the blacktop into Uravan, a collection of slumping wooden houses beneath a hulking, rundown mill surrounded by tailings piles. Looks like a nasty place, but in search of some tap water, I detour off the highway onto an empty Main Street where a boarded-up community hall and company store sit next to an abandoned factory. One building has a cluster of pickups parked in front. An older man in a uniform emerges from the front door and strides purposefully toward me. His gray eyes are curious, but his mouth is firm.

"Afraid you can't go any farther," he states. "This place ain't open to the public."

"Just looking for some drinking water. What's going on here anyway?"

The security guard follows my gaze around the dilapidated town and explains, "This is Uravan...or what's left of it. One of the first big uranium mining and milling operations in the country. After World War II, this place was a boom town -- more than a thousand people living here. In 1983, they shut everything down. The government said that the town was loaded with radiation. Hot spots all over the place. Folks got moved out and lots of homes were torn down."

"What are you doing here?" I ask.

"A bunch of us locals from Nucla and Naturita work here cleaning up the mess. Been going at it for eight years and we've still got a long ways to go."

"Aren't you worried about the radiation?"

"Some," the guard replies, shifting his weight to the other foot. "But the work's steady and there isn't much happening 'round here since the mines closed. We don't have any tourist business like over in Telluride or Gunnison. You still want some water?"

I follow the man into the building where a few dour workers sit around a table and stare at me through the blue haze of cigarette smoke. I fill my bottles in the bathroom sink, thank the guard, nod to the poker-faced crew, and hightail it back to the highway. I was right -- nasty.

Beyond the town, huge, plastic-lined setting ponds sit precariously close to the channel of the San Miguel River. Razor-topped chain link fences corral piles of rubble. Radiation warning signs are everywhere. Another mess. One generation rips open the hillsides; the next generation works to clean it up. All this to make bombs against an unknown enemy half a world away. Industrial insanity!

The highway climbs away from the river, but I detour onto a dirt track which follows the San Miguel into a twisting, narrow canyon. After three miles, the canyon opens to a confluence where the rusty tan current of the San Miguel flows into the chocolate waves of the Dolores River. Both these waterways are liquid mud due to all the recent rain. Heading upstream into the canyon of the Dolores, I find what I've been searching for: a tiny ribbon of clear water trickling in from a small sidecanyon. Bath day at last. Behind a creekside tamarisk, I wash my clothes, scrub my body, then tackle my hair. The water is so alkaline that the soap leaves my head a stringy mess. Ignoring my new dreadlocks, I stretch out naked in the sand for lunch and a nap.

The afternoon walk up the tight sandstone canyon of the Dolores is an unexpectedly early taste of the Colorado Plateau desert: the pungent scent of a juniper baked by the sun, a delightful cascading echo of a canyon wren, the sensuous sheen of the mud-swollen river, the bite of hot sun on my shoulders. Most enthralling is the texture and shapes and colors of the sandstone cliffs ranging from subtle to sublime. The mountains may be my new home, but the redrock canyons remain my favorite temple.

The canyon widens, then abruptly opens like a giant gateway into the middle of a enormous cliff-bound valley of grass. The Dolores River does not turn into this valley as one would expect, but flows straight across it, emerging from another huge gap in the opposite valley wall. Thus the name: Paradox Valley. I cross the waist of this geologic enigma to the paved road running the length of the green swath of irrigated land and enter the tiny town of Bedrock.

The heart of Bedrock is the Bedrock Country Store. In fact, the large barn board structure makes up about ninety percent of the community. I climb aboard the deep, cool porch, slide my pack onto a wooden bench, and examine the choice of doors leading to different facets of the establishment. Bypassing the door for "Spirits" and for "Hardware", I push past the screen door for "General Merchandise." The store's interior is dark, its shelves half empty. Things clearly haven't changed much since Fred and Barney shopped here. A blond woman who spent too many of her younger years in the sun is stationed behind the counter, yippy dogs flanking her on each side. I'm here for reinforcement for my shrinking foodbag, but with total monetary reserves totaling seventy cents, I'm not too hopeful. I grab a loaf of blanched "air" bread, the only variety visible, and sidle over to the counter.

"How much is this?" I inquire, hoping the prices are as ancient as the merchandise.

"That'll be a dollar-sixty," the woman deadpans.

"Oh, shoot -- all I've got is seventy cents," I moan theatrically, giving the blond my best hang dog, give-a-starving-guy-a-break mug. No luck -- she shoots down my silent pleas for sympathy with a snap of her gum. I shuffle back to the bread rack like a whipped pup.

"Well ... " the woman starts, "I guess I could split that loaf and take the rest home myself."

Not exactly the magnanimous gesture I'm anticipating, but what the hell? A man with less than a dollar to his name can't afford to be choosy. The woman counts out seven slices and slides them into a ziplock bag. I hand over my two quarters and four nickels. A dime a slice for fluffy, pale, nutrition-free bread. Damn -- they drive a hard bargain in Bedrock!

I hit the hot tarmac and with all of a dozen steps, leave Bedrock in my wake. I'm shooting for Paradox, the only other town in the valley, but settle for a campsite hidden in a thick stand of cottonwoods set off the road. The soft twang of country music drifts into my camp from a nearby trailer. Insects trill and float in the hay-scented air. A souped-up coupe roars down the road with a load of teenaged boys in baseball caps. Another summer day in the Paradox Valley winds down.

Day 75, Twenty-two miles

A few days ago, I woke up on a mountain and marched through the ecosystems to bed down in the desert. Today I reverse the process -- another long day in my roller coaster tour of the Southwest.

The day's first stop is the porch of the Paradox Mercantile and Post Office. The store is dead; dusty, jumbled debris left by the last owners visible through the fly-specked windows. The closet that serves as the Post Office still breathes, but it's about the only spark of life left in this cluster of houses planted around a red, barn-like church. Another small farming town bites the dust.

As I walk to the head of the valley alongside irrigated fields, something feels different and out of place, but I can't put my finger on it. I snag a few tart apples that are foolishly hanging over a roadside fence into the public domain, and then it hits me. The rows of cornstalks reaching over my head are the first crops I've passed in almost eight hundred miles of walking. Try duplicating that east of the Rocky Mountains!

The agricultural fields end when I start climbing into the Manti-La Sal National Forest at the end of the valley. Graveled switchbacks snake between rust-colored outcrops and blue-berried junipers as a pitiless sun wrings the sweat from me. The shade under towering ponderosa pines helps, but only a midday dip in Buckeye Reservoir really cools things down. Not far beyond that, I cross a cattle guard and with little fanfare, arrive in Utah -- my fourth state. At my feet lie two dusty quarters. Eureka -- three steps into the Beehive State and I'm a man of capital again!

The road opens up and levels off when I reach my first aspens. The bulk of the La Sal Mountains fills the horizon dead ahead. Cowboys twirling hammers instead of lariats fix a bunkhouse on a private inholding in the federal forest.

Getting ready for the fall roundup, no doubt. Yep, back in cow country.

The chill of this evening's air at 9,000 feet belies this morning's sweatbath. Better enjoy it while it lasts because beyond these mountain lies the largest expanse of slickrock desert on the continent and I'm heading right into the heart of it.

Day 76, Fifteen miles

This morning's cool, buttery daybreak hearkens the beginning of an outstanding day. Not wishing to waste a moment of it, I make short work of the last four miles to a wide, spruce-covered saddle called Geyser Pass. The rocky pyramids of Utah's second highest mountain range rise on either side of me. No doubt about it -- time for another peak ascent!

I hide my backpack under the low arms of a spruce and walk south through a dense virgin forest of dark green conifers. Abruptly, the trees end at a sea of scree that sweeps up an imposing fifteen hundred feet -- Mount Mellenthin. Like an ant scaling a house-sized pile of pebbles, I struggle up the rubble and tackle several low cliffbands on an ascent that equals any of those in Colorado. Sucking wind with a vengeance, I reach the four-foot summit cairn at 12,645 feet and slowly survey one of the broadest possible views of America.

I stare long and hard in every direction, sorting out the incredible vistas. Eastward is the green world from which I've emerged. A skirt of aspens slides down to a petticoat of pines above the slender grassy legs of the Paradox and Sinbad valleys. The Uncompaghre Plateau rises beyond the crease of the Dolores and San Miguel rivers with Mount Sneffels and her toothy neighbors forming a jagged skyline in the far horizon. New Mexico is almost visible behind the reclining human form of Sleeping Ute Mountain near the Four Corners Monument.

My gaze shifts to the west and rests upon a vastly different world -- the eroded, desiccated, awful grandeur of southeast Utah. Painted with a palette of cream, crimson and umber, the slickrock desert is a landscape where the skin of soil and vegetation have been stripped away to reveal knotted muscles, stringy sinew and bleached bones of naked rock. I stand as if upon the headlands of a coast, staring at an ocean of petrified waves stretching to the western horizon. The technicolor spectacle begins to resolve itself into recognizable landmarks: the incongruous emerald patch of Moab's Spanish Valley at the foot of the La Sals, the sun-crisped, wrinkled visage of Arches National Park, the tawny wall of the Book Cliffs far to the north. South of Moab lies the broken vastness of Canyonlands National Park where massive terraces of cinnamon and bone sandstone hide the deep, convoluted canyons of the Colorado and Green rivers. My eyes slide up and out to the rolling ridge of the Henry Mountains, blue with haze and distance. How can I possibly reach those faint, shimmering islands across this tumultuous sea of sandstone on a single load of food? The immensity of the canyon country ahead inspires and frightens me.

Just when my brain reaches geographical overload, I spot a landmark that sends my pulse racing all over again. Far, far to the southwest, beyond the Henrys, is an innocuous, faded hump that has me baffled until I realize that I'm looking across a hundred and thirty miles to the 10,000-foot dome of Navajo Mountain on the Arizona border. This lone peak was the most distant point visible from atop Sugarloaf Mountain where my quest began. This glimpse of Navajo Mountain, however distant, connects me with my ultimate goal and for the first time, I feel that the backbone of my immense journey is broken. The La Sals are my northernmost point where my circle starts clearly curving back on itself. I'm headed home.

Why didn't I make my twin circles of thanks to honor this important summit? I pluck a raven feather from my hat band and admire its ebony sheen -- this will do. With prayers of gratitude, I tuck the feather deep within the summit cairn. As if on cue, I hear a croak above me and find a flock of ravens circling the summit. With upraised hands and sudden tears in my eyes, I acknowledge the arrival of my totem. Thank you, Brother Raven!

Now I'm camped on South Mesa, halfway down the western side of the mountains. Once again, I've stepped inside the elevator of biomes and pushed the "Down" button. Sitting poised on the brink of canyon country, I stare into this tangle of wilderness with a mixture of excitement and fear. In this season, the bone-dry landscape below can be as deadly as it is beautiful. Yet I can't deny the lure of the horizon and I'm eager to enter this new realm -- for better or worse. Onward, brave companions, for there lies the way ahead!

Day 77 & 78, Nineteen miles

Mountains to canyons. Wilderness to town. Alone to among friends. Hungry and dirty to stuffed and clean. The past two days have been filled with transitions.

The changes begin with my last night in the mountains when I sleep without the tent after nearly a month of cold, wet weather. Entranced anew by the celestial diamonds overhead, I feel my internal clock being reset to desert time -- a focus on dawn, dusk, and night. Noon is for the mountains; it is best forgotten in the desert.

The next day I drop into Moab via a jeep trail, slipping off the mesa into a slickrock wilderness of pastel sandstone. Smooth domes rise beside dramatic cliffs and pillars. Multi-hued fins conceal secret niches guarded by a battery of carved turrets. A hazy overcast bathes this extravagant gallery of sculpted shapes in a soft light that exaggerates their buffed smoothness. I have entered a world of sensuous stone and feminine geology, a land of living rock.

As magical as I find my new surroundings, the tug of town is even stronger and I push hard to reach Moab by day's end. Lunch is a nasty affair of lumpy brown sugar wrapped in the spongy pulp of my hard-won Bedrock bread; nothing else left and I'm starving. The jeep road turns to pavement where a pack of mountain bikers mill around the entrance of Moab's famed Slickrock Bike Trail. Only a mile to go. I click into "town mode" and wind down the last switchbacks into the green oasis of Moab.

My first mission is to find the post office and retrieve the money sent by Abby. I get directions and the time from a passerby: four blocks away and 4:30 pm -- no problem. A few minutes later I'm standing outside the Moab Post Office and rattling the door -- locked. Big problem! The sign reads: "Monday-Friday, 9 am-5 pm." What's the deal? I hear movement deep inside the brick building and bang on the door again -- nothing.

I slump down against the wall, stunned. I've fantasized about food for the last three days, and now here I am, a few blocks from a huge supermarket without enough money to buy a sno-cone. Suddenly, the door pops open and a woman, short-haired and clerical in bearing, steps out. Ignoring the heap of distraught hiker at her feet, she moves to the flagpole and lowers Old Glory.

"HEY!" I shout a little too testily. "Why'd you close early?"

The woman glares right back and snaps, "We didn't close early -- it's Saturday."

Saturday? Damn, I would have sworn it was Friday. The woman finishes folding the flag and starts to head back in.

"Wait!" I cry. "You gotta help me."

The postmistress listens with visible impatience as I plead with her to check inside for my letter. Interrupting my blubbering with an upraised hand, she ducks inside and returns waving an envelope in my face. "You're mighty lucky," the woman explains. "We should have sent this back to the sender five days ago. We only hold on to General Delivery mail for ten days, you know!"

I slobber eternal gratitude all over the poor lady, then hightail it to the supermarket with two fifty dollar bills burning a hole in my pocket and a huge smile splitting my face. Wide-eyed, I stumble up and down the grocery store aisles like a weasel skulking through a barn of sleeping hens. The cornucopia of grub is overwhelming. Somewhere between the produce and the frozen foods, I decide to spend a layover day in Moab to replenish my body before the next leg. The landscape shouldn't be just an obstacle between me and my next resupply box. I want to eat to live, not vise versa.

I veer into the canned goods, and for the second time within an hour, my jaw hits the floor. Twenty feet away stands Brian, my pal from Wyoming whom I'd hope to meet back in the Weminuche. His eyes bug out as he turns and spots me. Moments later, other shoppers are scurrying away at the sight of two tall, scruffy, bearded, weatherbeaten, reeking outdoorsmen clasping each other in a hardy embrace in front of the baked beans.

The obvious question flies out of each of us in unison: "What are YOU doing here?" Turns out that Brian is in town visiting friends between Outward Bound courses. Like myself, he has emerged from a long stint in the backcountry only hours earlier. I look in his cart and double over in laughter. There lies an open bag of cookies from the bulk bin that Brian has doubtlessly been raiding unobtrusively while cruising the aisles. My cart holds an identical set-up -- brothers in villainy!

We buy the grub and take Brian's beat-up jalopy across town to his friend's home. Soon, our non-stop conversation expands to include Brian's sweetheart, Gingy, and Steve, a neighbor and river guide from next door. The evening progresses into a full-blown barbecue with many of Moab's professional river rats in attendance. Between mouthfuls of salad and grilled chicken, I weave the story of my Southwest Circle Quest for a rapt audience. My thunder thighs and runty chest is a sharp contrast to this crew of barrel-chested, skinny-legged boatmen, but there is an instant and powerful camaraderie between us. The music, raucous laughter, and swirl of new faces is so different from my normal solitary, meditative evenings, yet I'm totally at ease. I guess a little human contact is just what the doctor ordered!

As the party winds down, Brian explains that he'll be gone before dawn on his way to his next course. We hug goodbye, still astonished by the wild coincidence of our rendezvous, then I follow Steve back to his house, where his couch is available for the next couple of nights. It's nearly midnight when I finally stretch out with one of Steve's cats perched comfortably on my chest. My exhaustion is complete, but my mind continues to spin through the day's events and my abrupt transformation from solitary pilgrim to "Mr. Life of the Party." Just when I think I've got this quest figured out, another unexpected twist appears. The steady purring of my companion quiets my thoughts and I finally drop like a lead sinker into the smooth pool of unconsciousness.

When my eyes open, I'm already sticky from the rising heat of midmorning. The house is silent; Steve is still asleep. I arise quietly and slip into the shower. In the cluttered kitchen, I build myself a sizable stack of buttermilk pancakes under the careful scrutiny of four shin-rubbing felines and a floppy-eared mutt with the pleading brown eyes of a doe. When the washed dishes are in the drying rack, Steve is still gently snoring, so I leave him a note and head into town.

Moab, like Telluride, is a dichotomous place. I stroll through a neatly organized neighborhood of single story ranch houses surrounded by manicured lawns. Backyards hold the standard accouterments of suburbia: hibachis, blond kids, an occasional cocker spaniel. I could be somewhere outside Sacramento or Cleveland if not for the sheer cliffs of umber sandstone soaring a thousand feet on either side of town. This neighborhood is the enclave of the conservative Mormons who generally regard the harsh desert outside their oasis community as a place that God made for mining, ranching, and maybe a little jeeping on the weekends.

The glitzy downtown area of bike shops, rafting companies, ice cream parlors, and T-shirt boutiques represents the new face of Moab that emerged in the mid-1980s when the desert town became a Mecca for outdoor recreation. An army of tourists in flashy lycra and wrap-around sunglasses descend upon Moab each spring to churn through the redrock country astride knobby-tired mountain bikes. A remarkable number of these urban refugees have moved into town to buy homes and start cappuccino shops only to find their liberal lifestyles at odds with the original inhabitants. Moab has become a classic example of the Old West begrudgingly succumbing to the ideals of the New West.

I retrieve my resupply box from a bike shop, pore over maps and guidebooks in the bookstore, and put away two or three lunches in the course of the afternoon. Like the Tasmanian Devil, I buzz through a variety of eating establishments; satisfying my sweet tooth, assuaging my protein hunger, and paying back my calorie deficit. My cast iron belly happily accepts all the strange food and begs for still more -- scary!

Finally, I step into a phone booth and call Abby. I hope to talk her into meeting me in Flagstaff, but her Park Service season has been extended, so we make plans to rendezvous in Durango. I want to voice my concerns about this next leg, but Abby is already worried enough about me, so I describe my serendipitous meeting with Brian instead. Our goodbyes drag on for ten minutes before one of us finds the strength to hang up.

With my belly full and all tasks completed, I return to Steve's bungalow on the outskirts of town. My host is in his backyard playing catch with his canine chum whom he introduces as Duncan the River Dog.

"Is this stuff all yours?" I ask, nodding towards the racks of red canoes, plastic paddles, orange life jackets.

"All that and more," Steve explains. "Got a couple of sixteen-foot rafts rolled up in the garage." Steve owns and operates his own river-running company called Humpback Chub River Tours after an endangered species of native fish. His specialty is conducting small, environmentally oriented, multi-day trips on the rivers of the Four Corners. Steve's (and Duncan's) water born explorations of this region are as extensive as my overland travels. During dinner, I quiz my host about the management end of the guiding business and answer Steve's endless inquiries about my walk. We visit late into the night, our conversation roaming across a wide range of topics. Steve's low-key style and dry wit mirror my own and I feel like I've found a long-lost brother.

Now back on the couch with journal, pen, and cat, my thoughts turn to the upcoming leg of my quest. Between Moab and my next cache box in Hanksville awaits some of the most twisted and remote country in the West. Backcountry travel is generally discouraged in Canyonlands National Park in August due to the relentless heat and lack of water, yet I'm proposing to walk the length of the huge park and more. One failed water source could quickly lead to a life and death situation. Images of my close calls in Arizona keep reappearing. Am I insane? Will this passage be an historic first or a tragic last? More than once today, I've seriously (although surprisingly calmly) wondered if I am about to walk into the desert to meet Death. I sense that this next leg will be the crux of the quest. Outside, the thunder rumbles and a light rain has begun -- a good omen. I just might make it.

Capitol Reef N.P
Hanksville
Dirty Devil River
Green River
Moab
Canyonlands NP
Boulder Mtn.
Aquarius Plateau
Henry Mtns.
Colorado River
Escalante
Escalante River
Abajo Mts.
Bryce NP
Paria River
Canaan Mtn.
San Juan River
Lake Powell
UT.
AZ.
Navajo Mt.
Monument Valley Tribal Park
Lee's Ferry
Page
Scale
20 mi
Kathi Sutton
11/97

WEST SOUTHWEST
Land Of Living Rock

The Lone Trail

Three or four years ago I came to the conclusion that for me, at least, the lone trail was the best, and the years that followed strengthened my belief.

It is not that I am unable to enjoy companionship or unable to adapt myself to other people. But I dislike to bring into play the aggressiveness of spirit which is necessary with an assertive companion, and I have found it easier and more adventurous to face situations alone. There is a splendid freedom in solitude, and after all, it is for solitude that I go to the mountains and deserts, not for companionship. In solitude I can bare my soul to the mountains unabashed. I can work or think, act or recline at my whim, and nothing stands between me and the Wild.

Then, on occasion, I am grateful for what unusual and fine personality I may encounter by chance, but I have learned not to look too avidly for them. I delve into myself, into abstractions and ideas, trying to arrange other things harmoniously, but after that, taking them as they come.

Everett Ruess
On Desert Trails with Everett Ruess

Day 79 & 80, Eighteen & Twenty-five miles
862 miles total

As the curtain rises on the final third of my Southwest Circle Quest, I am a naked prisoner confined within a fold of deep shade. My universe is silent stone and a screaming midday sun. Sizzling maroon sand is punctuated with the pale green of snakeweed. Above soars a dome of blue, hard and mercilessly clear. Only the restless wind stirs. I'm a day and a half into my Canyonlands traverse and have entered a tough chunk of country that doesn't take kindly to strangers. I have little doubt this wilderness of rock and heat will test my physical prowess, desert savvy, and unfailing good luck like never before.

A couple of days ago, my last morning in Moab began slowly. My worries about a Canyonlands traverse are undiminished and Steve suggests a last-minute visit to the National Park Service headquarters. We drive across town. The detailed maps at the NPS office are helpful, but I've learned the hard way that maps can lie. Springs dry up; roads and trails are abandoned. I need to talk to an on-the-ground ranger who knows the country and its water sources firsthand. I hit the jackpot when I speak via radio phone with the district ranger of The Maze, a remote section of the park. With identical maps before us, the ranger and I hammer out a feasible route of foot trails, jeep roads, and water sources. As we talk, the list of challenges grows: finding hidden off-trail springs, a downclimb which might require a rope, and long, waterless stretches. When I ask about North Hatch Canyon, I hear a snort on the other end of the line.

"Yeah, there's an old track down there," the ranger admits. "But, you know, every time I go in there, something goes wrong and I barely make it out in one piece. Seems that place is out to get me, so I pretty much avoid going there if I can."

"OK ... " I manage, questioning my sanity again.

After a last gut-stretching meal back at Steve's bungalow, I bite the bullet, heave my monstrous pack onto my back and bid my new "brother" farewell with a flurry of thanks. Never did I imagine that this quest would involve so many tough goodbyes.

Ten minutes of walking in the August heat and I'm already soaked in sweat. I head for The Portal, a massive notch in the sandstone ramparts where the Colorado River leaves Spanish Valley. On the edge of town, I fall in step with another guy with a daypack walking toward the river. Clomping down the road together, we fumble through introductions. Crazy Mike is a raw-boned, rough-cut fellow with a voice of gravel and hawk eyes that keep you on his good side. Those eyes flair as he recounts his situation. "I live out of my van -- well, I did -- until a "friend" drove it out on the salt flats up north when it was too hot. Ruined it good. But the road's been my home for fifteen years. Ain't no stranger to hitchhiking!"

We reach the banks of the Colorado. Mike's gray eyes soften as we both pause to stare into the swirls of the muddy current. I ache to coo a loving greeting to my favorite river. Instead, I turn to Mike and ask, "So, what brings you out here?"

Mike holds my eyes with his for a long moment, then whispers in a husky, conspiratorial voice, "GOLD!" He looks pleased with my surprised expression. "Yup, I learned the trade from an old-timer up in southern Oregon. Since I lost my rig, I've been hitching around with my sluice box, shovel, and pan. Just got back from a prospecting trip up there," he jerks a thumb at the La Sal Range, "but I was looking in the wrong place." His voice gets low again as he confides," The gold is right here!"

Our narrow road turns to parallel the river and we stride side-by-side into a high-walled canyon. Mike points to a roadside outcrop. "See that dirt up there? That's ancient river gravel stranded atop the sandstone shelf below it thousands of years ago. Gold's heavy. It washes through the gravel and ends up atop the sandstone. I ran a few pans yesterday and got dust and a few flakes. If there was a side creek here to run my sluice box, I'd be making some real money!"

After another mile, Mike ducks into a shady grotto and shows me a beautiful spring-fed pool with duckweed and tadpoles. "Ain't she pretty?" Mike beams. "I figured a backpacker like yourself would appreciate this spot. Where you headed anyway?"

We splash the sweat from our faces and share some trailmix as I explain my trip. Mike nods appreciatively and says, "I love it out here myself. There's nothing better than watching the river flow and seeing the cliffs turn all rosy at sunset. But I'm moving on. The Colorado has taught me to keep following my dreams. Just today I learned about three creeks south of here where a man can find nuggets. I figure I'll work those creeks until I can buy another car. I feel like this could be it this time!" Mike concludes, grinning with a prospector's eternal optimism.

We reach the miner's hidden riverside camp and he offers me a rough handshake. "I surely enjoyed visiting with someone else who's out here following his dreams. Good luck to ya!" Crazy Mike slips into the thick shrubbery and disappears, another victim of gold fever off to chase rainbows.

The road turns to dirt and swings away from the Colorado up Kane Spring Canyon. Feeling fresh and hungry for miles, I set my sights on getting to the far side of a low gap called Hurrah Pass. I twist and climb up the sidecanyon, pausing at another roadside spring with some weary mountain bikers heading back to town. Clear, cold water gushes incredulously from a crack in the cliff, foaming down into a delicate garden of moss and maidenhair ferns. "Looks like Moses was just here!" a biker jokes. I hope Moses has left me a few more of these miracles ahead.

Two miles beyond Hurrah Pass I return to river level, but the Colorado is hidden behind an olive green thicket of desert willow and tamarisk. I drop my pack and grab my empty bottles to fetch some cooking water, but to my amazement, the dense jungle proves impregnable. Dusk is fading to darkness while I struggle to slip, sneak, or barge my way to the river, yet the brush is too thick. I return to camp empty handed. Frustration cools to humor when I consider my predicament: a hundred feet away flows the Southwest's largest river and I have to settle for a dry dinner for lack of cooking water. "Pretty good joke, Rio!" I laugh aloud. "Is this any way to greet your ol' amigo?"

Daybreak finds the red cliffs dancing with the sunbeams and me moving with empty water bottles rattling ominously in my pack. Farther along the river, I try breaking through the jungle again and finally stand at the river's edge. Reaching down, I stroke the water's surface and celebrate another quest milestone -- from the jagged crest of the continent to the bottom of the Southwest's watershed. The expanse of thick, coffee-colored water is such a wonder in this parched land. A beaver patrols the shore and I wish I could drift with him through these canyons. Maybe Steve's right -- a boat makes more sense than boots for sanely exploring canyon country, especially in summer. I'd rather stick next to the Colorado, but sheer walls and nasty shoreline vegetation make this virtually impossible. My route for the next few days will have to be a rough track into Lockhart Basin.

The jeep trail soon climbs away from the river and skirts along the base of a 1300-foot escarpment. To the west, the world opens onto a vast arterial system of sidecanyons above the Colorado River's gorge. Navigation poses no problems, but progress is slow, hot, and arduous. The two-rut track dives and twists, tacking left and right around the head of every little drainage. Rarely have I traveled such a convoluted path.

Now, as I write and relax, the hottest hours of the afternoon have marched by until my shadow equals my height. Time to eke out a few more miles in the reprieve of dusk. Playing tag with a malevolent sun -- it's a game I can't afford to lose!

Day 81, Fifteen miles

Soon after I hit the road again yesterday, I locate a small cattle tank formed by a low earthen dam across a side drainage. The shallow pool is brick red and alive with desperate tadpoles and frantic fairy shrimp -- yummm! But hey, when you're sucking down water like a bluegrass lawn in Tucson, anything wet looks appealing. I tank up.

The cliffs blaze fluorescent, then fade to gray as the reality of a twenty-five-mile day under a sixty-pound pack in temperatures hovering near a hundred degrees finally grinds me to a halt. Cooking by flashlight, I'm so exhausted that I can fool myself into thinking that the red mess in my pot with the ramen noodles is actually tomato sauce instead of silt. I'm so hungry that I don't notice the difference.

With the raging, screeching sun gone, the desert turns cool, dark, and habitable. I lie naked atop my bag; the night air as comfortable as the noon was unbearable. A crescent moon slides between a few evening clouds. The Perseid meteor shower begins to slice across the Milky Way with a steady parade of shooting stars. I try to watch -- no chance. My eyelids thud closed and I'm gone.

When my eyelids slide open, the eastern horizon is already smudged with plum and ocher. Venus is just fading away as I force myself up and onward. The pink-tinged air is lusciously cool and I'm determined to wring as many miles as possible from the jeep trail before the heat clamps down. By the time dawn's first saffron rays are stroking the basin with molten fingers, I'm enjoying a breakfast break with five miles already under my belt.

Late in the morning, I reach the only two cattle tanks indicated on my map, but they are as dry as the last three I've passed. Damn -- I was counting on these water holes. The alarms start jangling in the back of my head as the sweaty miles unwind on the griddle of Lockhart Basin.

Now, I'm holed up in a shallow seam of shade at the base of the soaring cliff. Over a thousand feet straight above me, a paved road ends at a viewpoint called

The Needles Overlook. I bet some geezer from Iowa is up there right now, standing next to his Airstream as he videotapes the washed-out midday panorama.

"Gawd, Mabel -- ain't this sumthin'!" he's cackling to his wife. "Can you imagine bein' *down in* that inferno right now? Pass me another cold Fresca, would ya , hon."

And here I am, jammed in the rocks like a damned lizard, rationing my last quart of murky brew which I could pour down my parched gullet in a single slug, but can't because I don't know when I'm gonna see any more water and, and ... dehydration sucks!

Indian Creek is three miles of exposed marching ahead. I was told there's water in that streambed -- sometimes. If there is, I'm golden. If not ....

This one could be close.

Later: Yeehaa -- the ol' Canyon Coyote cheats death again! I sit in a pretty sidecanyon above pools of clear water. Around the corner, Indian Creek is an oasis of flowing, ankle-deep water sliding over silky river cobbles between cottonwoods and sculpted walls. Shaggy storm clouds rolling overhead provide relief from the searing sun. What a difference! Take that earlier cynical pilgrim, add a little water and shade, and -- "presto" -- a happy camper!

Day 82, Thirteen miles

I am camped in the middle of the most fantastical landscape I've ever had the privilege of entering. Stretching away for miles in every direction is an infinite variety of eroded slickrock formation: domes, slabs, cones, buttes, pinnacles, monuments, and fortresses. Alternating layers of blond and cinnamon sandstone are intricately carved into an immense fairyland of erosion. Soil is an afterthought here, yet a few tough junipers maintain tenuous footholds in the rocks and add their dark green to the incredible panorama. Welcome to Canyonlands National Park -- Nook and Cranny Capital of the World!

I reach the park's entrance road late in the morning. A nondescript trailer sits off the pavement near the shell of a large, low building under construction -- the Needles Visitor Centers, both present and future. Inside the trailer, I find a desk complete with pony-tailed ranger, a bookrack of field guides, a couple of maps, some dazzling posters, and little else. The young lady behind the badge is the first person I've seen since Crazy Mike, so I offer her a gritty grin. The ranger smiles back, then demands a dollar entrance fee (pedestrian rate) before issuing me a backcountry permit. She's a little startled by my plan to continue across the Colorado River into the Maze. I assure her that I've done my homework, but she makes me promise to notify the park when I get to Hanksville. Can't leave a corpse littering their slickrock without proper authorization and all that. Fair enough.

The trail beyond the Squaw Flat campground is my first footpath since the Uncompaghre Plateau -- a welcome change. A progression of stone cairns pulls me up into the slickrock and the hike becomes a whimsical tour contouring around domed ridges, diving through unexpected cracks, and striding out on giant whalebacks. The shallow waterpockets or "tinajas" carved in the sandstone are brimming with clear rainwater -- excellent! For once, Zeus and Thor are batting for my team!

I'm now king of a fabulous slickrock castle above Elephant Canyon. My front yard is a veritable ocean of inviting tinajas where I can flop on my belly and drink to my heart's content. Naked in the penthouse, I enjoy the caress of a perfect breeze while the setting sun magnifies the magnificence of my surroundings beyond words. The magic of this spot nourishes my soul. I wish I could hold onto this feeling forever. This is a sacred land worth every torturous step in Lockhart Basin to be here. Blessed again!

Day 83, Twelve miles

My first emotion upon awakening is unshakable delight in finding myself still encompassed by an exorbitance of beauty. The ramparts and facades that were backlit at sunset are aglow in the vermilion blush of dawn. Everything here appears so sensual at the edges of the day.

This choppy sea of slickrock was once an unbroken plateau. When a massive salt dome beneath the layers of sandstone slowly pushed upward, the surface rock split into an intricate checkerboard of deep cracks. Water, wind, and time have further subdivided the terrain into a celebration of erosion. Ironically, the underlying salt dome formation led the federal government to consider a site just east of the park for the national repository for nuclear waste. What a travesty! Only a soul-dead bureaucrat could consider this place a wasteland fit for a nuclear dump.

Just beyond my castle, the trail plunges into a slot two feet wide, yet thirty feet high and three times as long. My footfalls echo softly as if walking the aisle of an empty church. Indeed, what is this place if not a natural cathedral? Emerging from the groove, I pad silently through deep sand in the shadowy depths of Elephant Canyon, then follow cairns up toward a seemingly impregnable bulkhead of rock. Just when all progress looks impossible, another rift in the stone appears, leading magically to another chamber. Alice never traversed a wonderland more intriguing!

The trail dances on like this all morning. With their endless twists and surprises, these footpaths are easily the most creative I've ever walked. Imagine stone steps that lead you down a narrow crack to an apparent dead end -- the earth has swallowed you. Yet turn ninety degrees and dive deeper still, led by a sandy strip of trail between blackish walls. The passage narrows. Your pack and shoulders begin to scrape the tight, tunnel-like walls. With claustrophobia rising, you turn your face upward toward the light, but the sky is only a thin ribbon of blue fluttering far overhead. The groove widens into a series of cool, dimly-lit, room-sized chambers. Narrow side slots provide glimpses of the "outside" world now as distant as a dream. You have entered the womb of the planet. Everything has the surrealism of a fetal memory. The heartbeat softly echoing is your own.

Finally, another ramp of steps leads up and out. You emerge blinking and bewildered as a newborn into the pulsing heat and intolerable brightness of the desert. The string of cairns still beckons. And you follow, guilelessly trusting the rock piles to steer you to the next adventure.

Not everyone becomes so entranced. I stumble upon a young man slouched under a juniper looking dazed. After a short conversation, I discover he has wandered all morning off the trail without a map carrying a pitifully small supply of water. The hiker doesn't seem particularly worried or scared, just bewildered by the complexity of this bizarre landscape. I share some water and the map and point him in the right direction. As the young man heads back to his base-camp, I wonder what would have transpired if I hadn't come along -- another statistic waiting to happen. This beautiful cathedral can easily become a nightmarish maze without proper preparation. This point is hammered home when I climb upon a whaleback and find that all the waterpockets are now dry. Maybe that guy isn't the only statistic walking around out here!

I sneak across the remainder of The Needles through places with names like Devil's Kitchen, Cyclone Canyon, and Devil's Lane. Now I'm in siesta mode, waiting for the backbone of the afternoon to break before following Red Lake Canyon down to the Colorado River. Hope my sweetheart of a river is more hospitable than she was on our last "date!"

Day 84, No forward miles

It happened again. Life on this quest is turning out not an orderly unfolding of events. Activity and change seem to strike in random, intense pulses. A mere twenty-four hours have passed since my last entry, yet my lunch at the head of Red Lake Canyon seems like ancient history after a day of unexpected happenings.

It is still hot as Hades when I switchback down into Red Lake Canyon and follow it to the Colorado River. The sidecanyon teases with a bunch of tantalizing bends which hide the river until the last moment and I smell the Colorado's faintly salty perfume and hear her quiet murmurings before I spot her tawny skin gleaming beyond a veil of cottonwoods. On the muddy delta, a great blue heron -- the old man of the river -- bunches his body, then launches into flight. My heart also soars upon arriving back on the shore of my favorite river.

Across the water is Spanish Bottom, a half square mile of flat ground tucked between the cliffs and the water. From Spanish Bottom, a Park Service trail will lead me up into The Maze, but first I must get over there. Fortunately, Spanish Bottom is also a popular campsite with flatwater boaters whose journey must end here because the wild rapids of Cataract Canyon just downstream. Since there's no road access to this point, jet boats from Moab haul the canoeists upstream to civilization. My plan is to get a ferry across the Colorado from one of these boat folk.

Although I'm prepared to wait here for a day or two if necessary, I notice a knot of tanned bodies directly across the two hundred foot barrier of slow, muddy water. We exchange waves, then I cup my hands and holler, "CAN YOU FOLKS FERRY ME ACROSS?"

There's a pause before one man shouts back in an accented voice, "VEE CANNOT HELP YOU, BUT THERE ARE CANOEISTS UPSTREAM. ASK THEM!"

I squint upriver and spot the glint of aluminum a quarter mile away. After humping up to this second encampment, I wave and repeat my request.

"SURE," the voice floats back. "WE'LL BE RIGHT OVER."

A new plan blossoms as I wait and I pull off my boots, tug the sweaty shirt over my head, and empty my pockets. Two guys in their forties dock their canoe nearby with a hiss of aluminum on sand.

"Howdy," I grin. "What I actually need is a ferry for my gear. I just decided to swim across!" I haven't hitched a forward inch all summer -- why start now? My odd request hardly raise an eyebrow.

"No problem," the bowman says as he grabs my pack and boots and offers me their spare life jacket.

"Better jump in upstream a ways," the stern man advises as they push off. "The current is slow, but it's strong."

I grope my way over the rocks on soft, unprotected feet and wade in up to my chest. The water is lukewarm. I lie back and surrender to the brown current. Ahhh...I didn't know water could feel this exquisite. Buoyed by the life jacket, I backstroke across the Colorado like a sea otter, realizing that this refreshing swim is one of my finest ideas all summer.

Back on land, I sit with the canoeists in their camp and, between sips of soda, outline my travels. The crew, four good ol' boys from Texas, just shake their heads, pop open more beers, and resume their upriver vigil for the whine of the jet boats. Their three-day trip from Mineral Bottom has been fun, but it's clearly time for town.

"Four months -- Gawd!" one sunburnt hombre drawls. "I'm sure glad it's y'all out thar and not me!"

Thanking the Texans for the livery service and liquid refreshment, I move downstream in search of my own piece of beach. Nothing presents itself until the other end of Spanish Bottom. I spy a gorgeous swath of soft sand, then hear Germanic chatter drifting out of the nearby bushes. A fleet of kayaks is pulled up under the cottonwood trees -- so that's why they couldn't help me. I move to the far end of the large beach and contemplate the silty-skinned serpent of a river slithering massively past.

The Colorado River will always be "The River" to me. This grand lady wears many dresses during her 1450-mile dance to the sea. Born just a handful of miles from Abby's post in Rocky Mountain National Park, she is a clear, youthful, mountain river as she rushes through her namesake state. Forsaking the mountains and muddied by the inflow of several tributaries, the Colorado enters Utah and dives into a series of dramatic redrock canyons; her calm and gentle flatwater smile occasionally breaking into howls of furious whitewater. Just three miles upstream from here, she is joined by her lanky cowgirl sister, the Green River, who has moseyed down from Wyoming. Now twice as strong, she bashes through Cataract Canyon, then dies a ignominious, but temporary death in the stagnant pall of Lake Powell. Leaping to freedom from behind Glen Canyon Dam, the Colorado waltzes wildly for over two hundred miles down the Grand Canyon before pausing again in Lake Mead.

Beyond Hoover Dam, the Colorado is an old woman, her youthful exuberance spent, creeping southward across the Mojave Desert. More dams and aqueducts pool and suck her lifeblood into the greedy guts of Los Angeles, San Diego, and Phoenix. A mere trickle -- a ghost of her former glory -- reaches the river's mouth and often no water at all enters the Sea of Cortez.

But enough of her sad demise. The River here is the living heart of the Colorado Plateau -- a miracle of water and greenery in a corridor of dessicated rock and hard blue sky. Reaching such an enormity of water after traversing a bone-dry landscape is nothing short of an epiphany. Loren Eiseley once wrote, "If there is magic on this planet, it is contained in water." I can only add that there is no more powerful magic than water in the desert.

While my pot of bulgar and dried vegetables simmers, one of my neighbors comes down to the beach to get water. The blond man smiles broadly. "So, you found your vay across dee river! Are you alone?"

"Yup."

"Sorry vee could not help you. Our kayaks are too small. Ven your dinner is done, you are velcome join us by our fire."

My neighbors turn out to be five kayakers from Germany who have just finished a sixteen-day trip down the Green River and are awaiting their shuttle. The two older men, Wolfgang and Ernst, have the swarthy, rope-muscled look of Jacques Cousteau. Their wives, Greta and Erika, are equally burnished brown by weeks in the Utah sun. The younger man, Stefan, is tall, blond, and powerfully built. Over tea I learn that, once again, I've fallen in with a nest of hardcore river rats. Wolfgang and Greta have paddled on the Yukon River and other arctic waterways while Ernst and Erika have run rivers in Mexico, Chile, and Siberia. Between expeditions abroad, they all float the rivers of Europe together. As stories chase each other around the fire pan, any barriers of language, culture, or age slip away. We share the bond of lives spent in the wilderness. The fire is just coals before I wander back to my camp.

Beneath the dancing swath of diamonds, I lie in the soft sand, listen to the whispered lullaby of flowing water, and my contentment is complete. Tell me again why the mountains were so great? How could anything top this? I laugh aloud at my fickle heart, then make my second outstanding decision of the day: time for another layover!

The unexpected splash of three mule deer bravely swimming across the Colorado awakens me at dawn. I unzip the bag to get cracking, then remember I've declared today a "holiday." Like any good vacationer, I roll over to luxuriate the morning away, but the sun won't hear of such nonsense. The growing heat drives me from the sack and I'm sweating in the shade before breakfast is over.

One by one, my neighbors come down to the beach, get naked (being immodest Europeans), and bathe. The kayakers then break camp in anticipation of an early afternoon departure by jet boat. I examine the big, plastic boats -- a European hybrid between a roomy sea kayak and a stubby whitewater playboat. Wolfgang sidles up.

"Nice boats, jah?" he boasts, noting my admiring gaze. "But zey are old and vee don't vant to pay the freight charges to bring zem home. Better to sell zem here and buy new boats back in Germany."

My mental gears start turning. I own a beautiful cedar-strip sea kayak, yet Abby has no boat. One of these kayaks would be perfect for her.

"All vee vant is two hundred, maybe two-fifty dollars. Do you know anyone who vants a kayak?" Wolfgang asks with a wink, obviously telepathic.

The gears are really grinding now; that's an incredible price. "Well, I would," I stutter, "but what can I do"

Wolfgang sticks out his lower lip to think. "Jah ... too bad," he says absently.

I leave to scout my trail up to The Maze, but my mind is stuck in nautical mode. It's a golden opportunity, but how can I take advantage of it now? A possibility flashes before me -- Steve Arrowsmith, my newfound buddy in Moab. What if I write him a note and send it with the Germans to Moab? Wolfgang can sell the boat to Steve and I'll have Abby reimburse Steve. After all, the boat is for her.

Rushing back to the beach, I explain my idea to Wolfgang. He tugs on his short beard and nods.

"Sounds goot. Here, look -- zis is the boat," he explains, kneeling next to the orange torpedo adorned with stickers. "She's been around and is all scratched up, but she is still a goot boat. Do you vant to try her out?"

Moments later, I'm zipping across the surface of the Colorado River like a kid with new roller skates. Slicing through the water with a double-ended paddle, I remember just how much I love kayaking. These nimble low-slung boats allow such an intimacy with the water. Yahoo -- this is too much fun!

Wolfgang steadies the kayak as I climb from the cockpit, my face split with a grin. "Here is zee deal," the wiry man begins. "You can have zis boat and spray skirt for two hundred and fifty dollars. If your friend is not at home ven vee arrive, no problem. Vee leave the boat anyvay. You send us the money ven you finish your valk."

I'm deeply touched by this display of trust, especially to a crazy foreigner who stumbled into their camp only yesterday. We close the deal with a firm handshake and, just like that, I've "bought" a kayak!

By lunchtime, the sun is seething. The Germans sit on their packed drybags in the shade, slapping at ants and looking longingly upstream where the cold beers and hot showers of Moab are clearly calling their names. A low rumble grows into a roar as a thirty-foot silver jet boat flies around a bend and shoots towards our beach. In a flurry of activity, the Germans are loaded aboard; "my" kayak is strapped to a rack with the rest of the boats. The kayakers each wish me "goot luck" and the jet boat thunders back upstream. Quite suddenly, Spanish Bottom is quiet and empty except for one skinny, lonely, bewildered, happy inhabitant. Did all that really happen?

Later: No more than an hour passes before the upstream glint of distant paddles flashing rhythmically in the sun catches my eye. Soon, two canoes and a kayak are approaching my beach, the only sizable campsite in Spanish Bottom.

"Goot afternoon. Do you mind if vee camp near you?" politely asks one of the canoeists.

Good lord ... more Germans! "No problem," I holler. "Come ashore."

Another round of stories begins after introductions. When I mention my recent "purchase" of the Prijon-brand kayak, these boatmen assure me that I've gotten a great deal on Europe's premiere touring boat.

The rest of the afternoon is a casual affair of swimming, writing, and chatting. At one point, I wander downstream and sit mesmerized by the roll and crash of Brown Betty, Cataract's first big rapid. I can't wait. The River is so seductive. I'm almost ready to trade in my walking stick for a paddle. River Rat Fever ....

Day 85, Ten miles

I open my eyes. An exaltation of crimson brightens the eastern edge of a lavender sky. A circus of bats ending their shift wheels overhead on backward wings. The dark, sleek head of a beaver noses upstream, silently patrolling my beach a dozen feet offshore. Another dawn on the Colorado River.

Even after an extra day here, I pack with reluctance. The River is such a powerful presence that I can scarcely bear to leave her. Yet, with a last, lingering touch of the muddy water and a wave to my neighbors, I start climbing toward The Maze. Flowing water, beach sand, and languid tamarisk are abruptly replaced with dry wind, slickrock, and burly junipers. After nine hundred vertical feet, I'm back in the high, wide, and lonesome.

Resting in the shade of a shallow overhang, I discover a panel of faint pictographs near the tangle of sandstone outcrops known as The Fins. Painted in faded maroon on the beige rock face are four eighteen-inch "ghost" figures -- long rectangular bodies with small, rounded heads, but lacking arms and legs. Beneath the human forms frolic a small herd of delicately depicted bighorn sheep. What was life like here a thousand years ago when the Anasazi and Fremont cultures inhabited this landscape? Can the artwork, pottery shards, and crumbling masonry structures they left behind teach us anything? Did these people worship the Colorado River? What did they call her? The wind and rock offer no answers.

My mission for today is locating a couple of developed springs left over from the cowboy era. The ranger had warned that these spring were hidden off the trail, but I'm barely able to detect any trail at all. Cairns are few and far between as compared to back in The Needles and several times I'm forced to backtrack. No wonder they call this place The Maze. Late in the morning, I find the first spring. Tucked deep in an alcove, a garden of maidenhair ferns clings to crumbling rock weeping precious moisture. Long ago, someone pounded an iron pipe into the soft sandstone and placed a metal-lined wooden trough under the pipe to catch the steady drips. I stick my face in this mini oasis and drink with the long sucking pulls of a horse. What a thing of beauty -- a miracle of water from the stone!

The second spring, two miles farther along, is my last known water for a long stretch, so I stop early and make camp in an alcove. A dull overcast tempers the blistering sun, so I take an unladen spin around my new neighborhood. As always, my mountain goat blood convinces me to scramble to a high point where I survey an endless ocean of undulating slickrock. It's a crime to traverse this intricate and beautiful land so quickly and I vow to return. How many years of return visits will it take to explore all the wonders revealed by this summer's walk? I'm looking forward to finding out.

Day 86, Sixteen miles

Mosquitoes. All night, the tiny blood-sucking choppers strafe my ears with their incessant whine. Who would have expected the winged horde out here? Filling up at the spring this morning, I see my chance for revenge. The water in my bottles is alive with swarming mosquito larvae. Alright, you vermin -- you bite me all night and I'll drink your children all day. Poetic justice and extra protein to boot! I load an extra gallon into my pack and head for the next spring over a dozen miles to the west.

Foot trails and jeep roads lead up two massive cliffbands as I climb away from The Maze basin. The sun is scorching and by the top of the Orange Cliffs, I am literally wringing sweat from my soaked T-shirt. The sixteen pounds of water I left with is going fast. Will it be enough? The trickle of wrung-out perspiration disappearing into the dust turns out to be the only water I'll see between dawn and dusk.

I chew up flat miles through a dense mesa-top forest of piñon and juniper. At one point, the ridge narrows to only a few hundred feet in width with a thousand-foot drop on either side. Huge expanses of eroded country roll away in every direction. The only hint of human existence is a handful of deserted jeep tracks winding like outsized game trails over sand and slickrock. What if this next spring is dry? How far away is help? Have I ever been this "out there" before?

Only an hour before sunset, the track edges under the lip of the escarpment and ends at Two Pipe Spring -- a tiny swamp of mud and old cowshit. Contrary to its name, there's no pipe or pools, just weeping seeps, but that's enough. Drop by precious drop, my drained bottles slowly refill. Lady Luck smiles on me again.

Day 87, Eighteen miles

The same ranger who told me about Two Pipe Spring said that I should be able to drop off the mesa here. "But you'd better have some rope to lower your pack," he'd warned. I scan the thousand feet of layered cliffbands for a navigable route. It won't be easy, but it might go. There appear to be breaks in each cliffband where I can safely descend to the next level. What I can't determine is if hidden obstacles lurking lower down could stop me cold, or worse, strand me unable to either climb back up or descend farther. No kindly string of cairns points the way as I enter this nearly vertical bushwhack. My progress goes something like this:

Find a break in the first cliffband.
Downclimb with care.
Pick my way down steep talus to the lip of the next cliff.
Look nervously left and right in hopes that another break exists.
Contour left seventy feet and scramble through the next cliffband.
Descend more talus.
Contour right three hundred feet.
Discover that the next "break" is actually a fifteen-foot overhang.
Curse a little.
Find another break.
Continue this walking chess match with the cliff and hope like hell that I don't get checkmated!

After several nerve-wracking hours, I manage to outwit all layers of the escarpment without incident. The tattered remains of an old uranium prospecting track promises smooth sailing to the Dirty Devil River and I start down the broad valley of North Hatch Canyon in a traverse reminiscent of Lockhart Basin. This is my third day without the sight of other humans in this huge, empty landscape. You could stick Manhattan Island in Hatch Canyon with room to spare and yet I've got all this space to myself. A yell hollered just to break up the silence is quickly swallowed by the vastness. Welcome to the American Outback!

The day begins screaming "AUGUST IN THE DESERT!" Drops of sweat spatter about my feet with every few steps. As reality grows increasingly uncomfortable, I mentally drift away to a gentler environment, envisioning myself afloat on a New England river. Just quietly paddling a cool, shaded creek through the emerald mountains and pastures of Vermont. No weight on my shoulders, no burning feet, no movement save the rhythmic dip of my paddle in the glassy water. And look -- there's Abby in the bow, turning to give me that dazzling smile. Maybe we'll just pull ashore under that weeping willow and ....

My radiator starts to boil and the pleasant fantasy fades back to a shimmering badlands of blackbrush and brown rock. Walk, walk, walk, drip, walk. Hours grind by. I am numb with heat by the time I stumble into the mocha-brown water of the Dirty Devil River.

Bill Dunn, one of the men of Major John Wesley Powell's pioneering descent of the Green and Colorado rivers in 1869, pulled his oak boat into the mouth of this tributary. The explorers were used to getting their drinking water from clear side creeks instead of the turbid Colorado. One of the men in a following boat hollered, "Have you found us a trout stream?"

Dunn looked into the smelly, extremely heavily-silted water and shouted back, "No, she's a dirty devil!"

A hundred and twenty-two years later, the Dirty Devil River continues to live up to its name. When I fill a quart bottle with the chocolate-brown liquid and wait an hour, over a cup of solid mud settles to the bottom. The refreshing dip in the knee-deep river leaves me with a powdery tan as I dry. The jeep track fords the Dirty Devil and continues up Poison Spring Canyon to Route 95 connecting Lake Powell and Hanksville. This difficult leg is almost over and it looks like I might survive it after all. No worries now as I lounge in the shade, lulled to lassitude by the narcotic of food and flowing water.

Day 88, Eight miles

My hair is clean. My butt rests on a wooden picnic table seat. Before me sits an eighteen-ounce jar of Jif peanut butter, newly emptied. With three quarters of my Southwest Circle Quest successfully under my belt, I'm sitting fat and happy in Hanksville, Utah.

Life was not nearly so grand after I finally dragged myself away from the Dirty Devil. The late afternoon sun slants directly into my face as I walk up the bone-dry creekbed of Poison Spring Canyon, draining bottle after bottle of purified river water. Despite its name, this canyon is supposed to contain a potable spring. Where? I'm wondering if supper will have to be another uncooked packet of ramen noodles before I spy a masonry structure under a mossy overhang just before sundown. Issuing from a pipe at its base is a steady flow of the coolest, sweetest water imaginable. Nirvana! I punch the clock and camp right there.

In the cool of dawn, I start cruising the remaining miles to the highway. At one point, I climb out of the wash and find myself staring at the inviting green humps of the Henry Mountains looking close enough to kiss. Could these really be the same mountains that looked so impossibly far away from the top of the La Sals? The cool forests ahead are calling, but first I've got to ride my thumb twenty miles north to get resupplied in Hanksville. The paved highway soon materializes like a mirage. I made it!

I plop my pack down on the asphalt and stick out my thumb. Surely a hero's welcome is in order after this unprecedented midsummer trek from Moab, but a few out-of-state motorists whistle by in their air conditioned rigs without giving me a second glance. Am I invisible? Did I enter the spirit realm without even noticing? For forty-five minutes, I haunt the tarmac griddle with no takers. I'm contemplating feigning unconsciousness when a Honda zooms by, reconsiders, and returns for me. The shirtless driver is a young French tourist named Paul. As I toss my pack in the backseat, I notice a hiking guide to the John Muir Trail.

"Have you hiked in California?" I inquire, struggling to adjust to the world accelerating to 70 mph.

"Oh, yez. I've done zee John Muir Trail twice!" Paul beams. "I love zee Sierras, but I decided to explore some of your famous desert country dis year."

Paul has just come from Moab and Canyonlands National Park and we are trading praises for the backcountry life when we cruise into the tiny desert hamlet of Hanksville. Paul pulls over in front of the post office and turns to me.

"You know, I am happy that I met someone like you," he says. "For me, Americans have generally been a disappointment. They just eat and drink and sleep and watch zee TV. I don't see much meaning in their lives. In Europe, things are much different."

"Maybe it has something to do with rootedness," I reply. "Europeans have it and Americans generally don't, especially out here in the West. Most of the towns out here didn't exist a hundred years ago. But what we lack in cultural history we have in a natural grandeur that remains largely untouched. This walk lets me establish a connection to the landscapes I want to call home. It's my way of sinking some roots."

A grin slowly spreads across Paul's bearded face. "Yes, this I understand."

Hanksville's Hollow Mountain Store is a tourist goods/gas station built into the hollowed-out center of a sandstone dome. The thermometer on the wall reads just under 100 degree in the shade. Stepping inside, I'm suddenly surrounded by air conditioning, Cheese Doodles, loud neon clothing, and children bawling for sno-cones. The "USA Today" headline is screaming something about a coup in the Soviet Union. Whoa, this is too much! Stunned by this rapid-fire return to the late twentieth century, I retreat empty-handed to the comforting reality of the desert outside. At Johnson's General Store, the other mercantile in town, the atmosphere is pure Mayberry -- OK, I can handle this. Mrs Johnson retrieves my cache box from her storeroom while I pick out some fresh goodies.

After shopping, I wander into "Buffalo Bub's Gifts and Tourist Information" next door. The shop is filled with chunks of petrified wood and quartz crystals with blue antique bottles and rusted farming tools cluttering the corners. Books, brochures, and maps are tucked in the remaining nooks. A rotund man with an extravagant moustache -- presumable Mr Bub himself -- sits glued to a portable TV behind the counter. I'm studying a collage of local topo maps papering one wall when Buffalo lumbers over.

"You planning a trip in the area?" asks the huge man eyeing my pack and walking stick.

I nod, busily tracing a possible route through the Henrys with a finger.

"You'd be better off going a little north of that."

I whirl around, ready to challenge the obese proprietor who has surely never hiked farther than to the donut shop. Buffalo looks at me calmly and asks, "Where exactly are you trying to get to, son?"

With a tone of superiority in my voice, I outline my summer's journey with particular emphasis of my triumphant leg from Moab. To my amazement, Buffalo is intimately familiar with everything I've seen. Tentatively, I quiz him on the country ahead: "Does this trail exist? Is this spring reliable? Can I make it up this canyon?" Without hesitation, the big man knows every answer.

"I just got back from my weekly tour of the Henrys. Been huntin' -- with a camera, that is," Buffalo explains with a grin. "I'm working on a photo essay of this beautiful black-faced buck that has a herd on the back of Mount Pennell." When I ask if people ever float the Dirty Devil, he says, "Oh, yes. I go all the way down to Lake Powell every spring in an inflatable kayak. Sometimes my buddies and I run it during a summer flash flood. Pretty wild ride!" As we talk, I learn that Buffalo grew up here and has been exploring the backcountry for decades; sometimes on foot, often by jeep, boat, or ORV. In addition to this shop, he runs tours in the Henrys and organizes local dig-your-own rockhound trips for Europeans. My lesson for today is that old favorite: you can't judge a book by its cover.

I'm glad to have the long, parched leg from Moab behind me -- beautiful, but tough. Things could have easily turned ugly out there. Tomorrow I'll call the Park Service and let them know I'm alive. Then up into the Henrys for another quick taste of the high country. The Great Yo-Yo Tour of the Southwest rolls on!

Day 89, Eleven miles

I'm bedded atop a hill overlooking Hanksville when my fitful slumber is shattered by the ragged crowing of a backyard rooster. From my perch, I watch as one of the loneliest towns in America wakes up. In two directions, Hanksville is seventy miles from its nearest neighbor. Head the other way and you'll find little human habitation for a couple hundred clicks. Crackerjack aluminum trailers sit interspersed with early Mormon homesteads of quarried stone. Empty cafes and boarded-up motels attest to an earlier heyday during the uranium boom. Perhaps another boom is on the way. The amazing collection of recreational and wilderness lands surrounding this community of ranchers and federal employees is attracting increasing national publicity. I imagine I'm looking at Moab thirty years ago.

On the other edge of town, I return to the Hollow Mountain Store, hoping to snag a quick hitch back to my route. A few powerful pickups towing shiny speedboats roll by headed for Lake Powell, but I'm way too scruffy-looking for this bunch. A lazy hour passes. When a ratty blue van finally pulls over, I hop in with a young European couple bound for Monument Valley. The woman in the passenger seat stares at me wide-eyed as I describe my walk from Moab. When we cross the unmarked wash at the head of Poison Spring Canyon, I ask the driver to stop.

"You want to get out *here?"* the young man stammers incredulously.

"This is my exit!"

The couple aren't smiling. Clearly, I must be insane, suicidal, or both to voluntarily march into this apparently endless wasteland.

"Thanks for the lift. And don't worry ... I know what I'm doing," I assure the ashen-faced couple. The woman is still shaking her head in disbelief as I wade into the sage to begin another week or more beyond the limits of the pavement.

On an old track leading to the foot of the Henry Mountains, a hank of rope stretched across the path reconfigures itself into a coil of rattlesnake. With a black tongue flicking at one end and rattles abuzz on the other, this two-footer is the third rattler of the summer. Less than a quarter mile farther, I freeze again at the sound of that unmistakable whirring. Buzzworm number four is hiding a few feet away under a bush.

I neither hate nor fear rattlesnakes. While I feel no special kinship with the reptiles like with Brother Raven or Señor Coyote, I don't meet these animals with dread. I honor and respect these powerful desert denizens and in return, rattlesnakes always seem to give me plenty of warning if I stumble near. Someday I hope to find the courage, trust, and willpower to allow a rattlesnake to explore my feet. But not today.

I climb into the foothills studded with aromatic piñon and juniper as storm clouds start sliding unobtrusively over the mountain's crest. Without warning, thunder crackles and tongues of brilliant lightning start tasting nearby ridgetops. I drop down next to a creek where the presence of a little water cranks the ecological transition into fast forward. One minute, I'm plowing through red sand between junipers; the next I'm slipping in rich, brown mud under aspens and spruce. No magic carpet ride could have been more abrupt.

Late afternoon finds me high on the mountainside pitching my tent in a murmur of aspens next to the delightful burble of Granite Creek. Below, the carved, surreal, naked world I've left behind is blazing scarlet in the setting sun. The highlight of the day? Ripe raspberries right here!

Day 90, Ten miles

Perky chickadees, like tiny cheerleaders in black and white uniforms tumble through the trees, encouraging me up the steep, wooded road in the morning. At Bull Creek Pass, I stow the pack and strike off for the 11,500 foot summit ridge of Mount Ellen. Soon, the tundra-coated granite is underfoot, a bottomless cobalt sky vaults overhead, and the planet is spilling away in all directions. Delight ripples through me. I'm back in alpine heaven!

My eye travels over the new country visible ahead to the west. Blood-red sandstone curls above bone-colored rock in a series of parallel ridges and overthrusts; a petrified tidal wave of geology called the Waterpocket Fold. Rising beyond this cacophony of erosion is the flat-topped dome of Boulder Mountain, the jutting prow of the Kaiparowits Plateau, and the faint, rosy cliffs of Bryce Canyon National Parks over a hundred miles away. Turning to the east, my gaze rolls back down Poison Spring Canyon, over The Maze and The Needles, to the slate-blue profile of the La Sal Range on the horizon. The idea of walking from there to here remains incomprehensible even after I've just done it.

Laughter bubbles from my gut -- what a flake! Less than a week ago, I sat next to the Colorado River and proclaimed it paradise. Now I'm a mile and a half higher and I can't conceive of a finer place than a mountaintop. I really must be the bastard offspring of a canyon coyote and a mountain goat! The air above me is alive with bird dance. Swifts and swallows whistle by, darting through aerial maneuvers that would make an F-16 pilot jealous. A trio of kestrels play tag. A red-tailed hawk hangs motionless above us all. In a moment of epiphany, I reach a major decision. One of my goals during this quest has been to discover my native name, one given to me by the wilderness itself. Several possibilities have come to me and I've been trying them on, waiting for one to fit. Now I have it! When I conclude my entry in the summit register atop Mount Ellen, I sign it "SwallowHeart." The swallow plays ceaselessly, soaring from the canyon depths to the mountaintops. My heart flies from one world to the other just as merrily. I am SwallowHeart!

Crouching down, I touch the mountain and gives thanks for the gift of a new name. The low, tough flowers of the tundra smile up at me, and with a jolt, I wonder if I'll be seeing my alpine amigos again this summer. I look around and realize that the wild places and their creatures have become my true home and family. How will I ever return to an normal indoor life when this is all over? I am now SwallowHeart, but what will become of Brett LeCompte?

I'm currently tentbound on the western flank of the Henry Mountains. Rain rattles the thin shelter of nylon while tremendous cracks of thunder shake the ground upon which I lie. With a good look at the country west of the Henrys, I feel the very real presence of the end of the journey for the first time and dread the conclusion of this deep immersion in the natural world. The trick will be to carry this world inside of me wherever I am. But how?

Day 91, Twenty-three miles

Another day, another environment. My return to the high country was all too brief. Hunkered in the paltry shade of a tamarisk at 5,000 feet, I'm hot, thirsty, and whipped. Nineteen miles today and I ain't done yet.

Early in my day-long descent to the desert, I come to a swath of bald mountainside that looks like a tornado disaster zone. A big sign offers the following explanation:

SOUTH CREEK HABITAT IMPROVEMENT PROJECT
In 1969, 600 acres had the trees and scrubs removed and reseeded with grasses, forbs and browse. A joint project between the BLM and the Utah Wildlife Commission to improve the range for deer, bison, and livestock.

What a joke! This devastation was accomplished by a popular technique in southern Utah called chaining. Imagine a massive anchor chain stretched between two bulldozers at ground level, creating a huge scythe that uproots every tree and shrub it touches. The result is a ravaged wasteland. Over twenty years after the slaughter, the gray ghosts of rot-resistant junipers still lie in heaps. The promised grass cover is minimal. Instead, a new generation of waist-high trees is struggling to succeed. How dare anyone associate the word "improvement" with this destruction. Appropriately, someone has gouged the words "deer" and "bison" from the sign to set the record straight. Disgusted, I turn to leave. Suddenly, a choir of yipping, screeching, and howling electrifies the air. Coyote seems to be screaming, "Don't worry, brother. The Earth is resilient. We have survived!"

On a hot, flat benchland lower down, a pickup towing a horse trailer bumps up the road toward me and stops. A wiry old cowboy, creased and weathered as his boots, eases out of the cab.

"Seen any cows back up there?" he asks with a squint.

"Yeah, I heard some cattle bawling up near that chained area."

The man dips his wide-brimmed hat in a nod and sets about backing his horse out of the trailer. Another man, younger and beefy with kindly eyes set in a face used to smiling, emerges from the passenger side. "Are you already moving the cattle out of the mountains?" I ask.

"Already moved most of 'em," the younger cowboy explains. "We're up here looking for strays. Only had'em on the mountain for five weeks this year on account of the drought and the buffalo over-population. We just spooked a herd of twenty-seven bison back down the road a piece." These bison are a wild herd of five hundred animals transplanted to the Henry Mountains years ago. I've been keeping my eyes peeled, but no sightings so far.

The old cowboy swings a surprisingly limber leg over the saddle and slowly rides up the road accompanied by his sidekick, a tri-colored bob-tailed Australian shepherd. The younger man watches the rider disappear and says proudly, "My father owns about seven hundred acres up here. He'll be eighty-two years old in a couple of weeks and he can still ride with the best of'em."

"Do you ranch, too?" I wonder aloud.

"I used to manage the Sandy Ranch down in the Waterpocket Fold. Now I work for Capital Reef National Park in the orchards; the ones planted by homesteaders a couple generations ago. The park still maintains the trees and the public can pick the apples, pears, and peaches for free at harvest time."

I must be drooling at the mention of fresh fruit since the friendly chap pokes his head back in the truck and says, "Sorry -- didn't bring any fruit. How about a cucumber?" He hands me a monster big enough to make a mare blush. Behind us, bawling bovines and clattering hooves announce the return of the octogenarian cowpoke pushing four steers toward us.

"Looks like time for both of us to get back to business," I drawl, swinging my pack up. "Thanks for the cuke."

The landscape turns into a John Wayne flick: tawny, broken, hot, and dusty. I half expect gunfighters and Apaches and hope for buffalo, but see none of them. The track dives into the tilted and sheared multi-colored sandstone of the Waterpocket Fold. The unusual geology is unlike anything I've encountered -- massive rock ribs with rounded backs and vertical faces separated by long, grassy valleys.

My mouth is cotton when the descent ends at the junction of Oak Creek and Sandy Creek. Both dry. Then a glint among the rocks catches my eye. From the stagnant puddle, I collect two foul, tepid quarts. Was I really strolling across the tundra yesterday? Would somebody please jerk my string and yo-yo me back up to the coolness of the mountains!

Day 92, Fourteen miles

The final four miles after yesterday's entry were hellish. I'm walking due west with the fiery fingers of the setting sun slapping me in the face, feeling like an ant beneath some brat's magnifying glass. I cross into Capital Reef National Park, shooting for Oak Creek which my map indicates should have flowing water. No such luck -- another dry bed of stones and silt. Damn! I start trudging upstream, aching to get off my feet, but needing water. Within two hundred yards, I reach another pitiful, uninviting puddle in a sandy depression. "This'll do," I mutter, pushing aside the surface scum to dip a bottle.

Not until my belly is full and my freed toes are sunk into the cool sand does my disposition improve. I'm hanging my food bag from a tree limb when I notice a bright light illuminating the cliff above me -- headlight? UFO? No -- the full moon! Exactly three lunar month have passed since I sat in my circle of stone. One moon from now, my circle of footprints should be complete. Circles spiraling with other circles. A quest for roundness.

I sleep well on the mattress of soft sand. Too well. In my dream, I'm kissing a tall, mysterious, curly-haired beauty so passionately that I wake up drooling. Aye carumba! These "woman dreams" are becoming disturbingly frequent. It has been a long summer in many ways!

The plan is to follow Oak Creek upstream to its source on Boulder Mountain, but where's the water? Half a mile farther, the mystery is solved. A diversion dam siphons ninety-five percent of the creek into an irrigation ditch -- more tinkering with the plumbing. Above the dam, Oak Creek is the delightful two-hop wide stream slicing an easy route through the western ridges of the Waterpocket Fold. The high sandstone walls drift from cream to cinnamon to pumpkin orange as I wander upstream.

My surroundings are stunning, but I'm feeling hot and bothered. My feet are complaining, my pack is an uncomfortable lump, and there's a painful crick in my neck. A lovely waterfall appears where the creek drops over a ledge, but I march on by until a little voice in my head whispers, "Hey, what's your hurry? Cool your jets! Enjoy where you are!" I listen and turn around. The refreshing water pounding on my shoulders is exactly what the doctor ordered. I splash and whoop and cavort like a duckling. Work becomes play. With my attitude properly readjusted, I sit naked in the shade and munch trailmix, realizing suddenly that I've just completed my 1000th mile. Yeehaa!

The high desert gradually becomes a sweet woodland as I leave the park and enter Dixie National Forest. A beautiful grove of ponderosa pines the likes of which I haven't seen since Flagstaff surround me. Dark trunks stand regal and ramrod straight on a carpet of buckskin needles. The afternoon breeze playing in the long, stiff needles create a satisfying deep "swoosh." Pines give way to aspens as I continue climbing the flank of Boulder Mountain. Coyly dressed in a dapple of heart-shaped leaves, the airy aspens are like milk-skinned maidens next to the swarthy pines. Tonight, I'm happy to be bedding down among these sylvan ladies in the cool comfort of the forest.

Day 93, Fourteen miles

Boulder Mountain is protected by a facade of high cliffs just below a broad, plateau-like summit. My map promises that a jeep trail will sail smoothly through the cliffs to the high meadows and lakes beyond, but when I reach the spruce zone, the track has faded to an intermittent elk trail. No problem -- the bushwhack is a welcome change after days of roadwalking. Gem-like raspberries crying: "Pick me! Eat me!" from the undergrowth slow my pace even farther.

The scramble through the palisades is like a magic gateway into a chunk of the Maine woods. The 10,800-foot mountaintop is a thick spruce forest broken by parks of open, rocky grasslands. Several sizable lakes and hundreds of ponds punctuate a landscape where a moose or loon would look at home. The illusion of the North Woods is complete when a chill, gray rain erupts from a dull overcast sky. I crouch under the arms of a spruce beside Halfmoon Lake and shiver my way through a wet lunch. Is this really southern Utah in August?

One indication of my true location remains painfully clear. Cows and cow pies are everywhere. Like the Hindus, Utah's ranchers seem to worship these graceless brutes, allowing them to trample every temple of wilderness. I pass near the canvas tents and horse trailers of a cowboy encampment planted in a meadow for fall roundup. "Get to work, boys," I want to shout. "Clear these bovine swine outta here!" But, the loaded gun racks in every pickup make me hold my tongue as I continue across a landscape mined with dung.

My grumbling subsides when I set up camp on the southern edge of the escarpment near Rim Lake. An impressive vista overlooks the arteries of the Escalante canyon system stretching away below. Distant storms and the setting sun alternately drench, then gild this wilderness of slickrock and I recall the beautiful week I spent with Abby down there this spring. That trip seems like a lifetime ago.

Perhaps it was.

Day 94, Thirteen miles

KABLAM!

What the hell was that?

I'm in the tent, dense with sleep that's just been shattered by an explosion. Poking my head outside, the first thing I see is a fat, shiny moon hanging innocently in the west. The eastern sky is a predawn red smudge. High, scattered clouds glide between fading constellation to the north.

I swing my eyes to the south and stare into the menacing teeth of a black thunderblaster about to swallow me. Thunder and lightning at dawn? The deluge erupts minutes after I batten down the hatches. For several hours, I'm a weather POW. Even when the patter fades and I break camp, the southern sky remains dreadfully ominous.

Yesterday, I "discovered" a chunk of the North Woods stuck here in southern Utah. Today I walk through a nasty Pacific weather system that got lost on its way to Seattle. Thick, steel-bellied clouds park themselves on the treetops while I knit together jeep roads, trails, and bushwhacks into a descent off Boulder Mountain. The storm pummels again with renewed gusto. Icy wind whips rain into my face and smears the nylon raingear against my body. To deal with these miserable conditions, I resort to a trick I learned when walking England's moorlands under similar skies. Gathering up all the fury of the storm, I begin to throw it back at the sky with lung-ripping screams and hollers. The harder the rain or fiercer the wind, the louder I yell. Instead of resisting the energy of the tempest, I let it fill and flow through me until I'm just a shade shy of berserk.

The heavens and I ease our monstrous duet as the trail heads into the shelter of the aspens. A tidy cabin appears unexpectedly in an opening in the forest -- the Jubilee Guard Station, built in 1905 and restored in 1989. The interior decor is only a couple of bare bunks and a wobbly table, but it's just the ticket for a break out of the weather. The walls are a register of cowboy and hunter names carved in the logs since the 1920s. Who else has sought out shelter here over the decades? What stories could this cabin tell?

Patchy sunshine has replaced the pewter overcast when the trail leads me face to face with a trio of bull elk sporting the impressive racks of late summer. The biggest bull stares me down while his younger companions spar and joist half-heartedly. The rut must be approaching. Is there any finer mountain music than the clack of clashing antlers and the bellow of an elk bugle?

The trail turns abruptly into an eyesore of a logging road which leads to a primitive Forest Service's campground where I punch the clock. The only other occupants are a family from Salt Lake City who inform me that heavy rains are forecasted for the next three days. Where's that Utah Tourist Bureau phone number ... ?

Day 95, Eight miles

After dinner last night, my neighbor, Randy, invites me to his family's campfire. He and his wife, Deborah, have been tramping around the southern Utah's backcountry for ten years. On this trip, they are introducing the wonders of canyon country to their two sons who sit with us, gleefully burning marshmallows into edible cinders. For a while, I answer questions about my quest for the eager faces aglow in the flickering, buttery light. Our conversation then turns to the idea of wilderness and the threats of grazing, logging, mining, and road construction. Randy has clearly devoted considerable time and energy to this issue.

"Do you realize that here in southern Utah we have the potential to create America's greatest protected wilderness outside of Alaska?" Randy asks passionately. "If we can get the Owens Bill passed by Congress, more than five million acres would get wilderness status. Of course, we're up against some powerful opponents. The logging and mining companies have the locals down here convinced that anyplace protected as wilderness will be 'locked up' and therefore rendered useless. The ranchers don't like the government coming in and telling them what to do with 'their' land which, in fact, is federal property belonging to us all. Environmentalist is a dirty word around here."

"Ever run into any hostility?" I ask.

Randy stares with intelligent eyes into the mesmerizing flames for a while before responding. "Nothing major -- a few cold shoulders is all. I used to be more radical in my views, but my thinking has become more holistic. Name-calling hasn't gotten us anywhere. The needs of the local communities are valid and need to be addressed. I've been working on plans to make low-interest loans available for the creation of a locally-owned guide service. Not much interest so far." Randy slides a loving arm around his closest son and says, "I owe it to these guys to keep working toward wilderness protection. What if someday they want to undertake a quest like yours? What if there are no wild places left to go?"

In the morning, I slip out of the campground and immediately enter the Box-Death Hollow Wilderness Area -- a fitting epilogue to last night's discussion. A faint trail skips back and forth across Pine Creek as it dives into a steep, narrow canyon. Progress is difficult and slow, but I'm in no hurry, savoring the beauty as if strolling through an immense art gallery. A delightful collage of trees -- aspen, spruce oak, maple, and pine -- line sun-dappled pools where tiny trout flit into shadows. The crumbling, cross bedded, chalk-white walls grow taller with every step until they tower a thousand multi-tiered feet above me. Stunted pines cling impossibly to fissures like wind-twisted bonsai trees. The canyon widens to an open glade of old growth ponderosa pines, a council of majestic grandfather trees. My walk becomes a pilgrimage into serenity.

Today has been my sabbath -- a day to slow down and worship the wilderness. It is no accident that the finest stretches of my journey such as San Pedro Park, the Rio Chama, the South San Juan, and the Weminuche, are protected wilderness areas. Randy is right. Perhaps the most important thing we can leave our children are the wild places, the original world. No amount of material wealth extracted from this land will ever equal its spiritual value. As Thoreau said, "In wildness is the preservation of the Earth." I feel the truth in these words to the core of my soul. We must protect the wilderness not just for ourselves, but for its own intrinsic worth. My love of Mother Earth deepens with every step.

Day 96, Eight miles

The harmony I felt during yesterday's meditative meander fades away when I leave the wilderness area and walk into the town of Escalante to retrieve my next cache box. My first glimpse of the town is a sawmill belching smoke. The clash and whine of heavy machinery rendering trees into boards is a dark contrast to yesterday's silence. Parked outside the mill is a posse of battered pickups, several sporting "SUWA Sucks!" bumper stickers (SUWA is the Southern Utah Wilderness Alliance -- the folks spearheading the effort for wilderness protection). Escalante, an old-time Mormon community of ranchers and loggers, has achieved national recognition for its anti-environmental stance. Several wilderness activists, including Robert Redford, have been publicly hung in effigy in this conservative town. What kind of welcome will this scruffy backpacker get?

The mixed cluster of trailers and brick Victorians looks friendly enough. Two grocery stores face each other across Main Street. The name of one, Griffin Mercantile, rings a bell; many Griffins had scrawled on the wall of the Jubilee Guard Station. Curious, I duck inside. A stringy lady in her fifties wearing a print dress cocks her eyebrows at the sight of my pack, then relaxes into a tight, thin-lipped smile. I grab a basket and pull a few goodies for the next leg off the shelves. While the woman rings up my purchases, I run a few of the names I remember from the cabin by her. This time her smile is genuine.

"Oh my yes! Those would be my husband's uncle's people. Used to be a mess of Griffins around here. 'Course, most have moved on. Where'd you say you saw them names?"

I explain my trek from Hanksville, figuring the full tale from Flagstaff would overwhelm the poor lady. Her eyes expand dramatically as I describe my hike over the Henrys and Boulder Mountain.

"My word!" she sputters. Her thin face bunches in confusion when she lifts the hunk of cheese out of my basket. "Now, how do you manage to keep this fresh out there?"

"The trick is to get rid of the plastic," I explain. "It's the oil that the cheese sweats out that goes rancid and spoils. I just wrap the cheese in a bandana that I rinse out every few days. The cheese kinda forms a skin and keeps just fine. Old desert rat trick!"

The storekeeper listens carefully, then exclaims, "Well, my husband -- he's a rancher, you know -- he's always coming back from the trail with a slimy pile of leftover cheese. I'll just have to give that bandana trick of yours a try. Thanks!" Score one for hiker/rancher relations!

The afternoon is a wild goose chase in search of route information for the next leg. Berry, the owner of Escalante Outfitters, the recently opened outdoor gear store which is holding my resupply box, is too new to the area to be very helpful. He directs me to the Forest Service office next door. The bearded ranger manning the information desk has little to offer as well, suggesting I visit the BLM office on the edge of town. An attractive ranger with a thick chestnut ponytail and a name tag that reads "Sue" stands behind the BLM counter. I flash her a smile and unfold my map before her.

"I hope you can help me," I plead, praying I don't smell as ragged as I look. "I need to get some information about viable water sources between here and the Paria River." As I explain my journey and trace my intended route on the map, Sue frowns at the maze of contour lines.

"Not much water out that way this time of year," she explains. "Let me ask one of the other guys."

Sue slips into a back room and returns with another ranger built like a line-backer with a beefy head sporting a crewcut. He pauses for half a beat to size up the skinny, sweaty, unshaven backpacker before him. "Whadaya want?" he demands gruffly.

"I need to know which springs are going to be flowing southwest of here. Where can I count on finding drinking water?"

Crewcut gives my map a careless glance. Stabbing it with crude jabs with his thick thumb, he sneers, "There might be water in this cattle tank ... and maybe this one. 'Course you might walk right by them without seeing them. Hell, you gotta be crazy to drink that stuff anyway."

I press the hard nosed ranger for more details, but Crewcut replies only half-heartedly, then mumbles something about "important work to do" and stalks off. From the back room, I hear his laughter as he resumes joking with "the guys."

Ranger Sue shoots me an apologetic look, understanding that my life hinges on locating water in the unforgiving country ahead. Together, we scrutinize the map again, piecing together a plan from Crewcut's scanty information. When my route strays beyond her district, she phones her counterpart in Kanab and grills him with my questions. What a lifesaver! I thank my new friend for all her help.

"No problem," she smiles. Lowering her voice, she adds, "Some of the range management guys around here aren't very sympathetic to hikers." A sudden idea brightens her pretty face. "Hey, you should talk to Bill next door. He's always off traipsing around in the canyons."

Bill is painting signs behind the National Park Service office next door. A medium-sized man with a salt and pepper beard and inquisitive blue eyes, he listens nonchalantly to my questions about trails.

"Sure, I've been in Hackberry Canyon," Bill says. "Which way you going in?"

"Don't know. I'll be walking to there from Escalante ...."

"Walking from Escalante!?"

Bill lays down his brush and slowly breaks into a wry grin as I tell him about the thousand miles I've already covered. Impressed and intrigued, Bill carefully details several routes into Hackberry Canyon, then ventures a few questions about my quest.

"I haven't hiked too much outside this area," the ranger admits. "Too much to keep me busy right here." His eyes begin to twinkle as he recounts his latest adventure. "My buddy and I have been eyeballing this remote slot canyon near the Escalante for years. The only way in turned out to be a three hundred-foot rappel. At one point, we were swimming in this long, icy-cold pool where the walls were only a foot apart. We struggled through that place for two hard days and covered only about a mile. Let me tell you -- that was one incredible mile! We figure we are the first people to get in there. Yep, enough amazing country right around here to occupy me for a lifetime or two!"

When I finish talking with Bill, the afternoon has vanished. I rush to the post office to fire off a few postcards, then commandeer a picnic table in a deserted park on the edge of town. The hectic search for information has drained me -- or maybe it's the massive Mexican feast I just handily put away. Still, if I wasn't broke again, I'd probably head over to the burger joint across the street for dessert.

The next two or three days are looking pretty dry. So, what else is new?

Day 97, Eighteen miles

Lunchtime in a furnace called Death Ridge. Boulder Mountain and the Henrys float behind me like a mirage -- oases of coolness and moisture. Yet, their lush forests seem as distant as a dream as I plow through another merciless desert. Sitting here in the shade, I think about Everett Ruess, another wide-eyed wilderness traveler who stumbled into Escalante back in 1934. The young man caused more of a stir than I did when he arrived in town riding one burro and leading another. The local ranchers had never seen anyone quite like the baby-faced, twenty year-old artist and writer hailing from southern California. A self-proclaimed vagabond for beauty, Everett had already spent three summers wandering the Southwest. Alone or with a brace of burros, the artist sought remote country, drinking in its beauty as he pursued his dream of oneness with the natural world. In a series of passionate letters to his family, Everett wrote of discovering in this land "such utter and overpowering beauty as nearly kills a sensitive person by its piercing glory."

Although he never made it to the Rocky Mountains, Everett traveled much of the same country as my Southwest Circle Quest: Navajoland, the San Francisco Peaks, the Grand Canyon, and southeast Utah. He encountered Navajo and Hopi families, early archeologists, and Mormon homesteaders. Yet mostly, the artist enjoyed solitary adventures and private communion with his surroundings. He was a footloose idealist in love with everything wild and beautiful. If I have a spiritual ancestor, undoubtedly, it is Everett Ruess.

Perched here on Death Ridge, I pray that the similarity between Everett and myself is not absolute since Escalante was the last town that Everett ever saw. The exuberant wanderer lingered in Escalante for a few days, taking in a movie and flirting with the local Mormon girls. He then rode into the maze of canyons along the Escalante River with vague plans of crossing the Colorado River and visiting Navajo Mountain. Everett Ruess was never seen again.

When his family stopped receiving his regular correspondence, they contacted Escalante town officials and a search party was organized. His camp and burros were found in Davis Gulch, but there was no sign of Everett. Some say the young explorer was killed by outlaws. Most believe that Everett, in his overzealous exploring, fell to his death in the labyrinth of slickrock. Subsequent investigations found that an Anasazi ruin had been inscribed with "NEMO 1934". A few think that the young dreamer, seeking ultimate freedom, staged his own disappearance like Jules Verne's nefarious Captain Nemo. Legend has it that Everett Ruess is still out here, an eternal vagabond roaming his beloved desert wilderness. His disappearance remains one of the great unsolved mysteries of the Southwest.

Everett, be you dim specter or wizened recluse, I hope you will join me around tonight's campfire. What a time we'll have recounting our common experiences and sharing of love of wild country! We are blood brothers across the ages, for I, too, am a vagabond for beauty. If anyone can understand my quest, it is you. Come, my friend, share your secrets with me.

Later: Another camp beneath the swoosh of ancient, wind-kissed pines. I've climbed to 8,000 feet on the side of Canaan Peak in search of water. A lucky bushwhack from Death Ridge leads me here to the clear, cold gush of Horse Spring.

All afternoon, I continue my vigilant search for a "ghost" almost as elusive as Everett. The remote, broken country around Canaan Peak seems an ideal place to finally glimpse a mountain lion. Ever since I was a small boy in New Hampshire, I've been deeply intrigued by this reclusive predator. Spotting a wild cougar has become one goal of this summer's quest. The tawny, sleek feline represents everything that is wild and powerful and mysterious in the Southwest. There have been times, like today, when I can sense the big cat's presence; feel the great, green eyes watching me pass. I pray that this "spirit cat" will reveal herself to me this summer. Time grows short.

Day 98, Seventeen miles

Dawn tiptoes down Canaan Peak, dusting the magnificent pines with fairy light as I bushwhack to its 9,200-foot summit. The southern face of the mountaintop is a precipice of the same orange and apricot limestone so deftly displayed in Bryce Canyon National Park, visible twenty-five miles due west. Here begins the "great staircase of geology" that steps down in massive cliff-bands reaching all the way to the bottom of the Grand Canyon. A shiver of anticipation shoots through me when I spy the low, massive, blue bulk of the Kaibab Plateau far to the south -- my home last summer. Returning to familiar country.

Setting my immediate sights on the scrubby uplands of the Paria River watershed, I bushwhack off the mountain to an unexpected jeep road that leads past a queer, concrete-covered quonset hut. Curious, as well as eager to top off my water bottles, I amble up the dirt drive. Even from a distance, I can tell the structure is no seasonal cowboy camp, but a real residence. Yet the homestead's air of funky self-reliance is marred by piles of trash strewn everywhere. A shiny pickup is parked in the yard.

"Hello? Anyone home?"

No answer.

A sliding glass door is open about eight inches. I utter another tentative "hello?" and steal a peek inside. The dark interior is cluttered, but homey. Nothing stirs inside. I'm about to knock, but my fist freezes in midair. Posted next to the door is a computer-printed sign that reads in English and Spanish: "COME THROUGH THIS DOOR AND YOU WILL BE KILLED."

My heart flies to my throat. I glance inside again and spot a Desert Storm-style camo jacket draped casually over a chair. Every story about half-crazed Vets holed up in the backcountry flashes through my brain. A downpour erupts, but I barely notice. Stiff with panic, I step away from the doorway and jog back down the driveway. Hightailing it down the road, I nervously keep checking my backside, painfully aware of my clear tracks in the wet sand. When the road veers west, I continue south in the bed of a dry wash where my footprints are invisible on the cobbles.

With each step down the wash, the surging adrenaline subsides and the thoughts come tumbling out. How easy it would be for someone to put a bullet in my forehead and dump my body in the rocks! Nobody knows where I am except Abby and she only knows I'm somewhere in the vastness between Escalante, Utah and Marble Canyon, Arizona. I would simply vanish just like my old pal, Everett. Hell, maybe that was old man Ruess's hideout back there. Did the eager, innocent artist turn mean and bitter over the decades as he witnessed the flooding of Glen Canyon, the carnage of uranium prospecting, and the poisoning of the air with coal smoke? Perhaps. For the first time all summer, I feel vulnerable and threatened by another human.

The morning does not improve. I hit another jeep road that has been recently "maintained" with a bulldozer. Raw gashes in the earth are everywhere. Uprooted junipers, still green, lie tangled and bleeding off the roadway as if some evil ogre pulled them up and cast them aside. I spot a patch of gray fur under a bush. It's a coyote pup, long dead and mummified, its skeletal foreleg still locked in the jaws of a steel trap. The bad vibes of this area are almost palpable. What have I stumbled into? Not until I abandon the track for the dry bed of Horse Creek does the foreboding fade away.

Late in the afternoon, I reach the gravel road that serves as the back way into Bryce. Once again, I'm out of water and the next known source is a half-day's walk away in the wrong direction. Time to gamble on the best water source after springs, seeps, and cattle tanks: passing vehicles. My wait is mercifully short. An ice-blue pickup with California plates is coming up fast, spewing a roostertail of dust. I jump to my feet, waving my arms in the middle of the road -- ain't no way I'm gonna be ignored as a grubby hitchhiker this time! The truck slows, but keeps rolling as a clean-cut, round-faced oriental man peers nervously out his window. He stares at me as if I'm Butch Cassidy and my gang is lurking nearby, ready to plunder his rig.

"Could you spare me some water?" I plead, trying to look harmless.

The palc man screws his face into a knot. "I dunno -- all I got is a gallon..." His truck has almost eased by me and begins to accelerate.

"WAIT!" I cry desperately. "You've only got about ten miles to the next town and I'm on foot and ...."

"On foot?!" the man blurts out. The truck jolts to a full stop. Minutes later, I'm plunging back into the desert, tanked up and grinning. Behind me, the tourist continues on toward Los Angeles with a story for his buddies back home about the "crazy bastard" that he saved in Utah.

Three more miles across sagebrush flats and I stand on the lip of a narrow, deep chasm. Following Bill's directions, I ease down a faint, treacherously steep trail into this tributary of Hackberry Canyon. Once on the sandy canyon floor, I realize I've entered another natural cathedral. Every sound softly echoes in this chamber of fluted, ivory-colored sandstone and I feel as welcomed here as I felt threatened this morning. What an emotional day!

Day 99, Eleven miles

I awaken to a duet of bird song. The gargled baritone of Raven underscores the refined, lilting soprano of Canyon Wren -- a delightful piece of chamber music to usher me into September. At first, upper Hackberry Canyon is a disappointment. The last human visitor down here rumbled around illegally on an ATV. Three parallel lines of knobby tracks disgrace the dry creekbed of this Wilderness Study Area. Then I cross paths with an "animal grazing unit" -- BLM lingo for a beef cow and her calf. They lumber awkwardly ahead of me, unable to scramble out of the canyon and too stupid to stop and let me pass. We play tag for over a mile. "Keep this up, you brainless morons, and you'll be seeing Arizona!" I holler at the two shit-caked butts swaggering before me.

A low, slate-gray sky weeps fits of rain throughout the morning. I crouch in shallow alcoves, sitting out the heaviest showers and watching swallows twirl through their aerial ballet. The creekbed becomes glazed with sticky mud, but this annoyance is offset by the collage of wet, smooth cobbles that glisten like magic eggs. A little farther, a subterranean creek rises to the surface and my day and a half dry passage is over. I relax, knowing I'll follow flowing water for the rest of this leg.

What an amazing difference a tiny thread of surface water makes. A dry canyon has the austere grandeur of a museum of sculpture, but a watered canyon is a verdant, linear botanical garden. The clattering echo of footfalls is replaced by the music of water sliding over slickrock, insect chatter, and the whisper of cattails and cottonwoods in the breeze. The sun emerges with rain-sharpened clarity to give this strip of life the sparkle of Eden and I pause often to absorb the magic: the rattle of a tiny forest of stiff, olive-green horsetails, the dance of a water strider gallantly navigating two inch rapids, a mob of tiny copper toads moving resolutely downstream on unknown missions. I feel as lucky as Adam to find myself in this paradise.

Day 100, Seventeen miles

It is almost dark. My desk is a battered picnic table tucked under a pot-bellied juniper in the BLM's Paria River Primitive Campground. A hundred yards away, a gaggle of loud kids scramble, spider-like, over a jungle gym of sandstone. Their parents, standing around a roaring "white man's" campfire, nurse beers and watch nervously. Before me is a rumpled heap of aluminum foil and a greasy corn cob -- the remains of the barbecue dinner kindly offered by this family upon my arrival. Today I stumbled from one drama to the next. New places, new faces, and new twists pile together until I don't know where to begin.

Let's start back at Hackberry Canyon. My passage in this sensuous hideaway continued this morning as the stream cuts through the creamy Navajo sandstone and the brick-red rock of the Kayenta and Moenave formations into the soft shales of the Chinle layer. The narrow canyon expands into a small valley of sage and a line of deep paw prints swings in from the undergrowth. I kneel to examine a track, then touch the large pug mark in wonder.

Felix concolor -- the ghost cat.

The sign is fresh, perhaps only minutes old. I scan the rocks for a white-tipped muzzle or a careless tail flick. If the mountain lion is still nearby, she remains invisible, teasing me.

Hackberry Canyon abruptly bends east to join Cottonwood Wash and the canyon ends with a magnificent narrows where all the previous rock layers bend upwards and reappear in rapid succession. As mysteriously as it surfaced, the flowing water sinks back beneath the sand. The mouth of the canyon, where I return to the gravel roadway, is dry, modest, and forgettable. Like a beautiful princess dressed in rags, Hackberry Canyon reveals none of her secret glory to passing motorists. Only a walker will find the verdant beauty hidden in her heart. The dusty road passes The Cockscomb; a bizarre configuration of vertical stone slabs like colossal dinner plates jammed upright in the ground. By lunch, I reach the Paria River, a fifteen foot-wide sheet of ankle-deep hazy water that will lead me all the way to the Colorado River.

In the afternoon, my attention shifts to the atmosphere. Ahead, the sky is friendly -- small, fluffy cumulus sheep chasing each other around an azure field. Behind me, all hell is breaking loose. A seething stack of purple-black thunderheads dumping rain and lightning is bearing down fast. The road is wide open, offering no protection.

Two voices begin arguing in my head. One says, "Keep walking; the sun is shining and you're cruising. If the storm hits, just throw up the tent and crawl in. No problem. Quit worrying!"

A deeper voice advises, "When that storm comes crashing down all around you, don't be stuck out here in the open. Use a little foresight. Forget the destination for a moment and find solid shelter NOW to sit this one out." After a hundred days out here, I've learned whom to heed and beeline a quarter mile cross-country to some house-sized boulders at the base of a cliff.

No sooner have I ducked under a deep overhang than the fiercest wind storm of the summer slams across the land. Damn -- my tent would have been shredded and hurled to Mexico in that first blast! Sheets of horizontal rain cut down with a vengeance, bending the sagebrush like a firehose. Even tucked under ten feet of solid rock, I'm splattered with spray. For ten minutes, the tempest rages with biblical fury, then disappears as rapidly as it broke. Soon, the sun is drawing steam from the sodden, mahogany-colored soil. Nothing like a pocket hurricane to enliven a dull afternoon!

An hour later, I top a knoll and stare at the heavy flow of trucks and Winnebagos zipping along Route 89, the first paved road since Escalante. Like Rip Van Winkle, I'm slack-jawed at the sudden appearance of the modern world. So fast. So loud. Like a frightened deer, I skitter across the asphalt and dive back into the safety of the desert beyond.

The nearby BLM Paria Wilderness ranger station is closed. The outside water pump is on duty, however, so I stop to tank up. Two pickups pull up and I'm joined by a man and a woman, neither of them the absent ranger. Tom looks like a city slicker slightly toasted by too much Southwestern sun. My attention is riveted on Liz, a wonderful configuration of deeply tanned limbs and casual grace who looks as at home out here as a pronghorn. When she offers me her dazzling smile, I almost melt at her Teva-clad feet.

Liz and Tom are both professional photographers who have spent the day doing a shoot together. Liz is also a Grand Canyon boatwoman (oh my!) who's about to embark on a special photographer's expedition down the Colorado in dories. I describe my summer's adventures, answering the barrage of endless questions and an hour of gab quickly passes between us.

When it is clear that the BLM ranger isn't going to show, Tom hops back in this truck, eager for a shower and a beer in Page. When Liz starts heading back to her own rig, I amble along behind like a lost puppy. She opens a cooler and hands me a cold juice, some cookies, and a cucumber.

"You might as well enjoy these," Liz says brightly. "This stuff is just gonna go bad sitting in my truck while I'm on the river." I grin foolishly, struggling to think of something, anything, to prolong my encounter with this goddess, but too much time alone has rendered my few social skills inoperative. Mute and helpless, I watch as Liz drives away, skewering my heart with a final breathtaking smile.

As the sun slips toward China, I strut the two miles of rutted road to the BLM campground lost in a lustful daydream. My revelry is suddenly broken by a loud, deep, roaring hiss somewhere to my right. The odd noise is coming from the Paria creekbed several hundred yards away. What the hell ... ? Then I remember the storm and run, pack and all, to the arroyo's edge.

I smell the flash flood before I see it -- a pungent aroma of churning earth and liquid mud. The sight of the raging river stops me cold. Only a few hours earlier, I had hopped across the Paria in two easy bounds as the six inch-deep stream meandered weakly down its expansive bed. Now I stare thunderstruck at a dense, bank-eating monster thirty feet wide and several feet deep. The torrent is so heavy with silt that the foaming crests of the powerful waves are not white, but brown. The naked stonescape upstream must have shed incalculable gallons of rainwater into the canyons of Cottonwood, Hackberry, and Paria, flushing everything downhill past this point. What if this flash flood had caught me in the narrow confines of Hackberry Canyon? What does this mean for my planned descent of Paria Canyon, a notoriously tight chasm which begins just ahead? The deluge continues to rip by indifferently as my brain fumbles once again to catch up with reality.

At the campground, I meet Mike, the BLM wilderness ranger who drives up after a routine four-day patrol hike through Paria Canyon. Mike is also dumbfounded when he sees the flashflooding Paria; thirty-five miles downstream, he had enjoyed clear, sunny skies all day.

"How long will the water stay high like this?" I ask the ranger.

"Should be almost back to normal by morning, but the mud's gonna be just awful," Mike explains. "The Paria flashed lower than this about two weeks ago and I still had mud up to my knees in places down there. The goo almost ripped the soles right off my boots." I glance down and start laughing at the sight of the painfully familiar arrangement of parachute cord holding Mike's boots together. When I explain my trip and my plan to start down the canyon tomorrow, the ranger looks me in the eyes and says, "Listen -- the chances are real slim that another major storm will dump in this drainage over the next few days. But if it does, you could be stranded ... or worse. I can't really stop you, but keep a close eye on the weather and be prepared to climb to safety. Even without another storm, you'll be slogging through the worst mess you've ever seen." Mike climbs back in his pea-green truck. "I'll run down here first thing in the morning and give you the weather forecast."

Paria Canyon is the first place along my route where I've hiked before. Abby and I spent three days in a partial descent of this popular canyon two springs ago. But the flooding of the creek -- I can still hear the ominous dull hiss from a quarter mile away -- strips much of the familiarity from this place. Just what am I going to find down there? Will the Paria flash again? What other choice do I have?

Day 101, Twelve miles

While I'm working on last evening's entry, another visitor arrives in the campground. Between paragraphs, I watch the lone woman assemble her turquoise tent a few sites away. She heaves a milk crate of food and cooking gear out of her yellow hatchback and plops it on the picnic table. After lighting a Coleman lantern to push aside the dark, the woman fires up a white-gas backpacking stove which ignites with the characteristic "whooof". With my writing completed, I'm eager to crank out my second dinner, so in search of illumination and conversation, I amble over. "Howdy!" I begin. "Couldn't help noticing your light. Do you think I might cook at the other end of your table? I promise not to make a mess."

The woman is in her twenties with light brown, shoulder-length hair framing an attractive, bookish face. While I speak, she studies me with shrewd, hazel eyes behind large glasses. "I guess that would be OK," she replies with a half smile. Over the combined roars of our stoves, I learn that my neighbor, Jeanne, has spent the last three years working for several national environmental groups and is now pursuing her own version of a vision quest.

"I was doing good work, but got burned out by the whole political scene," Jeanne explains. "So I quit and decided to spend this summer traveling around the West. I wanted to get to know the land I'd been working so hard to protect. A few days camping here; a short backpack there -- it's been great. I love it out here!" I begin describing my trek to Jeanne and we talk long into the night.

At dawn, Ranger Mike pulls his truck into the parking lot just as I'm washing my breakfast dishes. The forecast is for more widely-scattered thunderstorms -- the usual late summer stuff on the Colorado Plateau. I promise to call Mike from Lee's Ferry with a report on the conditions I find. Jeanne has decided to forgo the muck of the Paria and is headed north to search for less messy hiking near Escalante and I give her a warm hug before she departs. OK -- no more delays. Time to see what the flash flood left in its wake.

The Paria is still liquid mud, rich and sensual as a river of Ghirardelli chocolate. The flow, however, is a fraction of yesterday's torrent. Adjoining the cocoa-colored creek are broad fields of unbroken mud and silt left by the receding water that look both treacherous and oddly appealing. For a mile, the trail jogs safely along a bench above the flood zone. At the first creek crossing, I stop to pull out my secret weapon -- the sandals that I bought in Pagosa Springs and mailed to Escalante in anticipation of stream-walking in Paria Canyon. The taupe straps encircling my snow-white ankles look nowhere near rugged enough for the thirty-seven miles between me and the mouth of the canyon, but still hopeful, I step into the murky brew and begin weaving back and forth down the creek.

The water and mud ranges from ankle-deep to just under my kneecaps. The flimsy sandals provide little traction, turning the hike into a tenuous tightrope act. The bulky pack, clinging to my back like an oversized baboon, doesn't help much. It is almost a relief when one of the straps breaks after a couple miles. What did I expect for $2.18? I strip off the muddy sandals and the mud sloozes deliciously between my toes. Hmmm -- this ain't so bad. I reshoulder my pack and for the next two and a half miles, I walk barefoot down Paria Canyon, a coating of sticky mud acting like a protective second sole. Able to detect the nuances of the creekbed, my footing is greatly improved. I become an Aborigine stalking dingoes; a bushman tracking wildebeests. My sense of freedom and connection to the environment has never been better. What a difference!

This experiment ends when I reach the head of the Narrows, a stretch of tight passages that makes Paria Canyon one of the premiere hikes in the Southwest. Two hundred-foot walls close in on each other, forcing the creekbed to become too rocky for this pink-footed Paiute. Slowly lacing up my boots, I savor the last moment of dry comfort my feet will know for days, then wade into the Narrows.

For the rest of the day, my attention alternates between the stunning beauty around me and the challenge of the river channel beneath me. A combination of adventure, risk, and beauty give an unforgettable sharpness to the hike. Sandy beaches and all vegetation disappear completely. I move into an elemental world of Rock and Water and their mischievous offspring, Mud. My pace slows to a crawl as I tentatively probe each new pool and mudslick with my trusty staff. I quickly learn which banks will support me and which turn to bottomless Jello under my weight. Obscene sucking noises echo with each step as I rediscover a simple fact known to every six year old, but forgotten by most adults: mud is fun! There's a giddy pleasure derived from painting the first footprints across a glistening canvas of creamy virgin goo. I traipse on through the quagmire, getting dirtier and younger with each squishy step.

The world above the creekbed offers a different delight. Above me soar clean, sheer, sandstone walls of rust and beige. The cliffs climb to five hundred feet high, yet stand only twenty feet apart in some places. The delicate interplay of light, shadow, and reflection illuminate a fantastical sculpting of arches and alcoves, flutings and fault lines. The flood has erased any traces of earlier travelers in this surreal groove through the earth. I am alone in a primal wilderness.

When the canyon narrows even farther and the creek covers the floor with wall-to-wall water, my enchantment becomes wariness. The trail map warns of pockets of quicksand down here, assuring me that they are more of a nuisance than a true danger. However, these are unusual conditions and who's gonna pull me out? Images from old Tarzan movies of hapless explorers sinking to unspeakably horrid deaths haunt me as I wade into thigh-deep murky pools. A skin of wetness extends five feet up both walls -- the crest of yesterday's flood and I realize that had I been a day early, I could have drowned right here. Even higher are the ancient silt lines left behind by unimaginable hundred-year floods faintly visible twenty feet overhead.

At midday, I pass the narrow mouth of Buckskin Gulch, Paria's largest tributary, and the canyon widens a little. High, dry benches of sand begin to appear on the inside corners of every meander. These pockets of stability rooted together with vegetation are the only safe campsites above the wildly fluctuating river. I eat lunch across from the bench that Abby and I once called home for two nights. That trip, exploring the upper Narrows and Buckskin Gulch, was my first introduction to Utah's canyonlands and I still remember the awe and amazement that pulsed through me. Now, the thrill of discovery is replaced by the quiet joy of recognition and reverence. A bittersweet loneliness threatens to seep in as I think of sharing this spot with Abby, but this melancholy is dispelled when I realize that I've just crossed into Arizona. Back in the state where it all began!

I'm now camped on a large, sandy bench cloaked with maple saplings. Across the creek flows the finest spring in Paria Canyon -- so beautiful and perfect that it looks like a Hollywood creation. Cool, crystalline water pours miraculously from a crack five feet above the river, cascading brightly over emerald moss and delicate crimson monkeyflowers. A moat of nearly impregnable quicksand guards this desert jewel, but I manage to fill my bottles. Sunset is just the slow fade of daylight in this narrow confine. Bats and toads, the companions of witches, have joined me on the bench with the approach of dusk. Sapphire stars are snapping on in the swath of lavender twilight overhead. Life is good.

Day 102, Eleven miles

It is late afternoon. The sun is obscured by a bank of khaki clouds tinged with rouge. Thunder growls, lightning snaps, and rain seems imminent. Yet this stormy weather poses no threat as I sit, safe and protected, deep within a fold of stone. No tent to leak or blow away tonight -- my roof is solid rock. Cave life ain't so bad. It's a secure feeling rarely known to us nomads.

When the canyon walls blossomed dull gray to buttery gold this morning, I faced the grim task of persuading my warm, dry feet to climb back into the clammy, sodden boots. With a shiver of revulsion, I pull on two sets of damp, disgusting socks -- ugh! No matter that I'll be wet to my shins momentarily; the initial shock is the lousy part.

The morning's walk is a continuation of yesterday -- hellish from the knees down; heavenly from the knees up. The river still runs thick, but the silt has shifted from chocolate brown to tomato juice red. The shoreline has solidified somewhat after a day in the sun and coyote and deer prints are etched in red silt on a gray mudbank as larger stretches of benchland begin to line the river. Platoons of small spadefoot toads, their glistening obsidian eyes too precious for their warty hides, litter the trail.

My curiosity turns to the tiny creatures that live in this unstable river. What becomes of the water striders who dance spider-like on the surface tension when a three-foot crest of liquid mud sweeps over their eddy? What of the one-inch darter fish whose universe consists of the two feet of clear water at the mouth of the larger springs? Where do they hide when flood waters inundate their homes? Forty-eight hours after the largest flood of the season, I find both striders and darters enjoying themselves as if nothing happened. Ahhh, the mystery and miracle of life!

The canyon continues to widen. At Judd Hollow, I pass the first sign of humans since the trailhead -- the rusting remains of a 1940s scheme to pump Paria water straight up hundreds of feet to irrigate the surrounding plateau for grazing. This folly was happily short-lived, but the abandoned machinery continues to litter this wilderness. Another monument to the cow-worshiping cult of the West.

At lunchtime, I detour up a broad sidecanyon filled with cottonwoods, willows, oaks, and cattails to check out Wrather Arch. The well-muscled span of rock is impressive, but I'm even more intrigued by the surrounding walls. The thousand-foot, sheer face of pale Navajo sandstone is striped darkly with desert varnish. Chunks of rubble lie along the base of the facade like chips of marble carved from a sculpture.

Dozens of swallows dart and glide along the massive cliffs. Looking as tiny and bunched as gnats, the blue and white birds swoop and twirl, then dive straight toward the rock face, disappearing at high speed into tiny cracks containing unseen nests. I close my eyes, imagining myself capable of such joyous flight. I am SwallowHeart!

Day 103, Fourteen miles

Six feet from my toes flows my beloved Colorado River. Translucent green, she wears a different dress than during our last "date", but it sure is fine to meet up with the ol' gal again. Her friendly face at the end of a long day is always a joy.

By midmorning, I emerge from the Narrows into a wide valley where the towering walls straighten and spread apart like the opening of a colossal gateway. After quick ten miles, I know the trail's end at Lee's Ferry is at hand when I meet a couple of dayhikers heading upriver, looking clean and smelling fresh.

The confluence of the Paria River with the Colorado is a spot rich in history.

Here I cross paths with the route of the first European expedition to penetrate this region. In July, 1776, while a bunch of Yankee rebels were signing a revolutionary document in colonial Philadelphia, two Franciscan missionaries -- Fathers Dominguez and Escalante -- left Santa Fe and headed north with an unassuming expedition of ten men. Their goal was to establish an overland route from Santa Fe, the northern capital of New Spain, to the Monterey Mission on the California coast. For months, the peaceful friars traveled north and west, staying on friendly terms with the tribes they encountered while skirting the western slope of the Rockies. Upon reaching the Wasatch Valley near the Great Salt Lake, the expedition veered south in search of the mythic Rio Buenaventura thought to cross the western desert and empty into the Pacific. Instead, Dominguez and Escalante found themselves in the harsh basin and range country along the present-day Nevada border. By October, winter was nipping at their heels and the missionaries decided to head home via a more direct route back to Santa Fe.

The men reached the barrier of the Colorado River here at the mouth of the Paria. For six days, the Spanish explorers attempted to cross the river on crude rafts, but the current proved too strong. In search of an easier crossing, the weary men climbed the eastern escarpment of Paria Canyon a few miles up from the Colorado through a gap now called Dominguez Pass. They successfully crossed the Colorado in Glen Canyon and arrived back in Santa Fe after six months and two thousand miles. Although the expedition failed to reach its objective, Dominguez and Escalante were the first Europeans to see and describe the intermountain West. Their extensive journals and maps were the primary reference for this country well into the nineteenth century.

Almost a hundred years after the friars were foiled at this spot, a renegade Mormon named John Doyle Lee established a ferry crossing here. The Mormon Church offered Lee the remote post as a hideout after his leading role in the infamous Mountain Meadow Massacre where a wagon train of immigrants was attacked by Mormon pioneers. Federal authorities finally caught and executed Lee, but his homestead of hand-hewn cabins, the Lonely Dell Ranch, has been preserved by the National Park Service.

My trail ends here, but I continue along the Paria, determined to follow this creek to its bitter end. The tamarisk put up quite a fight, but at last, I stand on the spit of sand where the heavily silted Paria bleeds her ochre water into the icy, clear green current of the Colorado. For a half mile, the two rivers refuse to merge; half the channel is a tomato-soup red and the other half beer bottle green.

This bizarre sight perfectly illustrates the most recent events in the area. In 1963, Glen Canyon Dam began its stranglehold on the wild Colorado only twelve miles upstream from Lees Ferry. At this moment, a part of the soul of the Colorado Plateau began to die. Glen Canyon Dam changed the muddy Colorado into a mutant waterway of cold, clear outflow completely alien to the desert environment. The only time this section of the Colorado River lives up to her name is when her free-flowing tributaries like the Paria add enough silt. The mighty river's ebb and flow is now directed by an engineer responding to electrical demand in Phoenix.

Like all honest desert rats, I love to hate Glen Canyon Dam. That cursed plug of concrete represents all the wrongs that our modern society has inflicted on the Southwest. Glen Canyon and over two hundred miles of the Colorado and her tributaries were drowned beneath the resulting reservoir, Lake Powell (also known as "Lake Phowell" in certain circles!). Now the lair of the houseboat, jet ski, and bass fishing crowd, Lake Powell is admittedly attractive, but a stagnant recreational reservoir will never match the intricate beauty and harmony of the living ecosystem that was destroyed.

I meander over to the two boat docks where the Colorado is accessed by two human factions as different from each other as the red and green water in the channel. The left dock caters to the speedboat and trout-fishing crowd who cruise the twelve miles of flatwater upstream where huge, introduced trout have displaced the original mud-loving chub and catfish. No doubt these folks regard Glen Canyon Dam as a hallmark of progress and technical achievement. Next door, I watch sunbrown crews of boatmen and boatwomen unloading trucks and inflating rubber rafts in preparation for the 270-mile whitewater trip through the Grand Canyon. No doubt these folks share my opinion of the dam. I watch as a raft pushes clear of shore and starts drifting downstream. River rat fever returns. Someday I'll float the mighty Colorado, but for now, I'm happy enough just to be back in Grand Canyon country.

Ut.
Az.
Lake Powell
Glen Canyon Dam
Paria river
Page
Lee's Ferry
Vermilion Cliffs
Kaibab Plateau
Navajo Reservation
Kaibab Lodge
Grand Canyon N.P.
colorado river
Havasupai Reservation
Phantom Ranch
Hualapai Res.
Grand Canyon Village
little colorado river
Wupatki Natl. Mon.
Sunset Crater
San Francisco Peaks
Flagstaff
Kathi Sutton
11/97
Scale
20 miles
I 17

SOUTH
The Great Cathedral

People claim the land by creating sacred sites,
by mythologizing the animals and plants.
They invest the land with spiritual powers.
It becomes like a temple,
a place of meditation.

Joseph Campbell
The Power of Myth

Day 104, Six miles
1162 miles total

Unforeseen problems and adventures filled one of my shortest walking days. My thoughts and emotions have been as swirled and stormy as the ashen sky overhead.

The strange day begins with pancakes beside the Colorado River under a gentle morning shower -- what the Navajo call a "female" rain. Six miles of road-walking brings me to Route 89A and the Marble Canyon Lodge. This remote outpost tucked at the foot of the Vermilion Cliffs is a combination motel/restaurant/convenience store/gas station/post office/laundromat/airstrip. Since the "micro-city" is also serving as repository for my twelfth resupply box, I park my pack on the porch and head inside.

The first order of business is to pick up the General Delivery letter from Abby which contains a hundred dollars. The Navajo woman behind the counter in the shoebox post office looks up and down her array of cubbyholes. Nothing has "Brett LeCompte" written on it.

Damn!

Panic-striken, I hurry next door to the lodge and ask the front desk if they are holding any mail for me.

Nothing.

I slump onto the weathered wooden bench on the deep porch of the lodge. Didn't Abby get my postcards asking her to send money? Has something happened to her? She couldn't have forgotten, could she? From a nearby pay phone I call Abby's home number at the park.

No answer.

I dig out my wallet and check inside -- thirty-two cents. Even with the stuff from my cache box, I can't continue without buying fresh supplies here. The groceries I need are twenty feet away inside the store, but without those slips of green paper, they might as well be twenty light-years distant. Feeling penniless and powerless, my frustration grows into a tight, black knot twisting my insides.

This can't be happening ....

Over a skimpy lunch of two leftover stale tortillas, I idly watch the tourists emerging from air-conditioned cars and heading for the restaurant. A balding man in a peacock polo shirt walks past, studiously ignoring me, while his wife shepherds curious kids away from me and through the door. The truth is that I'm as dirty and destitute, transient and troubled as they believe. How long am I going to be stuck here?

My sulking is interrupted when the dark clouds building all morning finally organize into an enormous squall. Even the semi-oblivious tourists stop their shopping and step outside to gape at the monstrous sky. The storm crashes into the outpost with a fury even more demonic than I witnessed four days ago. Slashing rain pummels down in thick, gray sheets. A powerful wind rattles the hoses of the gas pumps and spits spray all the way to my bench. The violent deluge is a clearly a Navajo "male" rain. A sudden thought strikes me. Had Abby's letter been waiting, I would be out in the open in the teeth of this tempest. Ouch! Maybe my delay is some sort of crazy gift. Time to relax and go with the flow.

After thirty intense minutes, the squall slides east. The parking lot is a small, dirty lake shimmering as the sun breaks out. An innocuous dry wash bordering the lodge is now brimming with four feet of churning, chili-red runoff. Suddenly, I remember that the lip of Marble Canyon is only a quarter mile away. I grab my camera and rush over to Navajo Bridge, a graceful steel arch dramatically spanning the gorge nearly five hundred feet above the Colorado.

The rumble I hear while still a hundred yards from the lip of the canyon is electrifying. I edge out onto the limestone precipice. Across the high, narrow gorge is the outlet of a sidewash which usually would be bone-dry. Now a furious mahogany torrent twice the normal volume of the Paria River shoots explosively from this groove in the rimrock. The dark, mud-laced cascade arcs gracefully out and down, plunging twenty stories to dissolve in a roar of foam and spray in the Colorado. Scanning up and down the length of the canyon, I spot two more transitory, Yosemite-scale falls -- one mauve, the other maroon-- plummeting into the depths. Delighted by this rare phenomenon, I'm manic as a mongoose, racing between viewpoints and snapping pictures and thanking Thor and Zeus for arranging this exhibition of erosion. Within thirty minutes, these ephemeral waterfalls are half of their original strength. In another hour, the show is over as the sidewashes run dry. Now I'm sure my delay has a silver lining. I may be broke, but I'm not poor!

Unfortunately, my euphoria is as fleeting as the falls. The afternoon at the lodge drags on interminably. Ensconced in the laundromat, I read my way through a pile of old newspapers -- economic forecasts, holiday movie previews, the dissolution of the Soviet Union. Little of this "real world" stuff seems very real. How will I ever fit in again when my Southwest Circle Quest is over? Every hour or so, I walk out to the pay phone and try Abby's number. After a half dozen futile attempts, I punch the digits for Steve Arrowsmith, my chum in Moab. He picks up on the second ring.

"Yeah, I got home after a trip and there was this new boat in my backyard with a weird note," Steve exclaims.

I grin into the receiver, remembering I now own a boat capable of running the Grand Canyon. I describe my adventures since Moab as well as my current dilemma.

"Hang in there, buddy. If you can't get in touch with Abby, call me back. Maybe I can help you somehow." The sound of Steve's calm, nasal voice is a soothing comfort. As I hang up the phone, I realize that understanding friends like Steve will be the ticket to easing me back into society when my quest is over.

It's evening and pouring rain when Abby finally picks up her phone. After I blurt out the obvious question, there is a pregnant silence.

"Are you there already? I guess I just lost track of time. I'm so sorry. I never mailed your money."

I stare at the receiver as if clutching a snake. "You never mailed the money?!" I finally parrot back through gritted teeth. Sucking in a deep breath of wet sage mixed with diesel fuel, I try to rein in my anger, but the frustrations of the day flow into the phone. Abby is upset, then defensive. Lightning begins to flicker across the line.

"Listen," I finally sigh. "Mistakes happen. But what am I going to do now? I can't just hang around here. Help me think."

"Do you think you could get cash from the lodge with a credit card number?" Abby asks.

"No idea; might work," I mumble dejectedly, knowing neither of us own any "plastic".

"Why don't you go find out and I'll call my mother and get her card number."

Shot with this arrow of hope, I hang up and head for the lodge manager's office. The cheerless, silver-haired woman behind the desk listens to my plight with vacant eyes. Undoubtedly, she's noticed me loitering around her place all day. The weary manager drums her pen and agrees to the cash advance probably just to get me out of her face. Another quick call to Abby for the magic digits, and voila, I'm no longer a vagrant. Gleeful over my early parole, I buy my supplies including a handful of tiny pecan pies. After today, I deserve a sugar buzz!

Now I'm holed up in an empty hogan in the shadows behind the lodge. This juniper log and adobe structure was built as a prop for tourists eager to photograph themselves standing in front of a "genuine Navajo dwelling". I'm sure the management wouldn't be too keen to find me camping here, but the clean, dry floor is too convenient to pass up on this stormy night. "Don't worry, Sheriff. I'll get myself the hell out of Dodge first thing in the morning!"

Day 105, Nineteen miles

The trail out of Dodge turns out to be a day-long road walk along the base of the Vermilion Cliffs. I hit the asphalt under a sky of pearly haze and headwinds -- perfect weather for a shadeless stroll across a vast prairie where nothing grows higher than my knees. Mile after mile, I gobble up pavement with a steady stream of vacation traffic in overdrive speeding past my elbow. Oddly, the long road walk is a nice change from the confines of Paria Canyon, allowing me to stretch out my stride and walk head up, enjoying the expansive view.

The Vermilion Cliffs are a two thousand-foot palisade of ochre and rust cliff-bands to my right. Rolling away to the south is a flat desert plain of undulating salmon-pink sand studded with a pale green crewcut of blackbrush, sage, and rabbitbush. The scrubby desert appears unbroken, yet the mile-wide gash of Marble Canyon lurks somewhere out there. Beyond the invisible gorge, the dry plateau continues, forming the northwest corner of the Navajo Reservation. Ahead is the dark bulk of the Kaibab Plateau with familiar landmarks: Dog Point, North Canyon, Saddle Mountain, and The Cockscomb. This beautiful plateau was my home last summer and I envision the open, grassy glades and the deep forests of pine, spruce, and aspen that cloak this glorious "island in the sky". I'd detour up there for a visit except that the siren song of the Grand Canyon is even louder.

As the Vermilion Cliffs begin to glow warmly in the late afternoon sun, I leave the highway and head toward the escarpment. My goal is to find an historic spring called Jacob's Pool, named for Jacob Hamblin -- a pioneer explorer and trader often called the "Mormon Leatherstocking." The pools were an important stop along the Honeymoon Trail, a Mormon wagon road that extended from St. George, Utah, into Navajo country. A small ranch was eventually established at Jacob's Pool by the second wife of ferryman John Lee.

I follow shallow grooves left from countless wagon wheels to an abandoned stone ranch house next to a modern corral. Sure enough, an incongruous muddy pool sits ringed by thick grass -- excellent! I'm still exploring the spread when I notice a pickup bouncing down a rutted track that leads from the highway. Hmmm -- company's coming. Hope it's friendly.

The large truck, its bed filled with a shiny, four-wheeled ATV, skids to a stop in the dusty yard. Out leaps a big guy in his forties wearing chinos, a plaid shirt, a baseball cap and a huge grin. Looking like some overgrown kid who just won his first Little League game, he galumphs up and vigorously shakes my hand.

"Hey there! My name's Bill. I saw ya from the highway with my spotting scope. When I didn't see any fresh tire tracks at the turnoff, I got real curious. Figured I might know ya since I know everybody in these parts."

Bill is a schoolteacher from Flagstaff whose passion and second career is working as a hunting guide. He's heading home after a weekend of scouting the plains for pronghorn. When I ask the hunter about springs and cattle tanks along tomorrow's cross-country route, Bill grabs my map and enthusiastically begins slashing **Xs** at potential water sources. Then he notices the empty water bottles in my hand.

"Hey, you don't need to drink that nasty old stuff in that pond," he says, twisting his big, open face into a comical grimace. Bill fills my bottles from his jerry can, then hands me his card.

"When you get to Flagstaff, I'll bet you'll be ready for some of my wife's fine homecooking. Drop by for a visit -- especially if you see any big antelope along the way!"

After another high energy handshake, Bill pops back in his rig and takes off flying. His plume of dust recedes as the silence of the forlorn ranch rushes back in. The rain that has threatened all day finally arrives as a wispy pink curtain connecting earth and sky. I'm a long one-and-a-half day's walk across open desert from the rim of the Grand Canyon. Hope this cloudy, cool weather hangs with me a while longer.

Day 106, Twenty miles

The day dawns as crystalline as the previous morning had been murky -- so much for another cool day! I aim my sights for the low hump of Saddle Mountain due south and set sail across the desert. The scrubby plain offers little resistance as I head cross-country. The September sun is blazing, but could be much worse. Walking this stretch on a clear day a month ago would have been suicidal. Except for the cliff-bound horizons, I could be back on the empty prairies east of Winslow. The sense of unlimited freedom returns and I walk lost in sky and distance.

The locals make their appearances: Rattlesnake, Coyote, Pronghorn, Raven. Jackrabbit is the most conspicuous. The lanky speed demons stay hidden under the bushes until the last moment, then explode from cover with a heart-stopping flurry. The gray blurs race away in wild, zig-zagging sprints, leaping porpoise-like with unexpectedly grace over the sagebrush. Of course, that ubiquitous interloper, Cow, is also stumbling around out here.

Scrambling up a small knoll to get my bearings, I'm surprised to find the hillside covered with flint chips and pottery shards. No doubt about it -- I'm getting back to the country where this quest began. At North Canyon Wash, I reach a jeep road that leads to Buffalo Springs. At first I think I'm seeing a mirage -- a knee-high circular metal tub twenty feet across and brimful of clear water. But the cattle tank is real and right where Bill said it would be. Hallelujah!

Time for a long overdue bath. With only occasional rinses since Moab, my shirt is a batik of sweat, grime, and Paria silt while my shorts reek with the foulest of aromas. As the cowboys say, I'm considerably whiffy to the leeward side! Groaning with delight, I lower myself into the cool water.

After the soak, I'm enjoying lunch unfettered by clothing when I hear the light tap of approaching hooves. A lone pronghorn prances toward the tank. He stares at me unabashed and approaches to within a hundred feet. If the beautiful antelope recognizes the lean, pink biped before him, he shows no concern. Finally, his nostrils flair from a whiff of human scent and he bounds away, thirst unslaked. I guess I'll have some advice for Bill after all: stalk your bucks buck naked!

Two miles farther, a long fenceline marks the edge of the Kaibab National Forest. The scrubby desert stretches away on the other side unchanged -- there's not a tree visible within five miles. The fence also forms the northern boundary of the House Rock State Buffalo Ranch. Buffalo ranch?! Yep, seems that back in 1907 a certain Mr. Charles "Buffalo" Jones -- no relation to "Buffalo Bub" of Hanksville -- transplanted a small herd of bison to the grass-filled parklands of the Kaibab plateau. Buffalo ranching wasn't as much fun as Mr. Jones had figured, so he sold his herd to "Uncle" Jim Owen who was the first manager of the Grand Canyon Game Preserve (which predated the national park) and reportedly killed over five hundred mountain lions in that capacity. Owen was somewhat loose in his management of the shaggy beasts who migrated off the plateau down into House Rock Valley. In 1927, the state of Arizona bought the herd and established the current ranch where a hundred and twenty buffalo are overseen by a resident game warden.

The warden's house is my next water stop, and late in the afternoon, I spot a tall radio antenna with a ranch house tucked discreetly in a fold in the rolling prairie. I follow a dirt drive past a well-kept corral and hay shed to a neat, two-story stone house. An official-looking black pickup is parked under an apple tree. Plastic toys are scattered on the patch of lawn. Nobody's outside.

Dropping my pack, I chug some water and consider my next move. Folks in the boondocks rely on the noise of approaching vehicles to warn them of visitors. It would be quite a shock to find me sweating unannounced on your doorstep. My dilemma is solved when a pack of puppies scoot around the corner and discover a stranger in the yard. They voice a few obligatory yips, then bound up, all wagging tails and lapping tongues, and engulf me in a frenzy of love.

"Can I help you?"

I look up from the pups to see a tall, athletic man sporting a holstered revolver emerge from the house and stride purposefully toward me. With tanned, rugged features, dark, hawkish eyes, and a shock of black hair, he looks like a young Gregory Peck -- and he is not smiling.

"Well, I just walked from Jacob's Pool and I was hoping for some water and maybe a little information," I hastily explain, untangling myself from the pups and rising to face the game warden. The man continues scowling and pins me with his piercing gaze.

"What kind of information?" he asks coolly.

I produce my map and begin to explain my trip. Slowly, the warden's eyes soften. He looks at me with growing curiosity as I rattle off where I've been. Before long, we are squatting in the gravel, poring over my route on the map and exchanging life stories. Our intimate conversation continues to unfold until the stars are shining overhead.

The game warden, Chick Wayne, started out as a cowboy when he left home at the age of 15. Life as a ranchhand turned out to be a helluva lot tougher than it looked in the movies, especially for a scrawny kid -- long hours, low pay, and no job security. He had to get used to being thrown by flighty horses and stomped on by mean cattle. But the wilder the country, the better it suited the young maverick. Chick loved learning the land and living outside. He was fascinated by the stories of the old-timers with whom he worked, some of them the first Anglos to settle the hard country north of the Grand Canyon called the Arizona Strip.

Late in the sixties, Chick was all set to disappear into the Alaskan wilderness to stake himself a homestead. Just before he left, a friend suggested that he try his hand at being a game warden. The job fit. For the last twenty-four years, Chick has been working on wildlife refuges all over the state. He and his family have been stationed at the House Rock State Buffalo Ranch for six years where his primary task is maintaining a series of wildlife water tanks and the pipeline that feeds them from a spring on the Kaibab plateau.

When the sun is stretching out the shadows, Chick leads me up a hill above his home to show me the berm of the buried waterline leading straight to Saddle Mountain. We stand side by side admiring the beauty of the desert turned buttery gold by the last rays of the day. For several minutes, we are silent, then Chick turns to me and says softly, "Someday pretty soon, Game and Fish is gonna replace me with someone cheaper. My wife and I are already looking around for a new place to settle. Wherever we go, there has to be plenty of wildlife and wide open space with hardly any people. Wyoming maybe, or northeastern Oregon. This place has gotten too developed."

I stare at my new friend with raised eyebrows. His only neighbor is another remote ranch a dozen miles away and a trip to town is an all-day expedition. When I point this out, Chick nods. "But, I knew this country before Lake Powell and when there wasn't a Grand Canyon sightseeing plane buzzing overhead every few minutes," the warden laments. "Hell, the way I see it, there ain't much real wilderness left south of Fairbanks."

As we retrace our steps back to the ranch, Chick invites me to stay in the bunkhouse used by visiting Game and Fish employees. The long, low building with rows of bunks plus a gas stove, generator-powered electric lights, and flush toilets seems like a virtual palace. Chick waves off my profuse thanks. "Just don't let the dogs follow you in the morning," he warns. "I'm already missing three."

Day 107, Thirteen miles

The ranch is quiet as I get underway after a quick breakfast. A warm glow of first light combines with the cool air to grace the prairie with a soft beauty that's long forgotten in the hot glare of noon. I walk the berm, passing full water tanks strung out like shimmering pearls on a subterranean string. The land begins to slope gently upwards into a piñon and juniper forest and I peer through the trees, half-eager and half-afraid to sight buffalo. Chick warned me to show neither fear nor aggression should I stumble upon any of the shaggy locomotives. Tracks and "buffalo pies" are everywhere, but alas, I reach the southern boundary fence without even a glimpse of bison.

The ascent to the notch in Saddle Mountain is a stiff climb through scrub oak and ponderosa pine. I'm huffing from my first uphill grunt in a week when I top out and the world suddenly drops away. With an involuntary gasp, I gaze into one of the greatest natural wonders of the world -- The Grand Canyon. My heart soars -- I'm back! My eyes fill with happy tears that wash the tableau of sharp beauty into a blur of colors.

This magnificent chasm is so much more to me than unforgettable scenery. It was here that I first experienced and fell in love with the Southwest five years ago. For two glorious summers, I lived, worked, and played in the Grand Canyon, forging an indestructible bond with this amazing place. In this Notre Dame of canyon cathedrals, I feel most connected to what is real and essential in the world. The Grand Canyon, *The Canyon,* is my refuge and my temple. Two ravens fly just overhead, spiraling through wild acrobatics in the gusty wind. A sign of welcome -- I feel blessed.

Still trembling with emotion, I climb an additional thousand feet to one of my favorite lookouts, The Pulpit. This uncelebrated, rarely-visited viewpoint was the destination for a popular half-day guided hike I offered last summer at the Kaibab Lodge. From this elevated position, I can finally look back and see the two thousand foot gash of Marble Canyon splitting the plains of House Rock Valley. Farther north, Navajo Mountain is a smoky dome and Canaan Peak is a pink speck. The technicolor splendor of the Canyon falls away to the south where mountain-sized buttes and mesas are concealed in the mile-deep abyss. Beyond the Canyon stretches the pastel rainbow of the Painted Desert. My heart skips a beat when I notice the faint silhouette of mountains barely visible over the south rim -- The San Francisco Peaks! The end of my quest is literally in sight! Disbelief mixes with relief and sadness.

But it ain't over yet. Poised on the cusp of another Grand Canyon adventure, I can't think of a finer finish to my glorious summer.

Day 108, Fifteen miles

I sit on a sandy beach beside the Colorado River at the bottom of the Grand Canyon. Here, next to my favorite river in this glorious cathedral of nature, I've arrived in my Mecca. No place else makes me feel so happy, content, and harmonious with the world.

Far above me now, The Pulpit proved less hospitable when I camped beneath the pines near the exposed lookout. A rogue wind rakes the trees all afternoon and through the night. My buffeted tent snaps mercilessly and it's like trying to sleep on a runaway train.

I arise early, hoping to catch a classic Grand Canyon sunrise, but find scudding dark clouds and a thick, ugly haze obscuring the view. Current theories blame Grand Canyon air pollution on smog blown in from the Los Angeles basin and this windstorm out of the southwest seems to prove this hypothesis is correct. No wilderness is truly isolated from the human touch anymore. Everything is connected.

I backtrack down to the notch which gives Saddle Mountain its name and pause here to offer a prayer for a safe passage before descending into the Canyon. Although I've traveled hundreds of Grand Canyon trail miles, most of my planned route is across unfamiliar country largely devoid of footpaths. More than ever, my first mistake could be my last.

My descent route is the Nankoweap Trail, an historic footpath that descends six thousand feet over its fourteen-mile length. I've heard horror stories about this remote trail -- sections washed away, hand over hand scrambles -- but the rough, narrow trail isn't so bad. Familiar geology surrounds me -- Kaibab limestone, Coconino sandstone, Hermit shale, the Redwall. Each section of this enormous geologic layer-cake has its own color, texture, and personality and descending through each formation is like visiting different neighborhoods in my old hometown. At first, I move among old friends like Juniper and Raven, but as I sink deeper, new faces appear: Agave, Sotol, and Chuckwalla -- my amigos of the Inner Gorge. The hike becomes a homecoming.

Down, down, down! My knees are screaming from the relentless pounding. The skies have cleared and the chill of the morning is forgotten as I sink into the heat of the lower Sonoran life zone. Bottoming out at Nankoweap Creek, I gaze back up at The Pulpit jutting out from the rim a vertical mile overhead, and I can scarcely believe that I'm really here. Being back within The Canyon's folds is as sweet as a foot rub after a twenty-mile road walk. It only gets better as Nankoweap Creek leads me to a vast, stony delta in the main canyon. There she is: the Colorado, looking much more appropriate this time in her khaki dress of silt. Cliffs across the water rise a sheer three thousand feet in bands of orange, peach, and crimson. The River and The Canyon together! My God, it is good to be back.

The Nankoweap delta is famous for its Anasazi ruins and I soon spot three rectangular holes staring from an alcove five hundred feet above river level. A well-trod river runner's footpath leads up a debris slope to the masonry structures which are granaries used by the Anasazi to store corn grown below on the irrigated delta. A larger alcove nearby must have provided shelter as the roof is blackened from the smoke of ancient campfires. I scramble into this shallow cave, sit in the back, and imagine making my home here. Listening to the hushed roar of the rapids below, a deep sense of peace fills me. Yes, I could live out my life here; watching The River flow and the seasons change, dining on grandeur and drinking beauty. Romantic nonsense? Perhaps. Yet regular doses of natural beauty keep me alive as surely as food and water. As my body has been whittled away this summer, my soul has grown fat and happy.

I camp on a beach where the clean, white sand is edged with a curtain of tamarisks draped with strands of wispy pink flowers. Deep in the afternoon shadows of the high walls, the temperature is perfect. After a quick, icy dip, I lie back and melt into the soft sand. The band of indigo sky between the distant rims is alive with the silent dance of two hundred swallows weaving an intricate aerial ballet. The spellbinding performance lasts ten minutes, then in a flash, the sky is empty. My heart continues to pirouette. Magic happens!

Day 109, Ten miles

The roar of Sixty-Mile Rapid is so loud that I can scarcely think. I'm perched on a riverside boulder of polished gray limestone. Before me, the seething riot of churning whitewater is mesmerizing. The placid river constricts into a glassy tongue that dips into a stormy sea of four-foot standing waves. I wait on the brink of this aquatic chaos, eager as an ambulance chaser, in hopes that boats will appear. Watching rafts, dories, and kayaks challenge the world-famous rapids from the safety of the shoreline is a popular sport among us Grand Canyon hikers.

I spied my first bunch of river rats soon after completing yesterday's entry. One by one, small blue and yellow rafts splash through the tailwaves of Nankoweap Rapid and pull in a quarter mile upstream from my camp. At sunset, I wander over to say hello and glean information. The rafters' camp is a tangle of gear and exhausted bodies strewn lazily in the sand around a serious-looking kitchen. A thin, bearded chap strolls up to greet me. Steve is a boatman with Arizona Raft Adventures, a commercial outfit out of Flagstaff that's running this two-week, oar-powered float trip through The Canyon. The bronzed guide has spent thirteen seasons down here so I ask if he thinks I can hike next to the Colorado without getting cliffed out. Steve closes his eyes and mentally floats downstream, scanning the shoreline. Reopening his eyes, he says, "You won't find much of a trail and some sections will be tricky, but I believe it'll go." Excellent!

As Steve and I discuss desert hiking, whitewater rafting, and the guiding business, the aroma of superb cooking gathers around us. When another guide hollers the dinner call , Steve offers, "Hey, do you wanna join us? We got a ton of food."

"You'd better if you're gonna invite a starvin' pilgrim like me!" I laugh. I grab a plate and join the hungry passengers as the six guides serve up green chili enchiladas, fresh-baked cornbread, and steaming peach cobbler out of blackened dutch ovens. After four months of pasta, rice, and ramen, this feast is an unimaginable delight, especially here.

With a heaping plate, I sit with the guides near the water's edge where five boats are tethered like eager ponies. Conversation turns to the fluctuation of the waterlevel. As the engineers upstream at Glen Canyon Dam release or withhold water to generate electricity at a maximum profit, the Colorado can half or double her volume overnight. Guides must anticipate this artificial tide and adjust the lines throughout the night to keep their boats in the water.

Yet this tidal action has much greater implications beyond hassling the rafters. The rapidly fluctuating river is constantly gnawing away at the shoreline. With all the upper river's silt trapped behind the dam, the sandy beaches, which act as important wildlife habitat as well as camping sites, are no longer replenished by annual floods. Some of the campsites have shrunk by half since Steve started running the Canyon. Thankfully, this issue has recently gained national attention and a full environmental assessment of dam operations has been ordered with interim measures to limit release fluctuations.

With my stomach still in spasms of ecstasy, I wash my plate in a bucket of warmed river water and chat awhile with several of the participants, fielding the usual questions about my trip. After many thanks for a lovely evening, I retire to my beach and sleep like a babe beneath a canopy of stars and tamarisk.

Following the Colorado proves to be no simple matter. Easy beaches are restricted to small pockets with the rest of the shoreline impassable ledges, jungles, or boulder fields. Twenty feet inland from the soft sand and cool water of the riparian zone, the Sonoran desert burns hot, dry, and thorny. Game trails wind between extensive gardens of cactus -- the beaver-tailed prickly pear, the zucchini-shaped hedgehog, and the pineapple-sized barrel. Stiff, spiked limbs of mesquite trees snatch at my clothing and my pack. The Inner Gorge has the same climate as Phoenix so even in mid-September, the temperature hovers in the high nineties. But relief is at hand. When sweat starts pouring its sting into my eyes, I duck down to The River and hop in the forty-five degree water. Ahhh -- much better!

On the opposite shore, Coyote patrols a beach. With unblinking golden eyes, he looks right through me, then rushes for the thicket at the approach of a noisy raft. Señor Coyote -- you have followed me from the top of the Rocky Mountains to the bottom of the Grand Canyon. What a faithful companion you are!

Day 110, Twelve miles

Both Scorpion and Rattlesnake shared last night's pocket of beach with me, but neither interrupted another fine night's rest in the soft sand. Immediately beyond camp a new rock layer angles out of The River -- the five hundred million year-old Tapeats sandstone. At first I fear I'll be forced to climb above the riverside cliffs, but the face is broken into long, flat shelves. These sidewalks are directly above the whirling current and range from twenty feet wide to mere inches. Many times, I seem on the verge of being pinched off and forced into a tedious backtrack. At one point, I cling to a slightly overhung rock face inching forward on toeholds while my pack strains to pull me backwards into the hungry river. But, after two miles of "boardwalking," I near the confluence of the Little Colorado with the Mother River.

A major encampment with tethered rafts bobbing off the beach ahead surprises me -- my map designates this area as day use only. A small, bespectacled man is loading what looks like a fishing net into a sleek, outboard-powered Zodiac raft. He looks up in surprise at the crunch of my footsteps on the pebbled beach.

"Looks like an unsporting way to catch a fish!" I exclaim.

The man chuckles. "Yup, but we're trying to save the fish, not eat them." He then explains that he's part of a research team studying the endangered humpback chub, a native fish. Turns out the beaches aren't the only ones suffering as the result of that accursed concrete plug seventy-five miles upstream. Native fish that evolved in a warm, muddy Colorado have been nearly wiped out since the dam turned The River into a huge, cold, clear, trout stream. The warm, silty waters here at the mouth of the Little Colorado are a favored breeding ground and refuge for the beleaguered chub and the researchers are netting fish to establish an accurate population count. A few of the foot-long adults are even receiving surgically implanted radio transmitters so their movements can be monitored. Seems Grand Canyon research has become a hot item since the water release issue hit the national media.

I wander into the camp and find two women lounging in the makeshift kitchen tucked under a feathery tamarisk. The young, barefoot angel with a halo of frizzy blond hair is the expedition's cook and a boatwoman with O.A.R.S., the river company contracted to provide the researchers with transport and logistical support. The other woman, a school teacher from Wisconsin playing hooky, is a volunteer who is trading her labor for a free trip through The Canyon. I chat with the ladies over a second breakfast of cereal and fresh melon (the Mooch Master strikes again!) while the Grateful Dead sing "Truckin'" on a battery-operated boombox. The food and company are great, but listening to Jerry and the boys here at the bottom of the Grand Canyon is a bit much for me. I wish the crew good fishing and saunter out of camp for a peek at the Little Colorado River.

Could this major tributary be the same shallow, dry wash that I traveled along four months ago? The tremendous canyon of the Little Colorado enters from the east and rivals the gorge of her big sister. Under certain conditions, the Little Colorado River flows an otherworldly opaque turquoise from mineralized springs upstream, but today she runs a muddy brown that mingles with the olive green of the Colorado. Arriving at the mouth of the Little Colorado is another reminder how close I've come to closing my circle.

Hiking becomes increasingly more difficult beyond the confluence. The slickrock sidewalks disappear and I follow a faint bighorn sheep trail to a gravel bench a couple hundred feet above The River. Weaving between knee-high stands of blackbrush and agave, this is Grand Canyon bushwhacking at its "finest." Only five river miles separate today's camps, but I'll walk twice that before I'm done. The Inner Gorge thermostat is set on "broil". A myriad of small side-canyons force me to choose between a long contour around the heads of the drainages or steep traverses across the dry washes. Either way, the footing is loose and treacherous. Across the Colorado, I look longingly at the Beamer Trail, a white snake winding easily through the desert scrub. When I first walked that path years ago, it seemed rough and roundabout. Today, it looks like a freeway in comparison to my trailless struggle. This explorer business is rugged stuff! No wonder everyone sells insurance or punches a computer these days.

When I stumble upon a bizarre assortment of twisted aluminum debris in one drainage, I quit complaining. Back in 1956, two airliners collided above the Grand Canyon and crashed right above this spot. There were no survivors. The Park Service has removed most of the wreckage by helicopter, but scraps still remain. The mountainous Chuar and Temple buttes rise like twin tombstones above the place where one hundred and twenty-eight people were killed. I hurry on, unwilling to face any ghosts still haunting this rarely-visited spot.

Operation Desert Storm lives! Despite the disaster of 1956, air traffic above the Canyon has grown tremendously in the last forty years. A least a dozen companies offer scenic flights out of a large airfield just outside the park's southern boundary. Over the span of my short lunch break, I count eight planes buzzing above the confluence. Helicopters add tremendously to this racket overhead. The silence I've come so far to find is rudely shattered.

After hours of the toughest terrain encountered all summer, a sheer four hundred-foot drop stops me cold. Wearily, I trudge "inland" a couple of long miles until I find a break down which I can scramble. Even here, I must lower my pack on a cord and climb down after it. Thankfully, an easy river-runner's trail leads the final miles to the mouth of Lava Canyon. Beyond here, the terrain is rumored to be virtually impassable. My plan is to thumb a ride across the Colorado at this point and get on the trail system on the south side. But the Lava Canyon beach is vacant; my "river hitching" will have to wait for tomorrow.

Sitting naked in the sand to stretch after a well-deserved dip, I gaze across the Colorado and recognize a campsite from my earlier Grand Canyon explorations -- back in known country. The three thousand-foot Palisades of the Desert are a study of crimson and bronze in the setting sun. A crescent of milk-white moon lies on its back in the west. The River slides by carrying a scintillating reflection of the surrounding splendor. A tender conclusion to a tough day.

Day 111, Seven miles

My wait in the morning is mercifully short. Backpackers hitching rides across the Colorado from passing rafters are not uncommon, but I'm a rookie at this practice. Sitting packed and ready to go, I hear the labored chug of an engine and spot a dull gray, thirty-foot "baloney boat" motoring slowing down-river. This rubber monstrosity is one of the Greyhound buses of the Colorado, catering to folks who want only a moderate adrenaline rush as they buzz through one of the world's natural wonders in a week. Huge tubes and a powerful engine effectively render the rapids into showy, but safe Disney rides. But this is no time to be snobbish; the lumbering, fifteen-passenger whale could be just the ticket to get me across The River.

As the barge putts near, I wave, point to myself, then the opposite shore. The passengers wave cheerfully back, yet I ignore them, locking eyes with the lanky guide manning the tiller. The helmsman nods a stony OK and veers toward my beach. The crowd of geriatrics filling the boat look somewhat bewildered and confused as a scrawny, grubby, grinning pirate swarms over the bow and plops down in their midst. The guide tosses me a spare life jacket and we're off.

I'm pummeled with the usual barrage of questions, but my attention is riveted to the hefty rapid dead ahead. Just when the guide shouts "Hang on!", I realize everyone is wearing heavy rubber raingear -- except me. I brace for a drenching as we slide down a silky tongue into the throat of the whitewater, but with the prop running in reverse to control our descent, the big beast muscles through the five-foot waves with hardly any bucking.

My ride ends much too soon as the guide steers his rig across the tailwaves to the south shore. I hop out, heave my pack after me, and thank the stoic helmsman who allows himself the faintest of smiles as he gives me another nod. The life-jacketed seniors smile and wave: "Good-bye! Good luck! Enjoy your hike!" As I slip away into the tamarisk, I hear one elderly man ask another, "Who the hell was that guy?"

With an excellent trail running along this side of the Colorado, there's none of yesterday's nasty footing and sidecanyon headaches. The bottom of the Canyon here is broad and open as soft shales and sandstone in brick-red, sage-green, and lavender form rounded slopes instead of precipitous cliffs. I've walked this trail, known as the Escalante Route, on three occasions over the last five years and the landscape is alive with happy memories. There's the lone redbud tree where I once shared precious shade with a rattlesnake one sweltering afternoon. Here's the slab of sandstone embedded in the trail looking exactly like a manhole cover. I stop for lunch on the beach where Abby and I were once serenaded by a river rat who turned out to be a professional Flamenco guitarist. This backcountry memory lane of a trail stretches all the way to Grand Canyon Village on the south rim. My plan, however, is to work my way downstream back on the unexplored north side. Once again, I hang my thumb out in hopes of snagging a passing boat.

At mid afternoon, I wave down a small, two-person Zodiac -- more fish researchers. To my surprise, my request is denied. The bearded scientist smiles coldly behind mirrored sunglasses. "Sorry. We're not supposed to do that sort of thing ... especially if you don't have a life jacket." He eases the boat back into the current.

"But, wait, I just ......"

Too late. The boat drifts away, its captain smirking as he waves.

An hour later, I look up from my journal and am surprised by a lone kayaker playing in the mid-river current. I watch enviously as he skims and surfs, dancing with the waves and eddies. That's the way to experience the Colorado: the water at your fingertips as you dance with all the subtle nuances and frightening power of the current. I know this kayaker can't help me, but surely the support raft hauling his gear must be close behind. Moments later, another kayak appears flanking an overloaded red raft. I wave my arms and relay my request across the wide, noisy river. When the raft captain pivots his boat and pulls hard toward my beach, I know my passage is assured.

The inflated boat scrapes its scarred nose onto the wet sand as I tug on the tossed bowline. Topping a small mountain of rubber dry bags and loose gear is an upright driftwood pole flying a full-sized Idaho flag. Perhaps the Jolly Roger would be more in order judging from the sun-darkened, scurvy knaves in ripped cutoffs and floppy hats manning the vessel. Brandishing a goofy grin, the shirtless pirate behind the oars booms, "Climb aboard, matey! We'll take ya as far as ya want to go. Wanna beer?" Clearly my lack of a life jacket isn't gonna bother these guys. I throw my pack to the gear pile and perch atop it as we shove off. What a delight to once again find myself afloat in the Grand Canyon! My hosts, Brad and Henry, are from Boise and are enjoying their biannual float with friends through the Canyon. We drift past the beached Zodiac where the researchers who snubbed me are busy seining an eddy.

"Research -- bah!" Henry spits out, obviously disgusted with the idea of working down here. "We're doing our own research -- how much beer can we drink and still navigate the rapids!" Although tempted to sign on with the jovial buccaneers, I disembark on the north shore after a half-mile float and watch the soused sailors drift toward the foaming maw of Unkar Rapid.

After claiming another empty beach as camp, I drop my pack and climb a lower butte to scout tomorrow's route. Five hundred feet above The River, the view is spectacular. I am a full mile into the Earth. A quarter of a billion years of geology rise in a triumphant rainbow of rock all around me. Side canyons and buttes which would be national parks themselves anywhere else are lost in the boundless grandeur. Can this be real? The forms, the colors, the light -- it's all too sublime, too perfect. I fear I've slipped into an insurance company calendar photo. Even the clouds look painted on. I am immersed in The Sacred.

Day 112, Nine miles

It ain't over 'til it's over! With less than two weeks remaining in my four-month journey, today proved to be one of my greatest challenges. Despite her beauty, The Canyon is a strict taskmaster and she's offering me a tough lesson or two to ponder.

I'm climbing away from the Colorado at first light. Riverlevel hiking beyond last night's campsite is again impossible. The alternative is to continue down-canyon on the Tonto Plateau -- a flat benchland about midway between the Colorado and the rim. Since the scrub-covered plateau is virtually waterless and my next definite water source is two difficult, trailless days ahead, I leave camp loaded with two gallons of water. I might find some waterpockets in the sidecanyons I'll traverse, but then, I might not.

The first trick is reaching the Tonto Plateau. After humping fifteen hundred feet up a slope paved in peach-colored slate, I reach the cliffband of the Tapeats sandstone; once my ally, now my adversary. Luckily, a few deer pellets on a faint game trail reveal a hidden passage through the cliffs and I climb up to the vast tableland. Rising above me are the massive, sheer-sided buttes which fill the breadth of the Grand Canyon with such magnificence. Many of these monuments to erosion were named by Clarence Dutton, the protegé of famed explorer and geographer Major John Wesley Powell. Awed by the grandeur and inspired by an interest in Eastern religions, the young geologist named the formations for the ancient gods. Thus, in the course of the day, I pass near Solomon Temple, Sheba Temple, Krishna Shrine, Rama Shrine, Wotan's Throne, and the towering Vishnu Temple.

Side canyons that slice across the Tonto Plateau between these peaks prove to be incredible obstacles. Asbestos Canyon is the first challenge. Same old canyoneering dilemma -- do I scramble down, then up eight hundred treacherous feet to cross directly the narrow abyss or endure an endless contour around every little side drainage to the head of the canyon and back? This time I opt for the tedious, but safe contour.

Safe? Only one out of every ten footfalls lands on a stable surface. The other nine are a constant test of balance and patience on gravel and fractured slabs. The sun grinds down, except now there's no icy river close at hand. The collapsible plastic jug holding my second gallon of water is leaking profusely and the steady drip on the back of my legs feels like my lifeblood seeping away. Annoyance and frustration build until I release it with raging screams. The impassive walls echo my shrieks right back. Nothing improves.

After several hours of rigorous hiking, I stand on the opposite side of Asbestos Canyon. All that effort for a bloody half mile of forward progress. How about some swallow wings now! Fortunately, the afternoon sees better progress on a long, level section of open, stony benchland where I zig-zag between cactus, blackbrush, and the needle-sharp, fleshy bayonets of agave and yucca. Except for darting lizards and a handful of rock wrens, nothing stirs in the heat.

I reach the brink of Vishnu Canyon which looks twice as big as Asbestos and my heart sinks -- not another contour! One place looks crossable, but halfway down the nasty, thousand-foot descent, I'm wishing I'd gone around. Everything is loose. So many opportunities to wrench a knee or snap an ankle. One bad mishap here and I'm a dead man. At the bottom, Vishnu Creek is a stream of dusty gravel. Not good. I had hoped to find water here. Things look promising down-canyon so I drop my pack and scout ahead. Two six-foot drops in the creekbed end in basins of sand. The next dry falls is a smooth, sheer drop of a hundred feet. Damn!

But I ain't a goner yet. I remember an old canyoneer's trick: scramble up the side of the canyon, then down around the pouroff. Luckily, this works, but only after a violation of my "no climbing" rule. A seep at the base of the dry falls proves useless -- wet streaks on the rock -- but the moist gravel below looks encouraging. Armed with a cottonwood branch, I try a new tactic and dig. After a dozen six-inch deep holes, two slowly fill with a palmful of water. For the remainder of the afternoon, my life narrows to a simple routine:

Lie on my belly and stick my facc in the shallow depression.
Suck up the lens of water along with a mouthful of wet sand.
Swallow the water and spit out the sand, avoiding the reverse.
Move to the next hole and inhale more slurry.
Try not to think of the total lack of purification.
Roll onto my back.
Watch the afternoon storm clouds teasing overhead as the sumps fill.
Repeat.

Mouthful by mouthful, I rehydrate, calm down, and focus until my world narrows to a couple of small pits in the wet gravel. Inches from my nose, the miracle of water trickles magically up from the Earth. Time stands still. Finally, I'm finally in tunc with my surroundings. My senses are alive and I'm oddly at peace. Another lesson: patience and intelligence will triumph over blind anger and despair. Zen and the Art of Sucking Gravel.

Day 113, Eight miles

Twenty-four hours ago, I was frantically sucking wet gravel. Now I recline; carefree, cool, and content, next to a sparkling pool in Clear Creek. This marvelous brook has been flowing in, over and around me for the last hour as I completely rehydrate. Life, once again, is a blessing instead of a curse.

After four consecutive evenings sung to sleep by Colorado River rapids, last night's camp in the dry bed of Vishnu Creek is coldly quiet. Only the echoing hoots of an upstream owl break a stillness which settles on me like a heavy blanket. The stars are still out when I break camp and scramble back up to the Tonto Plateau. My goal is Clear Creek, a perennial stream where the trail system resumes. Two major sidecanyons stand in the way. Two quarts of water left. The race is on.

The first drainage proves simple; I cut straight across. Atop a small rise, the familiar formations come into view: Brahma, Deva, Buddha, Isis, Shiva, and my favorite, Zoroaster. I also spot the thin line of a trail which I'll follow out of Clear Creek Canyon as well as a section of mule trail dropping off the south rim. Glory be -- back in my old stomping ground!

Almost. The second sidecanyon is quite a bear, requiring a long, rough contour to its head. Up over another ridge and I stand on the lip of Clear Creek Canyon. At the bottom of the chasm of dark, igneous rock, a glistening silver thread is stitched with ribbons of greenery, but twelve hundred feet of precipitous cliffs and house-sized boulders still separate me from the oasis. Down to two cups of water and parched as a mummy. It's gonna be close! Three miles, two hours, and one outrageous downclimb later, I stand beside the delightful chatter of water tumbling over a smooth terrace of stone between a garden of cattails and cottonwoods. Could anything be more beautiful than this perfect creek of clean, flowing water? Praise be the simple gift of water in the desert!

After my epiphany at the pool, I meander upstream to the camping area. With a good trail entering this drainage from the west, Clear Creek is a popular backpacking destination, but surprisingly, the flattened and packed tent sites are all empty. I've visited Clear Creek on five previous occasions including leading three expeditions here as a Grand Canyon Trail Guide. More memories rush in as I recall those heady months as a guide -- living in Grand Canyon Village and leading daily interpretive hikes for small groups of tourists. Half-day and full-day hikes were the meat and potatoes of the small guiding business, but we guides lived for the multi-day expeditions. At times, I couldn't fathom that someone was actually *paying* me to have so much fun in a place I loved so dearly! But there were moments of sadness and frustration as well. People came to The Canyon and would look and look, but never see. Often they dragged their high-powered, rat-race lifestyles down into The Canyon with them.

One client, a Florida attorney, was quite obnoxious during the first two days of our Clear Creek trek. He was impatient, always rushing to the next camp or rest stop, cracking stupid jokes and oblivious to the beauty and quiet rhythm of his surroundings. Then, on the morning of the third day, as I led the group on a dayhike to some ruins, the endless banter behind me stopped. I looked back and found the lawyer staring with childlike wonder at the mesmerizing play of light on a small pool. He reached down and gently caressed the water. The Canyon had finally worked her magic. My clients would emerge after five days in the backcountry filthy and exhausted in the flesh, but glowing and revitalized in spirit. Who can doubt that our greatest strength and wisdom and inspiration comes from the natural world?

Day 114, Ten miles

If someone asked me to name my favorite spot on this planet, I would say right where I now sit. To some, this nook would be a prison -- a tight chamber in Phantom Canyon where towering walls of pink granite and lead-gray schist nearly pinch off the sky. But perched next to a triple cascade where Phantom Creek splashes delicately over and through a landslide, I am suspended in a bubble of happy memories and subtle beauty. The tinkle and hiss of falling water create soothing music. Scarlet monkeyflowers lean over the stream to smile at their own reflections. The prince of this pocket paradise, the effervescent water ouzel, dances his bobbing ballet. I discovered this spot on my very first day in the Grand Canyon five years ago and I've been returning ever since. There are lovelier places on this globe, but none I hold more dear. What a joy to visit here during my Southwest Circle Quest!

With an excellent trail guiding me across the Tonto Plateau west of Clear Creek, this morning's nine miles to Bright Angel Creek is a breeze. Around noon, I reenter "civilization" when I reach Phantom Ranch, the only major development in the bottom of the Grand Canyon. Built in the 1920s, Phantom Ranch is nestled near the mouth of Bright Angel Canyon. An oasis of cottonwoods shelter this cluster of attractive, unobtrusive cabins built of native stone. The central kitchen/dining room that serves hikers and mule riders is provisioned daily by mule packtrains from the south rim. Also strung out along Bright Angel Creek are a large Park Service campground, mule stables, and two ranger stations. There are even flush toilets and pay phones here. Although many other hardcore Grand Canyon backpackers scorn this busy outpost in the Inner Gorge, I've always enjoyed its blend of civility and rusticity. Phantom Ranch is a throwback to the early days of the Park Service where generations of hikers, mule riders, boatmen, and rangers have converged in the shade to compare their Grand Canyon pilgrimages.

I join the dozens of other backpackers -- the first I've seen since Canyonlands National Park -- as they slough off their loads and duck into the cool, dark comfort of the cantina. Heat-dazed and reeking, we sit together at the long wooden tables and sip icy beer or lemonade, happy to be off our feet and out of the sun. The conversation is a swirl of European tongues. I watch and listen, but do not mingle as my ability to be sociable has slipped away again. Perhaps I fear that if I start talking, I'll never stop.

Eventually, the roof overhead and the mob so close become too much, so I retreat into the glare and head for the broad beach where Bright Angel Creek joins the Colorado. The scent of toasted tamarisk and sun-blistered sand mingles with the salt-tinged breath of the great rolling river -- what a sweet perfume! I move to a particular smoke-colored limestone boulder tucked in seclusion at the water's edge. For years, this rock has served as my private diving board; I strip naked and clamber atop the chest-high perch. With three running steps I fling myself over the muddy swirls. For a moment, I am flying -- a great pink swallow swooping over the water. Then everything is dark, thick, bone cold. Every nerve explodes at once as I grope away from The River's clutch and return to the surface. Bursting back into the heat and light, every fiber of my being shouts "I AM ALIVE!" My love of this place and this life knows no bounds.

Day 115, Ten miles

A finer beginning to my twenty-ninth birthday is impossible to imagine as I awake to another sensual September sunrise in the Grand Canyon. The first order of business is a dedication of the double hoop gift of two thanks I made yesterday afternoon. Standing at my lowest point all summer at 2,500 feet, I gaze lovingly over the rolling, brown, liquid mirror and thank The River for her life-sustaining water and beauty. With a flick of my wrist, I toss the symbol of my gratitude into the well-muscled current and watch as it drifts away.

If yesterday's route from Clear Creek seemed like a highway after the two-day pathless stint, today's Bright Angel Trail to the rim is a veritable freeway. Climbing nearly a vertical mile over the span of nine miles, the Bright Angel Trail is one of the most heavily used footpaths in America. On a busy summer day, as many as five hundred pairs of feet plus dozens of mule hooves pound up and down the dusty switchbacks. Even in mid-September, I encounter more than a hundred backpackers and dayhikers -- more than the total I met all summer.

Over the years, I've hiked these sinuous nine miles dozens of times and the wide trail is another linear treasure chest of memories. Today, moving uphill at a comfortable, steady pace, I focus on the incredible diversity of pedestrians strung out along this classic route into the Grand Canyon. The faces come in a wide assortment of flavors: caramel, fudge, toffee, coconut, cherry. Most are beginning to melt. Conversation snippets are in German, French, Japanese, Spanish, or English smeared by Australian or British accents. Good ol' Yanks like myself are clearly outnumbered.

I encounter the fit, the fat, and the feeble. Lean runners streaking downhill pass overweight weekend warriors practically crawling back up to the rim. Footwear runs the full gamut: boots, sneakers, loafers, sandals. I begin to spot victims of the "The Bright Angel Vacuum" -- that seductive force that sucks unprepared tourists down the easy, steep trail, drawing them deeper and deeper beyond their abilities. It all seems so easy and alluring in the cool sweetness of early morning. But as midday heat cranks up, these poor bastards will find themselves stuck down here with no food, no water, and facing a three-mile staircase of stiff switchbacks to get home. I nod and smile wryly as I pass them: an older couple in matching sea-green tennis suits lugging a monstrous video camera, but no waterbottle; a clean-shaven man with his gurgling, two year-old daughter perched on his shoulders with his wife following in crepe-soled moccasins; a gaggle of giggling Japanese schoolgirls snapping pictures of each other. All these folks grin and laugh as they merrily spin down the convoluted trail, oblivious to the struggle that awaits them when they must turn around. Nothing I see on the Bright Angel Trail surprises me anymore.

After a trailmix break at Indian Gardens Campground, I start up The Headwall, the final three and a half miles where the trail roars up a lung-busting 2,800 feet. A string of familiar landmarks unwinds: the Redwall, the Three Mile Resthouse, Two Mile Corner, One Mile Arch. Here's the perennial brown-green puddle of rank mule piss where entire packtrains loosen their bladders en masse and the foul, bushy alcove where waterlogged hikers discreetly do the same. There's the hidden cove of petroglyphs and the tame bighorn boldly cornering hikers in hopes of hijacking a snack. It's another homecoming. All at once, I top out and am immediately engulfed in a world of crowded blacktop, crass souvenir shops, idling Greyhounds, clicking cameras, and sunburnt tourists -- Grand Canyon Village. For once, I don't resist the crush of civilization. Hey -- it's my birthday -- time to celebrate!

Time to eat! My withered stomach begins doing backflips as I review my culinary options. After the initial plunge of a double scoop chocolate raspberry cone (my first ice cream all summer) I lose total control and the afternoon digresses into a delirious blur of grease, spice, and sugar. When the shadows begin to stretch between the pines, I waddle to the Camper's Services building and enjoy a splendidly hot shower. Clean and shiny on the outside, my gut remains an insatiable black hole. I skip across the street and buy fixings for a Mexican dinner from the supermarket.

Surprisingly, I enjoy this afternoon foray in the modern world. Grand Canyon Village is crowded, tacky, and unnecessary ... but I like it. Maybe it's because this was once my home. Unfortunately, the buzz and hustle of the hotels, trinket shops, book shops, restaurants, and museums lure both residents and visitors away from the main reason they're here. The Grand Canyon becomes a surreal, scenic backdrop for another shopping expedition.

The highlight of the day comes when I retrieve the small package I'm expecting from Abby at the post office. Along with an important map is a birthday card and photos. My heart thunders as I read her sweet words and gaze upon her face in the pictures. One more look at that smile and I swear I'll run the last leg to Flagstaff! All told, a most memorable birthday.

Day 116, Fourteen miles

Yesterday, I awoke at the lowest elevation of the summer. Today, I watch the buttery light of dawn pouring into the mighty chasm from the westernmost point along my grand circle. I have come to say goodbye. The first few pilgrims are starting down the Bright Angel Trail and part of me longs to join them and never climb back out. My love affair with this marvelous gash in the planet hasn't ever grown stale. Yet my quest remains uncompleted. I gaze over the hotel rooftops and the rolling blanket of pines to the steel-blue San Francisco Peaks beckoning to the south. Time to begin the last leg of my long journey.

When I finally tear myself from the rim and enter Grand Canyon Village, something is clearly amiss. The area around the venerable El Tovar Lodge has been cordoned off. Patrol cars are everywhere. People with cameras are lined up behind police barricades facing a strangely empty road.

"Hey, what's all the fuss?" I ask an old man in Bermuda shorts and a pork pie hat. He grimaces at me like I just asked which way is up.

"The President, kid!" the geezer spits out. "Air Force One just landed at the airport. He'll be here in a few minutes!"

Turns out that George Bush is making a three hour visit to the Grand Canyon today, ostensibly to reaffirm that he is still "the environmental president". Aye carumba! Eager to avoid all the hoopla, I try to escape south to the Kaibab National Forest, but my route is on a collision course with the presidential motorcade. The normally docile park rangers are as nervous and testy as riled rattlesnakes. A small army of county police and state troopers is providing additional muscle. Here and there lurk ominous G-men in bulging dark suits and opaque sunglasses. They glare at me and mutter into their lapels. My every move is blocked. The entire park is on hold.

Trapped!

Not so easily foiled, I resort to the network of obscure footpaths known only to residents, sneak around the last barricade, and start cruising again. The footpath dips near the road where a herd of deer are foraging in the dappled sunlight beneath the pines. The liquid-eyed does lift their heads at the racket of approaching motorcycles. Together, we watch the parade of flashing patrol cars and skulking black limousines roll by.

What a circus! All this commotion for one man. Bush may have the fame, power, and prestige, but he is clearly a prisoner of his celebrity. Few humans are as time-poor as the President of the United States. Thus, in regards to the two things I value most -- personal time and personal freedom -- I am infinitely richer than this man.

After the President is safely within his bubble of security at the rim, Grand Canyon Village is allowed to exhale. Traffic resumes. Returning to the park entrance road, I face another blockade of heavily armed civil servants and can almost hear their thoughts as they huddle between a couple of patrol cars: hmmm ... a foot traveler ... highly suspicious ... could be a small thermonuclear device in that big pack! It takes every ounce of charm I can muster to persuade these "gentlemen" to allow me to continue walking down the road.

A few hours later, I'm in the Kaibab National Forest Ranger Station in the gateway community of Tusayan gleaning information about water sources from the rangers, but Smoky's finest have precious few words of wisdom about my route through their forest. The problem with rangers these days is that they rarely get out and *range* anymore! Too much paperwork to process. My research is abruptly interrupted when the chief ranger announces that The President is on his way back. The silver-haired bureaucrat kicks me out and closes the station, then assembles his entire staff next to the highway to hold up a huge banner proclaiming: "The Kaibab National Forest Supports President George Bush". Everybody waves and cheers as the motorcade rumbles by. Minutes later, Air Force One thunders directly overhead trailed by another jumbo jet of media bloodhounds. The whole parade wings away to lunch in Salt Lake City.

Poor George. Did you even get a chance to really see The Canyon? Did you savor the rich vanilla aroma of the ponderosa pines bathed in warm September sunshine? Will you ever linger long enough to witness the miracle of sunrise or sunset? How can you be "the environmental president" when you are so isolated and protected from the environment?

Leaving the asphalt for an obscure Forest Service road beyond Tusayan, I quickly leave the crowds and chaos behind. My company narrows to my few old forest friends: Ponderosa, Red Squirrel, Piñon, Chickadee, and Juniper. With the Grand Canyon now in my wake, I set my sight on Arizona's highest point.

Day 117, Seventeen miles

After a week on a world of wildly-eroded rock heaped into spectacular vistas, today is an easy tromp through a flat, green, monotonous landscape as I cut across and drop off the Coconino Plateau. The dirt track unrolls before me and I chew up the miles, passing a flock of wild turkeys, a few bowhunter encampments, one private ranch, a handful of cattle tanks -- pretty tame stuff compared to yesterday's commotion. Once this route rattled with stagecoach traffic as early Grand Canyon tourists braved the twelve-hour ride from Flagstaff. Just reaching the rim of the Canyon was an adventure in those days -- nothing like Bush's buzz in/buzz out whirlwind visit. At Red Horse Wash, I pause for lunch at the crumbling foundation of the old Moqui stage stop, one of three stations where drivers changed horses. The majestic groves of ponderosa pine give way to a scrubby piñon/juniper woodland as I slowly lose elevation. The bulk of the San Francisco Peaks slips into view and looms larger with every step. When a truckload of curious cowboys grinds to a stop at my elbow, I ask about a possible water source ahead and the amiable cowpokes give me the lowdown. These guys have a better handle on the country than the rangers who are in charge of managing it.

Late in the afternoon, I pull up to the Lockwood Canyon Tank, but the stock pond is a gruesome stew of fairy shrimp and cow piss. Fortunately, a metal tub behind the corral holds a few inches of stale rainwater. Inside a boxy tarpaper shack nearby, I find another register of previous visitors scribbled on the plank siding. The best "entry" is "Britt and Benny ate bobcat here during a horrendous snow storm, 11-17-77." Classic!

Day 118, Eighteen miles

At dawn, I'm startled awake by an unearthly wailing that sounds like the ungodly offspring of a goose and a dinosaur! I pop my head out of the tent and spot elk grazing only a quarter mile away. A magnificent bull tips back his antlered head and bellows out another bugle; his breath forming white jets of steam in the chill air. What a wake-up call!

A track follows Lockwood Canyon down to a grassy plain where I briefly dip into Navajo land. Smooth, symmetrical cinder cones rise like immense stepping stones to the San Francisco Peaks towering nearly a mile and a half above the plains. Twin sets of powerline towers looking like huge, spindly space aliens shackled together with massive cables march from horizon to horizon. The crackling wires are alive with energy streaming from Glen Canyon Dam and the

Navajo Generating Station toward some insatiable metropolis to the south -- a space-age umbilical cord stretched across a prehistoric landscape. The morning is a flashback to the first leg of the journey as I trudge ant-like across a vast, lava-encrusted skillet.

The plain eventually begins to tip up toward the dark ponderosa forest which girdles the peaks. Tucked at the base of a low escarpment is the Cedar Ranch, home of the roving ranchhands I saw yesterday. With my water bottles rattling empty, I decide to make a social call on this outpost. A pudgy black and tan Australian shepherd lurches to his feet as I enter the yard. Two cowboys loitering next to a split rail corral call the mutt off and squint in my direction.

"Howdy! Any chance I could fill my water bottles here?" The lads looking me over appear every inch the mythic cowboy image -- pointy boots, faded Levis, checkered shirts, huge bandanas loosely knotted around their necks, floppy, sweat-stained hats. One cowpoke's mouth twists upwards into a tobacco-yellow grin.

"Yer makin' pretty good time. Saw ya yesterday from the truck. Come on into the bunkhouse. We'll fix ya up." I follow the fellas, their spurs a'jangling, into the long, low cinder block building. The bunkhouse has all the homey comfort of a block of prison cells. Dusty duffels are stuffed under peeling steel cots while denim jackets hang from nails under bare light bulbs. Boxes of white bread and canned goods are set on wide counters flanking a bleak kitchen.

"How long you guys been living out here?" I ask as I fill my bottles at the sink.

"Well, I been cowboying for eight years," explains one of the hands. "But I just signed onto this outfit last week. It's one of the three ranches owned by the Babbitt family that runs cattle from the Havasupai Reservation clear over to the Little Colorado. Most of the guys are up in the national forest rounding up the stock to move it down toward the Navajo Reservation."

"Why aren't you guys up there?" I inquire. The two cowboys exchange a glance.

"The cook quit," the other cowboy says with a sheepish grin. "We was elected to come back early and fix supper."

Beyond the ranch, I follow a jeep track angling up an escarpment of lava. Out on the plains, dust devils dance before a black wall of rain while the brick and lavender hills of the Painted Desert shimmer in the sun beyond the crease of the Little Colorado. The peaks are now hidden by the forest, but I can feel the presence of Dooko'oosliid, the Holy Mountain. Climbing to the summit of these sacred peaks will be the last challenge of my summer-long journey. What a finale to my quest!

Day 119, Sixteen miles

I'm living up to my new name once again. My flighty fancy has forsaken canyon country and is now singing the praises of the high mountains. Camped here among the spruce high on the slopes of the San Francisco Peaks, I'm in seventh heaven. SwallowHeart lives!

This morning is a long road walk on Route 64 beside Grand Canyon-bound tourist traffic. Eventually, another dirt track tacks more directly toward the foot of the peaks and I enter one of the most beautiful forests of the entire journey. The September sun bathes this gorgeous woodland of stately ponderosa pine intermingled with smooth, twinkling aspen in bright, warm light. A gentle breeze scatters the first golden doubloons of fall and a rich, intoxicating aroma fills the air. I am enchanted to the point of tears.

The forest opens and I gaze at a wooded wall rising a steep four thousand feet to the craggy summit ridge. Mount Humphreys, the highest point in Arizona, forms the northern end of the ridge while Mount Agassiz, scarred by ski slopes, anchors the southern terminus. Ignoring my original plan to camp in this meadow, I impulsively start bushwhacking straight up the mountainside for an alpine camp. Unrelentingly steep elk trails weaving through thick aspen groves set my thighs on fire as I crank up the fearsome slope. Once in the spruce zone, my progress slows to a crawl as I navigate a sea of deadfall. Panting like a coon hound, I lean heavily against a Douglas fir and wonder if I've been too impulsive. There's nowhere to camp in this tangle of downed trunks.

Suddenly, I hear voices. Who else is bushwhacking up here? I contour towards the conversation and hit a well-developed trail absent from my map. Two college students are surprised when I emerge from the thicket like a wild man, but assure me that the newly constructed trail leads right to the summit ridge -- perfect!

I'm now camped above 10,000 feet on a tiny, flat niche grooved in the severe mountainside under a sky gloomy with storm clouds. My fingers are growing numb in the cold bite of dusk even though I lie in my bag bundled up like a mummy. Was I really sunbathing at the bottom of the Grand Canyon only a few days ago? Can Sugarloaf mountain be only a half-day's walk away? Am I prepared for this walk to end? Do I have any choice?

Day 120, Eight miles
1360 miles total

Today it all came together. Exactly four months -- a third of a year -- has elapsed since I stepped off the bus in Flagstaff. Tonight, the moon comes full again just as the summer officially gives way to fall at the autumnal equinox. And today my fourteen hundred-mile line of footsteps come back to where they began. My circle is complete!

What a day! After a frosty breakfast, I'm moving upwards, eager to be the first pilgrim atop Mount Humphreys. Clearing the trees and switchbacking to the scree-covered ridge, I peer into the Inner Basin at Sugarloaf Mountain -- there she is!. My journey will be complete when I stand before my circle of stones atop that hill. But first, the summit. I head north along the dramatic ridge noticing my wildflower friends of the tundra are all but gone while the tough shrubs clinging to the volcanic rubble have the scarlet leaves of autumn. The biting wind shoving me along is a dramatic contrast to the wilting heat of the Inner Gorge only a few days ago.

The 12,633 foot summit of Mount Humphreys is a small dome capping the end of the ridge. I remove my pack and retrieve the last of my twin circle gifts. This final offering is the finest of the summer. A ring of aspen encloses a hoop of spruce -- the trees of the high country. Bearing this gift, I climb the last few feet to the summit with the reverence of a priest approaching an altar, then raise my eyes to the amazing breadth of country visible around me.

To the north, the plains I just crossed angle up to the Coconino Plateau where an odd gap in the trees reveals little of the glorious chasm hidden there. Beyond, barely visible in the haze, are the uplands of southern Utah. I have walked here from that impossibly distant horizon. My gaze swings east. The cinder cones around Sunset Crater rise above the thin ribbon of greenery tracing the course of the Little Colorado River. Farther still, the Painted Desert stretches hot and pink, seemingly forever. I have walked into that horizon as well. There are no faraway blue peaks left to beckon me, no remote vistas to urge me on. My universe lies encompassed before me. With a hint of sadness haunting my feelings of awe and gratitude, I move to the edge of the summit and dedicate my gift to the mountain.

An unbridled joy bubbles forth and I release an echoing victory whoop. Despite the odds and the obstacles and the moments of doubt, I made it back! Leaning against the summit cairn, I spoon a late breakfast of granola into my smiling face and watch as the view becomes even more breathtaking as the haze burns off. More pilgrims arrive at the summit. Two college students and a visiting father huff up the last pitch and collapse beside me. Their first question is the one I've dreaded answering all summer, "Where are you coming from?"

There is no simple answer. I try to explain my saga, pointing to the horizons, but the whole affairs sounds wildly improbable even to my own ears. Dad is alive with questions while the boys are stunned into silence. How many more times in the weeks and months ahead shall I be forced to squeeze my incredible adventure into an inadequate handful of sentences?

The mountaintop becomes crowded with new arrivals: more college students, two older women proud of their summiting time, an Olympic rower and his girlfriend. I enjoy the light-hearted swirl of conversation until I begin to drown in it. Swallow and Raven have also arrived, circling the peak in a dance with the wind so I ease away from the mob of mountaineers and commune with these winged friends who faithfully accompanied me all summer. Perhaps only they will ever truly understand me again.

The summit party breaks up when ominous clouds materializing overhead begin rumbling deep in their bellies. We are all thinking about the story someone told of a young man killed by lightning on this ridge earlier this summer. As we retreat, I glare up at the sky. Listen Thor and Zeus, don't you fellas even *think* about zapping me this close to the finish line! The gods listen for once and the storm passes quickly without claiming any new victims.

After retracing my steps to the saddle, I spiral down into the Inner Basin, lost in thought. I have traveled from the end of one winter to the threshold of the next. The aspens in the belly of this sleeping volcano that were just leafing out when I last saw them in late May are now slipping into their fall wardrobe. The seasons of my life have undergone undeniable changes as well. Will I be able to adapt as handily as the aspen?

Finally, I stand in Lockett Meadow at the base of Sugarloaf Mountain. Hoisting my trusty pack for the final time, I begin the last half mile of my fourteen hundred-mile journey. The elk trail leading to the top is rough and incredibly steep, yet I'm determined to make this last climb without pause -- a final blaze of sweat and oxygen debt. Perspiration runs into my mouth, my nose, my eyes, but I will not let up. I'll push my limits right to the end.

Panting and lathered like a racehorse, I reach the top and cross through the woods to my vision quest circle. Everything is happening too quickly, but my legs won't stop. Suddenly, the ring of rocks is before me and there is nowhere left to walk. Pulling my knife from my pocket, I cut off the worn and filthy woven bracelet which has encircled my wrist since the hour of my departure. With this simple gesture, my journey is completed and my circle is closed.

I ease my pack to the ground and retrieve the drum from the cache I left nearby. The instrument sounds as good as ever. I step into the circle and begin beating out a slow pulse. The drum speaks loud and proud and my body responds in a victory dance. Finally, an emotional dam bursts and I weep uncontrollably. Drumming and dancing, I cry in joy, in relief, in thankfulness. I've done it! I've really done it! I dreamed a dream and made it come true! My life will never be the same.

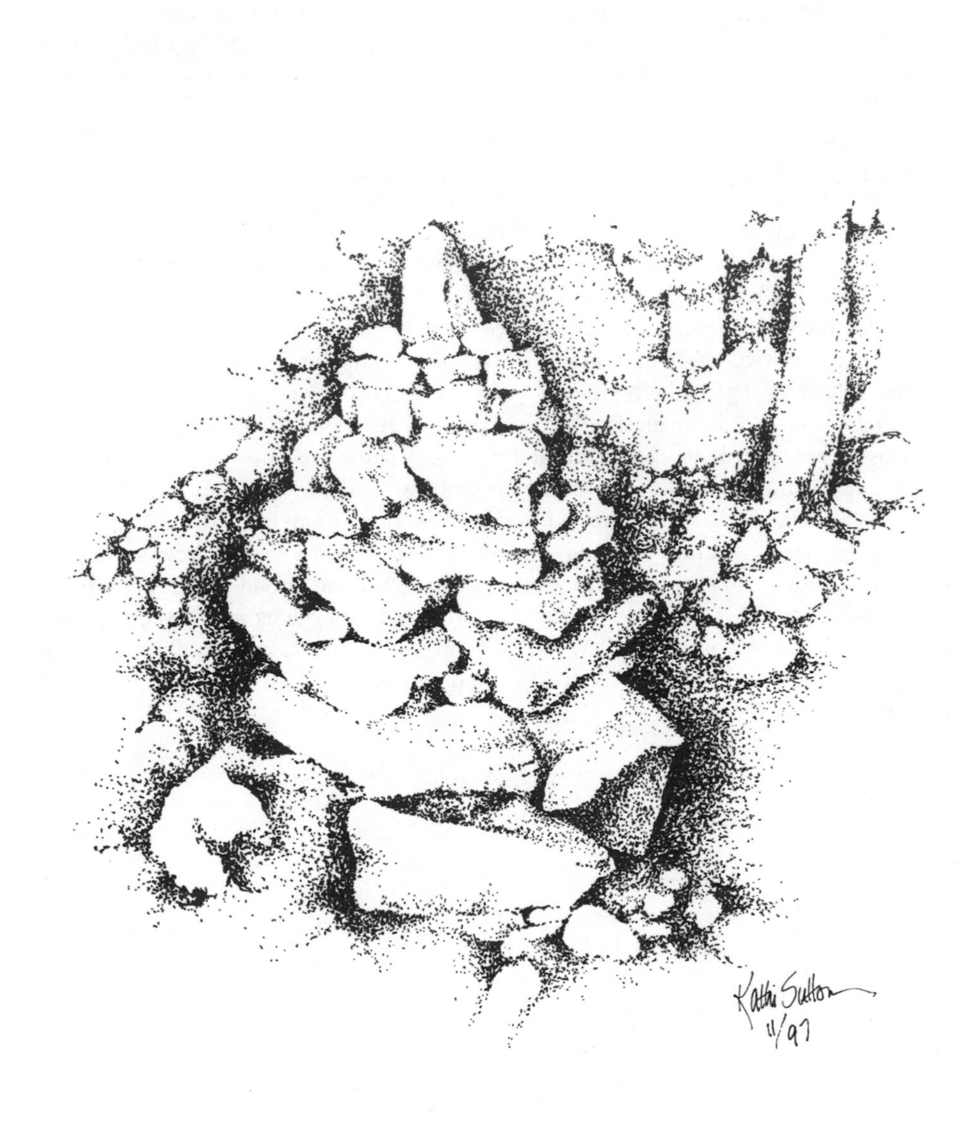
Kathi Sutton
11/97

THE CLOSING CIRCLE

The ultimate aim of the quest, if one
is to return, must be neither release
nor ecstasy for oneself, but the wisdom
and power to serve others.

Joseph Campbell
The Power of Myth

Day 121

After the emotional epiphany at my vision quest circle, I set up camp nearby in the darkening twilight. Watching the dancing flames in the same fire ring where I sat last May, the entire journey begins to feel shadowy and distant. Could the vast wonderland etched in my mind be just a magnificent dream, like that of Lewis Carroll's Alice, from which I am just now awakening? Did I spend four days in my vision quest circle ... or four months? Maybe I never left this mountaintop! I teeter on the edge of realities, unsure where I'll land.

Although my walk is completed, my quest continues. I have decided to conclude this experience with another stationary vision quest atop this mountain. My opening vision quest was a traditional test of physical and mental endurance. In retrospect, that challenge instilled the toughness and determination I needed to meet the rigors of the trail. My closing vision quest shall serve a different function: a time to review what I've learned and to prepare for my reentry into society. I'll allow myself full use of my camping gear, but restrict food to a single daily meal. My circle of movement will be the several acres of this mountaintop until the final night when I'll return to the circle of stone. I stand at an important threshold: leaving one world and entering another. This transition cannot be rushed.

Even before my eyes open to greet the dawn, my mind is already demanding: Get up! Get moving! Make some miles before it grows too hot. I throw back the bag, unzip the tent, then remember where I am. After four months of constant travel, I can scarcely comprehend being still. Hunting for water, seeking shade, plotting routes, plodding miles--this seems to be the only life I've ever known. Day One of my post-walk life and I'm already disoriented!

In the plastic cache bucket which remained here all summer, I find a copy of the announcement that I sent to family and friends last winter declaring my intention to undertake a quest. I reread my promise of "making a hero's journey" and "asking myself those big questions: Who am I? What is the proper way to live my life? What is my life's work?" Suddenly, my summer seems like a disappointment. Although my initial vision quest was profoundly insightful, the walk itself was alarmingly secular. Once I hit the trail, my thoughts we-

dominated by miles, not myths. I spent more time contemplating ramen than ritual. A wave of confusion washes over me. Did I forget my goals and fall from the spiritual path I intended to follow? Was the summer just a fun escape into the backcountry? What did I really learn? My cheers of success yesterday begin to ring hollow.

I move on to the stack of letters sent in response to my announcement. In my father's voluminous reply, I find that he anticipated this conflict between spiritual and physical realities. He asked, "How are you going to empty your mind and be with your heart when so much effort will be needed to meet the obvious physical and mental challenges?" He was right; I found it nearly impossible to be a monk and an explorer at the same time.

Morning slides into afternoon and thoughts and questions pushed aside since May begin to resurface. Then I realize all is not lost. I could have given in to yesterday's fleeting urge to continue immediately into Flagstaff and start hitching to Durango to meet Abby. If I had ended the summer that abruptly, my quest would ultimately be a failure. Now, by forcing myself to slow down and remain here, I have the perfect opportunity to seek new answers to the questions I originally posed. My body may rest, but my heart and mind and soul still have important country to traverse together.

Day 122

Last night, I huddled at my fire and stared for hours at the hypnotic flicker. Slowly, the answers I've been seeking began to flow into me like the heat from the flames. This morning, I am ready to put pen to paper.

First, was my Southwest Circle Quest a success? Yes and no. Last summer when I added the spiritual element of a vision quest to my original idea of a grand adventure, I quickly created many expectations for this journey. I led myself to believe that I would experience months of unbroken solitude in the wilderness where, through constant introspection, my journey would progress to metaphysical realms. I would emerge from the experience enlightened; a Four Corner's version of Castanada's Don Juan. Well ... that wasn't reality. Between the heat, the thirst, the bugs, and the average of fifteen miles of daily hiking, this vision of seamless contemplation proved impossible. I discovered that a single journey cannot function as both a deeply spiritual retreat and a challenging physical adventure. At first, this realization caused me great guilt. The turning point occurred on the summer solstice when I decided to focus on experiential education instead of meditative learning. Why retreat into my head when I was enjoying my closest contact with the greatest teacher of them all -- the natural world? With my guilt released, the journey took on a new vitality.

So was the summer just a long, exciting backpacking trip? Hardly! Had I chosen to undertake my grand adventure in some foreign, exotic location like Peru or Tibet, it would have been just that -- a grand adventure. Interesting, challenging, insightful perhaps, but still a distant wandering. Instead, I choose to explore the region which I intend to call my home. And this made all the difference.

What I really accomplished this summer was neither a metaphysical vision quest nor a pleasant trek, but a walkabout. This concept of walkabout is borrowed from the Australian Aborigines. According to this ancient culture, Australia is crisscrossed with invisible trails called songlines. Every topographic feature in the landscape is thought to have been sung into existence by ancestors and is alive with mythic meaning. A walkabout is a ritual journey across the outback which retraces the songline path of a person's totem ancestor. A young Aborigine on walkabout intimately learns the stories and the geography of his homeland as he literally sings his way across it.

My journey became a walkabout as I glimpsed the soul of the land and learned its songs. My understanding of the plants and animals and landforms of the Four Corners area has grown beyond appreciation into a passionate devotion, the deepest love I have ever known. This remarkable place is and always will be alive and sacred to me. My spirit has become a part of its spirit. I am now "owned" by the land -- the mountains, canyons, forests, and rivers -- by a bond that can never be broken.

In a very real sense, I have defined my universe with an unbroken line of footsteps. Like the Navajo, my world is bound by sacred mountains: Mount Taylor, the La Sals, and the San Francisco Peaks. I now hold dual citizenship in two worlds. Brett LeCompte's home is the human world which I left and to which I must soon return. But, as SwallowHeart, I am also a member of an older, larger world where my best friends include Canyon Wren and Raven, Elk and Coyote, Ponderosa and Aspen.

Did my quest result in enlightenment? Nope. I understand now that this process is destined to be a life-long affair. Yet my Southwest Circle Quest has given me something nearly as valuable -- a physical and spiritual homeland in the deepest sense of the word. I know unequivocally that the wilderness of my circle will always be my Source, my Center, and my Bliss.

What else did I learn? Many lessons were not new ones, but important affirmations of what I already knew and believed. Perhaps the most profound teaching is that anything is possible if you truly believe in it. A year ago, this journey was only a dream -- a whimsical line drawn on a map. Now, I have turned this dream into a reality. The secret was slow, steady effort combined with trust and an infatigable will. Many times, I gazed at distant peaks and wondered how I'd ever reach them. Yet, I simply put one foot in front of the other, and before long, that "impossible" summit was under my boots.

I learned not to become overwhelmed by impossible undertakings, but to break everything into manageable bites. I still can't conceive of walking fourteen hundred miles even having just done it! But I can grasp fifteen miles a day repeated again and again. By turning my dream into reality, I am filled with incredible inspiration. Right now, anything seems possible.

I learned that every problem, every difficulty is actually an opportunity for growth. My greatest appreciation of life inevitably followed my infrequent brushes with death. Even frustrations like my boots blowing out and running out of money proved to be boons in the final analysis. The trick is recognizing and accepting the gift that goes hand-in-hand with every problem.

I've come to realize that within me are two voices; that of the flesh and that of the spirit. Although the voice of the flesh often shouts loudest, it's the voice of the spirit that speaks to my soul. Throughout the summer, I tried -- not always successfully -- to allow the voice of the spirit to guide my actions. When I listened to this intuitive, inner voice in critical situations, it did not fail me. In fact, paying attention to this inner wisdom probably saved my life more than once.

Perhaps the greatest surprise of the quest was the realization and eventual deep belief that I was watched over, guided, and protected by some form of guardian spirit. I traveled alone across fourteen hundred miles of remote, rugged terrain with barely a scratch. When I needed water, I always found it. Shelter from an oncoming storm would appear just as I required it. Someone who knew a difficult stretch of country ahead would inevitably cross my path. Even human friendship was provided in regular doses. I simply cannot attribute my unflagging good fortune to my abilities alone. There were too many instances of perfect timing or unbelievable circumstances to be mere coincidence. Some force seemed to be ensuring that my quest ended safely and successfully. As to the nature of this guardian spirit, divine or otherwise, I'm not sure. Yet I truly believe that I was not alone out there.

Day 123

The final full day of my Southwest Circle Quest has arrived. On the eve of my return to human society, I must ask myself: Where do I go from here? Although my voice of the flesh is chattering eagerly about the soon-to-be-realized comforts of civilization, my voice of the spirit is already preparing for the inevitable letdown. I'll reenter a world that will whirl around me like a record at the wrong speed -- too fast, too loud, too meaningless. This wilderness world is a place of incredible beauty and harmony. Why go back to the fractured world of humanity?

Joseph Campbell discusses this dilemma of the "hero's return" in his classic study of mythology: The Hero with a Thousand Faces. Campbell explains that the hero's real mission is not the quest for the "boon" for which he has suffered long and hard. The hero cannot simply enjoy his hard-sought reward by himself. The ultimate goal must be returning to his society with the boon so that all may benefit. And yet, this return is often the hero's most difficult task. The boon he offers may not be understood or even accepted by his society.

Campbell's lessons from mythology speak all too clearly to me on a personal level. A big part of me simply doesn't want to go back. I could just hike back over the San Francisco Peaks, hop in the Arizona Trail, and head south. I'd be in Mexico by Thanksgiving. I've always wanted to see Central America ... the Amazon ... the Andes ....

But, no. My circle has been drawn; my walkabout completed. The time has come to return to the world where I ultimately must reside. These past four months in the wilderness have been possible only through an umbilical cord of food and supplies from the modern world. Despite my intimate spiritual connection to the land and its inhabitants, my day-to-day home and work must lie within the human realm.

What, then, is the boon which I must share? After much thought, I believe my gift is to act as an ambassador between the two worlds of which I am now a member. I shall dedicate my life to bridging the growing gap between human society and the larger natural world in which it exists. I will strive for peace, harmony, and understanding between people and their environment, particularly the environment of my new homeland. Although this is not an entirely new revelation, I am filled with a renewed strength and sense of purpose. I've received my vision after all! Truly, I am blessed.

Realizing my purpose is one thing; fulfilling it is quite another. I'm up against centuries of religious and cultural prejudices which view the natural world as simply resources to be conquered and consumed. What can I do? It's too soon to figure out all the details, but here are some immediate ideas:

*I shall use my life and lifestyle as an example of a responsible, harmonious, and sustainable way to live on this planet. Clearly, we must mend our overconsumptive, polluting, unsustainable ways. I vow to help my society make the difficult, yet inevitable transition to a more balanced civilization.

*I believe I can have the greatest impact as an ambassador to the natural world by returning to the field of outdoor leadership and environmental education. By leading trips into the wilderness, I can directly guide people in creating deeper, non-destructive relationships with the natural world.

*I shall use my writing as a tool to educate and inspire. By publishing an account of my Southwest Circle Quest, I hope to teach others to follow their dreams and to seek an intimate connection to the wild places.

I know my road will not be an easy one. To many, the concept of a living, breathing, animate landscape is almost unfathomable. There will be obstacles, setbacks, and frustrations. Yet I will handle these with the lessons I learned from my walkabout -- with a positive mental attitude and good humor; taking small, careful steps with courage and indomitable perseverance. Best of all, I know that when my work in the deserts of human society becomes too hot and exhausting, I can return to the cool, refreshing spring of my wilderness home and drink deeply of the life-sustaining elixir.

The Final Hours

As the pinks and oranges of the Painted Desert flares, then fades at the edge of day, I put aside my journal and my revelations and return to my circle of stone. My voice of the flesh rebels at the prospect of the cold, uncomfortable vigil ahead, but I am resolute. Wearing clothes, but no shoes and carrying knly my thin wool blanket, my drum, and my medicine bag, I enter the sacred circle.

Memories of four intense days and nights I spent on this spot pour through me. The intervening miles and months since my last vigil vanish. My universe narrows to this simple ring of rocks. I begin by drumming up the moon. An hour passes. My arm is aching. The steady pulse of the drum joins with my own heartbeat, echoing together into the gathering darkness. A saffron spark alights on the horizon. The moon slides out of the desert and climbs into the stars, slipping from rose to pearl, cool and round and rich. I put the drum aside, sit cross-legged in the dust, and the final night begins.

I close my eyes and begin a powerful prayer of thanksgiving that continues until dawn. Starting with my initial arrival on this mountaintop, I mentally relive each day of the quest. Landscapes and faces begin to unfold before me in startling detail. When I remember a situation in which I was given help, either from a human or non-human source, I offer a heartfelt thanks for this gift. So many debts of gratitude! So many blessings!

The night air grows cold. The spruce tree guardians surrounding me begin to sway and chant softly in the wind. I curl into ball on my side, a shivering, blanketed lump bathed in quicksilver light within a circle of stones. I do not sleep. My internal journey over the mountains and through the canyons continues. Sometimes I rest, exhausted by remembered miles, but I feel good.

Hours evaporate. I stand and stretch stiff limbs. The moon stares straight down at me. The blanket hangs from my shoulders and when I spread my arms, they become shadowy bat wings. Cat Stevens' song, "Moonshadow", leaps into my mind and onto my lips. Softly, I begin to sing as my numb, bare feet tap out a cadence in the dust. The lyrics quickly run out, but the song goes on as I use the melody to pray aloud. Every offering of thanks floats effortlessly from my heart to my mouth. My voice is strong; my steps sure. Energy surges up through my toes and shoots from my tongue and my fingers. I sing and dance away the midnight hour. Finally crumbling back to the ground, I am aglow. After a while, I hoist my imaginary pack and pick up the thread of my journey, murmuring the details to stay awake. Again, I slump to my side. Do I sleep? Perhaps. There is no dream.

When I next poke my head from its woolen shroud, a thin line of crimson embroiders the eastern horizon. As the false dawn begins to wash away the darkness, I huff down the last couple legs of my mental footpath until memory touches the present. I rise to my feet and face east -- time to drum up the sun! My final dance starts slowly, but grows stronger with the light. With my nightlong prayer completed, my soul is as calm and rippleless as a bottomless pool.

A peace such as I've never imagined fills me. No thought. No emotion. Just drumming and dancing.

Without warning, a spark of perfect fire touches the seam between Earth and Sky. Just as suddenly, an unbridled joy erupts in my heart. I explode into a crescendo of drumming and shouting. As the sun's warm face kisses mine, my final circle comes to a close.

One important ceremony remains. Relaxed and refreshed despite the sleepless night, I return to my camp. Spoken prayers are not enough to express the depth of my gratitude. I have decided to offer sacrificial gifts to Mother Earth and Father Sky. I think how Aborigines let their own blood flow from ceremonial cuts onto the ground to show their gratitude to Mother Earth. I, too, feel the deep need to offer something personal and precious.

After packing my gear, I build a large fire and reach for my homemade drum. Two black lizards chase each other around the deerhide face stretched over a cedar frame. Holding the drum up to the clouds, I ask Father Sky to accept my gift, then lay the drum in the flames and add more wood. The drum dies quickly and its spirit flies away in the spiraling smoke. The funeral pyre burns down to coals.

Now I take the medicine bag from my pocket and examine it lovingly. The sachet of soft, honey-colored leather was sewn for me by Abby -- her gift at my departure. Attached to the beautiful bag is the tiny white turtle she carved for me from soapstone. I smile. That's me -- walking slowly and deliberately with my home on my back, gathering wisdom as I make my long journey.

Tugging open the drawstrings, I reverently remove each of the sacred objects inside. Each item represents a section of my journey or an event of the quest. A lichen-covered cobble from this mountaintop traveled the entire loop with me to return here. A smooth green stone joined me as I sweated across the open plains of Navajo country. A porous lump of lava recalls my joy upon reaching the heights of Mount Taylor. A ptarmigan feather represents my three glorious weeks along the Continental Divide in Colorado. A pebble from the top of the La Sal Mountains reminds me of staring down on the land of living rock. A piece of pudding stone flashes back to the relief at finding water in the parched vastness of canyon country. Another smooth pebble plucked from the shore of the Colorado River quieted my thirst when I sucked on it in the Grand Canyon. A chunk of black ice -- obsidian -- entered my bag only a few days ago when I reached the San Francisco Peaks. Also in the collection is my worn bracelet, now free from my wrist. Finally, there are two locks of hair. One is long and chestnut; a gift from Abby from her own body. Throughout the summer, the touch and scent of these precious strands have filled me with comfort and love. Beside her locks I place a tiny braid of my own hair -- black and shiny as Raven. An offering from my body. I arrange these things in a circle and give them one long, last, loving look. My entire quest is symbolized by this collection of stones and natural objects. Nothing in the world is more valuable to me now than this medicine bag. This is precisely why I have chosen it as my offering to Mother Earth.

Slowly, I put each talisman back in its leather home and knot the drawstring. Moving to the fire pit, I stomp and drown the coals, then cover the ashes with a thin layer of dirt. In the center of the depression, I position a flat rock and place my medicine bag on this tiny altar. It might as well have been my heart torn from my chest lying there. With tears streaming down my cheeks, I ask Mother Earth to accept my gift. Gently, I cover the medicine bag with dirt and fill in the depression. Then, using the stone slabs of the fire ring, I mindfully construct a two-foot high cairn to mark the grave. This shall be the only evidence of my passage on this sacred mountaintop.

The sun is now burning bright several palm-widths above the Painted Desert. Skinny aspens frosted with splashes of gold tinkle in the autumn breeze. I gaze about me at the wilderness world that has been my home, my school, and my temple; I am ready. The faint whining of a truck grinding out of the desert towards Flagstaff drifts up from the highway a few miles distant. I turn toward that sound and begin walking. My true work is about to begin.

EPILOGUE

Five and a half years have now passed since I walked away from my vision quest circle atop Sugarloaf Mountain. Despite my mental preparations, the initial return to society proved immensely difficult. The most glorious summer of my life was followed by the most dismal and disheartening winter I have ever known. Desperate for money, I found myself living in Albuquerque, working for a temporary service, pulling eight-hour shifts in a hideous plastics factory. The contrast with my life on the trail a few months earlier could not have been more dramatic. Following my vision seemed an impossible dream.

By the following summer, I managed to get my life back on track. I began working as a trip leader for Deer Hill Expeditions, a family-run camp which provides teenagers with backcountry experiences and service work opportunities in the Four Corners area. By the next summer, I had added rafting skills to my hiking experience and became a guide with The Four Corners School of Outdoor Education as well. Thanks to these two fine organizations, I've been able to act as an ambassador for the country I so dearly love and make my vision a reality.

Abby and I eventually parted ways, but we remain close friends. I now live alone in a yurt on a sage field in Southwest Colorado. From my simple home, I can gaze at both the rugged summits of the La Plata Range and the mesas above the canyon country of Utah -- centered between my beloved wilderness worlds. The yurt allows me to live simply and close to the Earth even when I'm not in the backcountry with a group.

Leaning near one of the yurt's windows is the agave staff that accompanied me for every step of my Southwest Circle Quest. One touch of the smooth, golden shaft is enough to bring the memory of our adventures together flooding back. Although it's "retired" now, I keep this walking stick with the hope of one day passing it on. Someday, perhaps when I'm an old man, I'll meet a young man or woman in love with the Earth displaying that undeniable gleam for adventure in his or her eyes. I shall then pass along my staff and urge my young friend to "Follow your dreams!"

May the circle be unbroken.

SwallowHeart
April, 1997